Unfinished

Merrilee,

Meeting you on
the dock of the Cove...
I loved it! and your
story, I look forward
to hearing more of your journey.

Suzanne.

Unfinished

SUZANNE GRAVELLE

Design: Jack Steiner
Editor: Ann Fischer and Christina Konecny
Cover: Diane Kolar

Distribution:
Innovative Logistics LLC
575 Prospect Street, Suite 301
Lakewood, NJ 08701

ISBN: 978-1-927005-06-4

All the events in this book are true and the accuracy of the events are how *I* remember them and strictly from my point of view. Some of the time lines may be slightly off and I apologize if you find yourself not remembering the events "exactly" as I have written them.

Some of the names have been changed to protect the identity and privacy of some of the individuals.

I dedicate this book to my children Carly, Marc, and Nicholas. Their unwavering support, faith in their own survival skills and encouragement for me to keep driving further away, allowed me to be away from them for as long as I needed to be. Thirteen months is a long time! It has also shown me I can go again without the worry about them!

Besides the calls from Nick wondering if I could come home for "Just a Minute," you never made me feel as if I had abandoned you and that made all the difference in the world to my journey. Thank you, I am so very proud of you...You are Warriors.

Also, I want to thank my sister, Kathryn. Without your unselfish acts of love and support, putting plates of food in front of me, your words of wisdom and motivation for me to keep moving forward. I know I would not have come through this transition as quickly as I did with out you... I hope never to have to reciprocate but trust if you ever need me; like I needed you...I am there.

Thank you Katie! You are my rock! I love you.

And to Mr. Aswell...Thank you for allowing me to be me and for you always being you.

I would also like to thank all my friends and family for opening up their homes to me. You all made me feel so welcome and being with you distracted me enough to forget why I was "running."

Table of Contents

Unfinished

The Path of a Seeker

On the old trodden path, a seeker awakens
And rises to the call of the wind
Hastily she moves to the drum of her heartbeat
Shifting the sands off her feet.
The seeker her gaze on the farthest horizon
Crushes not, the rose in her hand
Or stifles the wind that caresses the grasses
Only things freely given, she takes on her path
The seeker, a wanderer with one destination
Heeds only the call of her soul
Who conquers each pain as if it's a jewel
To take to the heavenly throne.
The Path of a seeker never runs smoothly
Still she walks on the old trodden path
The rose in her hand, her only love token
She takes to faraway land.
Just like a rose in the hand of a seeker
So is God's precious gift of his love
N.P. JUNE 1983

CHAPTER ONE

Self-Imposed Exile

I am living in self-imposed exile. I have intentionally removed myself from everyone and everything that is familiar. Whether it is because we need to rest and rejuvenate our minds and bodies or we need to explore and work through an issue that is troubling us without distraction, interruption or influence, taking time alone, in my opinion, is important. This time away can be for a few hours, a couple of days, a few weeks, or in my case—indefinitely.

Self Imposed Exile... it sounded so peaceful when I first said it to myself. There was no question; I had to be alone, in exile, to figure out what was happening to me, to explore the choices, decisions, changes and challenges that were rapidly becoming my life.

Although I was actively taking part in making some changes while allowing others to just happen, I could not ignore the knowledge that I was suddenly thinking and feeling differently than I had been in the recent past. It was the challenges that came with the changes I was not prepared for. The challenges started to come about when it appeared to me that the plans I had for my future suddenly made no sense to me. They felt like were plans for someone else's life. When I realized I was in this confused state, not knowing the answers as to what I wanted for the next phase of my life, I did what I always do...I researched the problem and the conclusion I came to was that the research I had to do was on myself. And in order to do that I wanted and needed to be alone.

Professional therapy was suggested and it was something I considered. I may have pursued that option if I had stayed, but my desire to be alone and driving overpowered everything else. In the end I chose to take the professionals with me but they had to be compact. I had to be able to pop my therapists into the CD player when I was driving or open a book when I was sitting still, and this worked very well.

Clearly, leaving my forties and looking at turning fifty, was going to bring changes as it does with every one, every new decade of life brings with it unique changes and challenges. Not having a partner in life to consider my choices with, confide in or help me with this transition, I had no choice but to make my decisions by myself. Most people have to consider someone else before they make radical changes in their lives but the only consideration I had to take into account was how my actions were going to impact my children. They are now adults living on their own and well aware that I am going through a complicated transition.

As a person of action I couldn't sit around and wait for answers to appear, I had to get out and seek information. The only resources I had, like most people, were the examples of those people close to me. I paid special attention to people older than I was and in long-term relationships. I wanted to know how they made them successful and how they maintained their individuality while still having a successful relationship with their partners.

I watched them interact and paid attention to how they responded to each other. I would ask people in relationships I admired how they dealt with their personal transitions, their thoughts and feelings as they encountered their own fears when they realized they were restless, changing and growing towards another level of their lives. I wanted to know how they maintained their sanity enough not sabotage their relationships. The most common positive response was the expected, "respect for their partner's space, trust, faith and communication when issues arise." But more often than not the answers I got that disturbed me the most were, "It's too late now so I have just accepted that this is my life," or "I made this bed and now I have to sleep in it."

I was disappointed that I had access to so few examples of people who felt they were living their lives the way they really wanted to and hoped that once I went outside my circle of influence I would see something different. What I found was that there is an overwhelming number of people who accept their so-so lives, believing that what they have is all there is for them. I could not accept hearing things like, "This is how my life is. Period" I knew that wasn't what I wanted for myself and that I was living a life that had become unacceptable to me and had to change it. As a result, I chose to step outside my comfort zone, and take a huge risk to see if I could actually attain the vision of the life I had created for myself.

The dreams and plans we had for ourselves when we were young rarely work out, but does this mean we stop dreaming, stop working towards our revised, new and improved grown up visions and just accept life as it is? Not to me, so I started to really listen to my instincts when I found myself at an impasse and did not know what to do or know which way to turn. I stopped reacting in the moments of confusion and conflict, taking the time to question the thoughts and feelings I was having until they made sense.

Unable to give myself an objective outside point of view I started looking to experts. I began reading books, listening to CD's, and watching DVD's, searching for information that would help explain why I was confused and conflicted about making decisions that should have been easy to make. I began to realize that I needed to make change or I was going to be one of those people who simply accepted life as it was without question. Although I was living a comfortable life and could have sustained my life as it was, I didn't want to. I felt there was something more.

Sometimes it takes an unexpected life-altering moment before we see ourselves as we really want to be. It can spur us into making changes we have been hesitant or afraid to make. Some of these moments are tragic and others can be blissful.

I knew if I did not address the changes that were taking place and the challenges that began to surface because of all the new information I had, if I did not implement the knowledge and take action to change the things I found unacceptable for me, I would continue to act and feel confused and conflicted and that was not the woman I wanted to be or the example I wanted to set for my children.

My life was in a transitional state and major shifts were already beginning. But it was during a business development course I was taking to help improve and increase my business that I experienced the life-altering moment that forced me to make the drastic changes I have made. This moment took what should have been a normal life transition and turned it into a complicated, complex series of events that sent my world into a downward spiral that rapidly got out of control.

It was not the knowledge I was gaining for my business that impacted me, it was how this knowledge impacted me personally. I became aware that the image I had of myself on the inside was not the image I was projecting on the outside. This revelation took me well off the course I was planning for myself, which in turn made me take a long, hard, truthful look at my life. At that juncture it became apparent to me that I did not like a lot of what I saw.

Since that moment I have felt as if I awakened another woman who lives inside of me. And she was starting to make herself heard—quietly at first, and then gradually increasing in volume until I could no longer ignore her screams. She was starting to emerge, and my old self—the dependable, predictable self that kept me and everyone around me comfortable and safe, was fighting to suppress this unexpected new presence every step of the way.

I was fighting because some of the changes I was making scared me so much. They were not part of the original plan. They were foreign, reckless, out of control and took me out of my comfort zone. It was this new woman who was creating new visions and asking me to make decisions that made little sense to the old me, yet it seemed I was helpless to stop the process. At the same time because it was so scary and exciting, a big part of me did *not* want to stop it. I have always been an adventurous person, but having been such a structured individual during my entire adult life, the struggle to step outside of the safe environment I had created was the hardest step I have ever taken.

Long before I took this course I had been feeling claustrophobic, suffocated by my own thoughts and feelings and unable to understand why. I thought the feeling would pass but it did not.

Big indicators that something was happening to my mind had already started to appear a few years before my last child moved away from home. Responsibilities and activities I had once enjoyed started to annoy and frustrate me. Conversations I was having with everyone around me left me feeling sad and heavy and I would stay that way for long periods, questioning at every turn why life was so hard for everyone. All of this questioning and thinking became fuel for the new woman and she started pushing me harder, backing me into a corner, and making me think more. This fuelled my desire to get away even more, and I believed that if I could let her completely emerge from the shadows I could then give myself the opportunity to find my true, authentic self.

I found myself wanting space, wide open space—not just a drive out to the country. It had to be wider than that. I wanted to feel free, knowing that I would not be interrupted and could have all the time I needed to start and finish a thought. I was exhausted, tired of hearing about the troubles of others, thinking about my own problems and had no time to find resolution. It got to the point where I could no longer stand conversations about all the sadness in the world, or try to figure out the purpose of life, or listen to my friends talk about their own lives and how they wished for something different. Examining my own life, constantly overanalysing every aspect of it, and still coming to no conclusion as to how to make my world, my friends or myself feel better, is how I got to this place of feeling the need to drive into a Self-Imposed Exile.

We do not have to look very far to see the external influences that can overwhelm us. Every time I turned the on television, or caught a glimpse of a newspaper headline, I was aware of Mother Nature's destructive forces killing millions, children starving, people murdering people, the threat of nuclear disasters, wars, the demise of our world economics, and government decisions that made no sense to me. I felt helpless to make change and began to stop watching television and averted my eyes when I saw the papers but I could not get away from it. Every time someone called or walked through my door, they brought the outside world in with them. And because I worked with the public and had to know about many aspect of their lives in order to help them, conversations were often drawn to the sad state of affairs we found ourselves living in, how sad the world and our lives have become, and again, there never seemed to be any answers to make it better.

When in actual fact the world has always been in a sad state of affairs because of human decisions and Mother Nature is always going to exert her force upon those that appear to be in need even before she inflicts her deadly wrath. We have become immune, calloused to realities because we see it, read about it; bring it deliberately into our homes on the nightly news, every day. But if it does not immediately affect our life, impact us somehow, it is easy to shake our heads and say, "That's horrible, that's shocking, that's too bad, oh how sad," turn off the T.V., put down the paper and go back to eating our dinner that was just delivered to our door.

Life outside my front door was awful and yet I couldn't feel sorry about any of it. I found myself shaking my head and saying, "That's horrible, that's shocking, that's too bad," but in truth I felt very little and that was a huge indication that something was happening to my emotional state of mind and that concerned me greatly.

I am a sympathetic person and normally I could feel empathy for someone else's pain but now I found my lack of feeling and emotion extremely disturbing. I thought, "Well at least I understand I feel this way. Now I just want to know why and fix it."

I asked myself, "What happened to me? How did my life

suddenly become the most important sad topic of the day?" I was never this way. I was too busy to indulge in such drama. I was the steady one, the happy one. I was the strong one. I was the listener. Now it appeared to me, I was doing the very thing I despised…being dramatic and unable to stop the downward spiral of my emotional state of mind. And because I could not change the events that contributed to this despair, I just wanted to find a way to accept what I could not change.

I felt selfish for feeling weak and vulnerable and knew I had to do something to change my state of mind in a hurry. And removing myself from all influences that would continue to distract me from concentrating on myself seemed like my only choice. Exiling myself completely seemed drastic, but it was the only way I was going to be able to examine my state of mind and figure out what was keeping me in this place of despair. It was not an easy plan. When my focus for 30 years had been on others I had no idea how I would manage to focus only on myself.

Being such a private person there was no way I was going to start divulging and projecting this dark emotion onto my friends and family. I didn't want to hear anyone say, "It's okay, we all go through stuff and we need to talk with someone about it." That was not my way.

I felt like I was bleeding from every pore but when spoken out loud my sorrows sounded trivial. Knowing the rest of the world was falling apart and there was so much undeniable pain being suffered by so many other people around me and in the world, I asked myself how I dared to feel this way? How could I possibly feel anything but grateful for a life that appeared to be so full? But as we all know, even when logic dictates that we know differently, when it is our pain, regardless of what has caused it, it feels as if we are alone and there is no one who could be suffering as much as we are.

When my closest friends would ask, "What's going on? Tell me, maybe I can help." I had no idea what to say. "Oh I feel sad," or "I have a pain that's not caused by an injury you can see," or, "I'm losing my mind and don't know why." All this sounded so pathetic to me. Furthermore, how could I tell them what was going on with me when I could not fully explain it to myself? That was what I had to discover. I needed to know what would make me feel this way and how to get over it. All I knew for sure was that something *was* happening to me, something that I had never experienced before and I hated it to the point I had to leave. But not before I nearly killed myself—not intentionally, it just happened.

In the beginning of my self-analysis, before I decided to take the drastic steps to exile myself, I kept my issues to myself until it became apparent to those around me I was detaching from them as well as the world around me. When I was deep in the middle of it, my physical appearance changed drastically in a very short period of time and thank goodness I had people around me to recognize this was not because I was working out at the gym.

I am so grateful I have friends who "check in when friends check out"…and they bring soup! I had lost so much weight and the repercussions of not eating started to show. My hair was falling out and there were dry patches all over my body, I had no energy, my brain stopped functioning properly, my vision started to blur, and my physical strength diminished to the point where it was difficult to walk. Breathing became a laborious chore I had to consciously make the effort to do.

I could not afford this kind of analysis anymore. It took

all that was left in me to get up and fight to live. So what did I do? I got up.

My closest friend Don saved my life. He brought me food and forced me to eat and he stayed with me, taking vacation time from work to be with me. He knew some of what was going on but he did not care about anything except my deteriorating physical well being. He fed me back to a point where I had the strength to realize I had to get control of myself, I had to take action to get on with my life, and I needed to talk. And there were only two people I wanted to talk with—my cousin Roslyn and my friend Lee. They are the two most logical, stable women I have ever known and I knew they would listen without prejudice.

When we started to talk it was only about the obvious issues. And the only thing I was prepared to talk about with Roslyn on the phone and my friend Lee in my kitchen was the break-up that had broken my heart. For sure this was a reason for me to feel messed up and sad. The man I had been fantasizing about a life with and I could not make the fantasy come true. Looking at the big picture … yes, I had a broken heart…but I had had broken hearts before without falling into this state. Why was this broken heart now the focal point of my despair?

The most logical conclusion we came up with was this: The break-up was only the catalyst for bringing back the issues I had stuffed away, ignored, denied, and filed at the back of my mind, hoping I would never have to deal with them. This broken heart was just heavy enough to make my house of delay and denial come crashing down.

Self-imposed exile, to my mind, was the only way I was going to be able to separate the issues I had pulled out of my memory bank during my self-exploration and the crash of my soul. And to deal with them one at a time I was going to have to be by myself, alone with my thoughts. This idea immediately gave me a feeling I had not felt in a long time. That feeling was…quiet.

While I was in my mental decline, questioning why this was happening to me, I started to remember moments in my life when something not so nice had happened to me; not to my children, not to my friends, but to me. When a memory was triggered, I tried to remember it in as much detail as I could and try not to embellish it, making it better or worse than it was. I wanted to understand why these things had happened, and if I did deal with them, how I dealt with them. Now I wanted to know if they had had lasting effects on me and how those effects were now infiltrating my life, because it was clear to me by then that something apart from the end of the relationship had definitely affected me in a profound way.

I am fortunate not to have to include my childhood memories in trying to understand why I have suddenly become disconnected from myself. I, unlike so many people I know, had a "normal" childhood. It is the choices I have made as an adult that I want to explore. Why did I attract the people I did into my life, men and women, the ones that impacted me in negative way and left scars, and do I still continue to attract the same kind of people today? And if I do, how do I change the Law of Attraction to a more positive vibration to attract more positive people? Okay … I know all the gurus say it is a change of thinking that changes the vibration. Easier said than done, but I have done the research and know this is what I must do.

I have a variety of people in my life. Some of them have been really great influences and continue to be. It is the ones who show up and are not so great that I have a hard time recognizing as the problem. Even though they are not influencing me in a positive way I am generally having so much fun with them that I refuse to believe they are not good for me until it's too late. I want to know how I can attract the right people into my life *all* the time. I know this is almost impossible as how do you know whether people are good or bad influences until you spend time with them?

Sometimes we get a feeling when we first meet someone and we make decisions about them on the spot. For example we like them…but over time we come to find out our perceptions were wrong. Even when I came to the conclusion someone—man or woman—was not a good influence on me; it would take time for me to sever the relationship. I would delay doing this until something happened that was either unforgivable from my point of view or I would do something they would think was unforgivable and the relationship would deteriorate to the point of not even being able to be friendly any more. I want to change this.

The memories that I have started to pull from my memory bank are not pretty, they are not nice but they did not kill me or stop me from living my life, working or raising my children. I do not want to believe they have had lasting effects on me, but because certain behaviours and reactions continue to surface in my weak and vulnerable moments and I keep getting the same negative results in some of my personal relationships, they obviously left their marks.

I either did not want to or could not deal with these things when they were happening because I did not have the mental tools of experience and wisdom to help me work through the issues at the time. I did not have the knowledge to understand that the repercussions of not working it out could impact my future. I did not take the time to think about them because life was so busy and I did not have the discipline to stay focused when I did think about these issues and see them through to more positive conclusions.

Even having the tools I do today and using the resources that are available to me, (and I am sure there are many more I do not have) I am still reluctant to deal with past issues. But I have no choice because I believe these issues are obstacles stopping me from evolving into the woman I see in my mind and because I keep coming back to the same negative results. Today I want to do everything I can to ensure I do not continue this pattern.

We all are great procrastinators and want to delay or deny what we know will disturb us and bring us the pain we never wanted to feel in the first place let alone feel it all over again. I know now that I have become an expert at delay and denial. Who wants to keep injuring themselves? I have developed this great ability to push issues that disturb me to the back of my mind and I do it quickly, justifying it by telling myself they did not happen the way I think they did. I soften the memory by convincing myself that it was not as bad as I thought. I believe this action of softening a memory played a major part in allowing the repetition of bad choices, allowing my reactions and behaviour to continue to be detrimental. I suppose we all do this to some degree. Over time we soften hurtful moments. It is a survival tool that kicks in that keeps us from going insane and I am grateful to have it because it got me through to this present moment.

I did not want to delve into the issues when they were happening and I easily used the excuse that I was busy being a mother but I know now it was not that, it was because they evoked fear and doubt. But now I have the time and it appears I must address them. There is no doubt the issues were like toxic free radical cells, and they had been dormant in the dark recesses of my mind waiting for the moment when I was in a place in my life when I was weak, in a place of dis-ease, like having a broken heart. At that point they became active, racing through my body, attacking me and poking me like a metal dental tool hitting an exposed nerve. These painful moments were now lining up and taking turns, knocking the breath out of me, kicking me in the knees, hammering nails into my brain, making me think about them and attacking the most vulnerable parts of my body …my mind and my heart. They kicked me so hard I was knocked to the floor.

I knew I had to address these issues that had now become my truths if I ever wanted to be free of them. I also knew I had to get away from my friends and family in order to do it. For years my friends had told me how they admired my strength. Now I was weak and vulnerable and I had to get away from the embarrassment I was feeling, even though they said, "Don't be ridiculous. It is difficult for a person who has always been the one to hold everyone else together to suddenly find themselves falling apart. It's okay. This will pass." But it was not okay to me. Yes, I understood that this moment would eventually pass but I never wanted this moment to show up again. I wanted to know what had really happened. Where did the fearless, strong, take-care-of-everything, make-all-the- decisions, do-anything woman go? I figure if I keep asking myself these questions eventually the answers will fall off my tongue just as easily as the questions do and I will at least have closure.

Why did these other issues I was not going to discuss with anyone else have to surface at a time when I was most vulnerable? Why did they start to emerge when I needed my strength and energy the most? Because this is the party Fear and Doubt love to crash. It is not a "pity party"…it's a "life has taken its toll on you party" and the guests of honour … Fear and Doubt, have shown up and they are not alone. They have brought along a few of their friends—Truth, Sadness, Dread, and Loneliness…and right now, they seem far too comfortable in my body, the party has gotten out of hand and it is frustrating me because these feelings override all the other parts of my life that make me happy and I want to get back to those happy parts.

So I do as I do with everything I fear. I go to the source, just like I did with flying. I love to travel but I do not like to fly and I seem to fly a lot. I took a course to get my private pilot's license just so I knew why planes bump and drop suddenly. I am not saying I could fly a 747 jumbo jet but at least I could talk the language and hopefully get us down safely in a crisis, but this time I am the source. And before I can take care of anything else, I must take care of my broken heart because that is the issue that is overpowering every reasonable, logical thought in my mind and feeling in my body.

But first I wanted to put myself in a place where no one knew what was happening to me, where I would not have to talk about myself and I could figure out this problem because it was preoccupying me and distracting me from everything else. I wanted to go places where I would be somewhat anonymous, where I could be around other people but not intrude or be intruded upon. I needed to think without distraction, interference or influence … so, 30,000 kilometres and seven months after leaving my comfortable world behind, I have literally driven myself into the Self-Imposed Exile I had been seeking. And for the moment I have stopped driving in order to piece together all that has happened and all that I have learned.

Early in my journey, after stopping and spending time with friends I realized I did not want to stop driving because that was when I would start to think. But I was not in any frame of mind to think positively about negative issues of the past or my broken heart, as I had not yet processed and come to terms with the fact that I had just sold my home, packed up my life, kissed my friends and children goodbye and driven away, let alone trying to figure out anything else. After those first few days and visits, I only stopped when it got dark—to rest.

You would think that so many hours on the road would have been the perfect time to think things through and when I stopped to visit with friends and family I would be able to enjoy where I was but it did not work that way for me. While I was driving my mind would drift to the new unexplored destination I was heading towards and I was so busy trying to take in everything around me that addressing any issues of despair, although the feelings were still there, was not easy to focus on.

When I did stop for a few days, it was and continues to be, all I can do to sit still and try to enjoy the moment. I look around at where I am and who I am with, hoping and praying to find peace. But the whole time I am there, regardless of how peaceful and beautiful it is, regardless of whether I am with others or I am alone, all I do is look at the exit door and plan my next escape because driving has become my escape.

In the night, alone in another strange bed, I would *force* myself to pull up a memory, thinking this was the way I should do it, to try and figure it out. But it is difficult to bring up old memories and continue to think about them when recent ones are so fresh, so I have learned to allow whatever thoughts are most prevalent to take precedence. This is a revelation for me, understanding that I am taking care of issues that are still raw and fresh in my memory and dealing with them sooner than later, that I am not stuffing them away or ignoring them before a new crisis happens and I have to file them away. I am doing this because I do not want to have compounding issues. I am sure that is what has happened in the past and to repeat that again would make me crumble even more deeply under the weight of being presented with so many things at once.

The most pressing question was why I had derailed the goals that were in motion before I met Jack. I wanted to know how the plans I had for self-exploration beginning with minimizing the quantity of possessions in my life in order to maximize its quality had gone sideways. I wanted to know how and why the life I had envisioned when my children moved away from home was now not in place, and where had this new woman I was beginning to know and like had gone?

My goals and dreams were intercepted by the idea of a fantasy life I believed I was going to live with this man. The images of that future were incredible so why would I not go off track for them? After all, there is nothing wrong with getting off your own track and merging onto another one if you are both going to live happily on the same track. I understand now that instead of merging my vision with another's, I had collapsed myself completely into someone else's dream. I had changed my original vision to the point where very few parts of it were mine anymore, believing I would be happy doing this. I was wrong.

Another revelation came very quickly after my emotions

settled down that surprised me, concerned me and confused me. I discovered by listening to him and watching him—he who broke my heart—that he was going through his own transitions. He was making life-altering changes such as moving to a new city, changing his business, ending a long term relationship, and meeting me. There was so much that was affecting him mentally and physically too. Meeting me became the catalyst for him to make some of these changes but he was also unprepared for the personal challenges these changes presented for him.

When he described his thoughts and feelings, fears and doubts, it was as if he was describing me. It was then that I knew we were both in trouble, as we had no idea how to deal with ourselves let alone try to figure out how to fit into each other's lives nor were we in any position to support each other emotionally. So he left, he went back to a familiar place and for months I heard very little from him. He had some idea of how his leaving affected me but not to the degree it had. I never let him know.

I will always remember the morning my friend Lee and I were in my kitchen reading our Universal Law cards. It was four months before my house sold, and four months after he left. My cell phone was on the counter and it went "Blip." I nearly fell off my stool. He was the only one who text messaged me with that ring tone and I hadn't thought I would ever hear it again.

"Are you there?" I was staring at the message and looked up at Lee.

"It's him"

Lee smirks and says "Of course it is."

I text him back "Yes, I'm here"

"Can I call?"

"Yes."

I got off the phone, looked at Lee and said, "He's free, and he's moving."

That was the beginning of a whole new phase for us but we were cautious and very non-committal. He was living in a province thousands of kilometres away so it was impossible to spend physical time together and the cell phone became our life line. I was also able to follow his transition closely from afar.

Now that I am physically free and I can be anywhere I wish at anytime, I could have gone and hung out close to him, but for reasons yet to be explained, we continued to be apart.

We did manage to spend some time together although it was sporadic, but we were never mentally apart, and communication via text and phone was constant while I was driving around the country on my quest for answers. And what we both realized and continued to feed with conversations was that although we did not want to let each other go, we were not ready for the kind of commitment required to make a relationship last. Our conversations revolved around the fact that although we cared a great deal about each other, being so new in this phase of our lives, perhaps it would be a good idea if we allowed our selves some time and distance to get to know ourselves better and give ourselves a chance to settle into our new lives. I thought I would be okay with this as I was just starting to heal from the broken heart when he came back into my life, but again I was wrong.

Accepting that we were free to explore the world in any way we pleased, including other relationships, without having to consult or concern each other with the details, was easy in theory but it created more fragility in our relationship, creating a whole new set of fears and doubts for both of us. It became a case of my always saying, "I don't know when I'll see you again," because I was heading to another destination far away from him, or he was heading to another city for work that was far away from me. This created an air of independence, forcing us to believe we really didn't know when or if we would see each other again. I would say out loud so often, giving life to the idea that we were actually free of each other, that it seemed inevitable that one of us would begin to explore a new relationship. But deep inside me, it seemed unrealistic, that it would really never happen for either one of us. In our minds, the Universe keeps bringing us together for a reason. We were destined to be together … just not right away.

Not knowing what track to be on, not in a relationship but never out of it, was not only more confusing to me, it became an obstacle that I had to understand and put into perspective and get over before I could even think about what my next move was going to be. To create a new vision, to move forward, I needed clarity because I was not just going through a "normal" transition any more. It had become convoluted with the most powerful, undeniable, intense, desired emotion a person can ever feel … love …and I wanted to know if it was real and if I was in it or was this just a fantasy, a dream created via phone calls, texting and short visits.

In the beginning, while I was driving, I kept telling myself, "The next time I stop somewhere for a few days I will deal with that issue or I will write out that problem," but it was not easy to do when there were so many beautiful images in my head. I preferred to create scenarios of unimaginable bliss and think about the next time I would see Jack, rather than think about retracing or reliving moments of my life that made me unhappy and begin to understand why.

It did not take long for me to understand that I couldn't ignore the older issues that were so prevalent and always invading my thoughts and this awareness was the first step in separating my issues and dealing with them one at a time. When a thought was triggered, I would take the time to think them through, evaluate the impact they had at the time and the impact they have had on my present life. After processing past issues and coming to positive conclusions, it was easy and exciting to then allow myself to think of the fantastic moments I have had and the ones that have yet to happen and not allow my past mistakes to influence my current life. There is no question that understanding why I did what I did or did not do in the past and coming to successful conclusions has allowed me to close the door on the past and move forward. Thinking about the positive things, without the invasiveness of "having" to deal with the past has made me feel better and I sleep better, waking refreshed instead of tired and anxious. Giving myself permission to "let it go," and allow the thoughts that make me smile instead of forcing images into my mind that I had told myself I "needed" to address, gave my mind a much needed rest and dealing with ugly stuff, past images and thoughts when they arise, became easier.

I felt relieved after giving myself permission along this journey to think about whatever was on my mind at the moment. I knew when the time was right to think about the issues that had sent me driving into exile; that my subconscious would bring the thoughts and images to me. A name, a place, or a smell for example would trigger a memory I was supposed to relive. Then I would thoroughly analyze it until I was at peace with it. But in-between the triggers, I let these thoughts just be and it felt wonderful.

Since I have such an extensive relationship with my own state of mind I am aware that, in the past I have allowed myself to stay in an unhappy place for too long. One of my quests along this journey was to pay attention when I found myself dwelling on a thought that changed how I was feeling physically. I wanted to compare the two states of mind— negative and positive. I already know that positive thoughts make everything better but as it is nearly impossible not to have negativity impact our lives either through outside influences or closer to home, I experimented with the two emotions. I have purposefully thought about negative issues over several days and nights, and consciously compared how I slept and how I felt when waking up.

During the negative thinking period, I would wake during the night because my dreams were filled with anxiety. You know the kind, when you want to scream and no sound comes out, or you need to run from something that is chasing you and you cannot run, and then there was my " favourite" dream of being naked in some public place looking for something to put on and finding nothing. Those restless nights almost always came after a negative conversation, days of negative contemplation and worry about issues that made me feel confused and anxious and the feeling of anxiety did not go away when I woke up. If I allowed myself to continue thinking about these things it never took long before I found myself complaining of a physical pain that generally required a trip to the doctor and extra hours of sleep for many days before it went away.

The positive thoughts are not so easy to continue thinking about when fret and worry are much more powerful. It has been proven that stress is a major factor in causing many physical and mental disorders, and I know that unless I deal with the negative or sad thoughts I will continue to be susceptible and my mental and physical health will be affected. They already have been. I want to come to a place of peace, be at ease with the issues that are causing my stress, or at least learn how to manage the stress. I know the positive thoughts I force into my head, no matter how blissful and euphoric they are only mask the anxiety, tricking me into thinking I am okay, but this only lasts for short periods.

When I was in my positive thinking phase of my experiment, masking my negative thoughts with fantastic positive thoughts, was not easy to do, but I felt no physical pain, I was much more jovial, slept more soundly and my dreams were not dark and ominous. But my brain knew I had not dealt with or removed the negative thoughts and soon enough, a sign, a name, a smell, would trigger an old memory and I was right back in the dis-eased moment.

It would be nice to have positive thoughts all the time but we do not. It requires a conscious effort to bring the thoughts that relieve our stress to the forefront of our minds. At the same time we have to be aware of what is giving us grief and not procrastinate in addressing it simply because we don't want to deal with a painful moment.

I have conflicting thoughts that create emotions that are also conflicting. I find myself wanting to think about Jack while telling myself to stop thinking about him. I like thinking about Jack and the images of a life that has been created because of him. But because he is going through his own transition and needs to be on his own to figure out what he wants in his life, I have no choice but to remove the physical images of him and create images that include only me. This is not easy to do because since my children have moved out the pictures in my mind *have* included him.

Now I want to know that I can be happy without depending on anyone else to create an environment that I am happy to be in. After all, I had been doing it for many years so it's not like I don't know how. I was just never completely alone before ... having children you are rarely alone.

When I met Jack I let a very solid wall come down. I knew this would open me up to all kinds of heartache, but I thought I was ready. What I was not ready for was for my heart to be broken so soon afterwards. I was opening my mind and my heart to romance and he had a major role in unlocking that part of me that had been shut away for years ... the intimate part of my life that I would not allow myself to enjoy, keeping every relationship at arms length, never making a commitment that lasted more than three months. He broke through that barrier and even though I am happy this happened, confirming that I am capable of loving again, detaching from physical images of him and trying to find that place of peace alone is not so easy. This is where more confusion and conflict comes in, juggling the negative and positive yearnings.

The conflict starts when I wake up. The first thing I think about as I lay there stretching is how my life would be if he had not come into my life. Then I switch to thinking about how fantastic it would be if I could share this adventure I am on in this beautiful part of the country with him. Then I tell myself I need to stop including him in my thoughts because they are getting in the way of allowing me to get down to the root of why I felt the need to run away in the first place. The reasons were there long before I met him. I have to remind myself I can't include him in my goals and plans anymore and it has made me wonder why he was brought into my life in the first place as I know there is a reason.

Then I get back in my truck and continue driving myself closer to where I said I wanted to go, where, for some reason the Universe is guiding me to go …. Alaska, the furthest I can get from the only place I want to be, the only place that gave me peace in my heart, when I was wrapped up in his arms, just breathing. I drive further away telling myself I can't go there now. I can't go near any town he's in. It's not our time and I have to come to terms with the reality that it may never be our time. I have to find a place where I can think, where I can breathe, feel peace in my heart, and integrate the images of my new vision with the very best parts of the old one and not be so consumed by a life that may never be.

I know I will get there … someday.

Now that I have stopped driving and have come to a place of exile where I can sit and reflect for a while, I think back to my last winter in the Maritimes. I was shovelling my long walkway and cursing the ice and snow. To take my mind off the chore, I prayed to whatever gods may be and I was talking out loud to them, "When my house sells, please take me to a place where I don't have to shovel snow." I should have been more specific. I should have prayed for a place that was not too hot, not too cold, had rain only during the night and snow only in the mountains where I could go to see it when I missed it.

Now over 30,000 kilometres later, the Universe has brought me to a place which I have been heard to say many times, "I will never live there again." The weather here affects me in a grey way, but I am not always in control of my own destiny and now I can see why the Universe sat me down here. It is familiar enough for me to feel safe. And even though it took weeks for me to settle down and stop looking at the exit door, it was the very best place to be to contemplate and find resolutions.

I sit in a beautiful apartment on the South West side of Vancouver watching the rain, again, wondering how I got here and where the time has gone. I feel as if I just left home, but as I look back over the calendar that has tracked my daily travel since I left, it tells me I have been gone a long time. When I read through the pages of my travel journal, I can't believe it is me I am reading about.

Did I really go there and do that, with that person? Did I really go there and do that all by my self? And the most bizarre place I spent time to figure out issues that made some of my friends question my sanity, did I really have to go there to find the answers I was seeking about Jack and heal my broken heart? Did I really have to spend time there before I could find the peace of my mind that has allowed me to resolve past issues, to make decisions and get on with my future? Yes I did!

"Wow! Look where I was, Look what I did!"

It all seems very surreal to me now. I have tucked in for the Canadian winter to give myself the time I need to contemplate life now that I have opened my mind and my heart to all the healing I require. I am not the same woman I was when I left and I am not yet the woman I am going to be. The woman that was screaming to be let out, is now down to a dull roar as she has not fully emerged and I am sure there are a few more screamers inside me that will, in time, make themselves heard too but until that happens I will concentrate on the one that is right in front of me as she is still UNFINISHED.

Delay is the Deadliest Form of Denial—C. Northcote Parkinson

CHAPTER TWO

The Terror Barrier

Bob Proctor, who *is* he? The first time I paid attention to this man was when I saw him on Oprah. Bob is the co-author of the book "The Secret." I saw this program long before I met the man I hold partially responsible for the transformation of my life. Bob told me, as he tells everyone, that "I can have anything…I *Truly* Desire" and now I'm not sure if I want to thank him or poke him in the eye!

Oprah had been tempting us for weeks, telling us she was going to reveal the biggest secret ever! Of course, we all wanted to know what it was. I went home from work specifically to watch it. When she introduced Bob Proctor and he started speaking, I was captivated by what he was saying. I couldn't help but feel as if Bob was looking right at me through my television screen and speaking directly to me.

He was describing events that happen to all of us but few of us are aware of them or take the time to be aware of when they are happening to us. After the show was over, I went out to the book store and I bought the book. When I finished reading it I thought, "Oh my god … they wrote that book about me." I have that power; I have the "Secret."

Several months later I found that Bob had entered my life again when I enrolled in one of his programs aptly named, "Thinking into Results." Bob Proctor is an authority on the mind. He has written several books on the topic and designed programs to teach us how to be in control of the thoughts we have. Several decades of proof that this can be done intrigued me enough to venture in to town each morning for twelve weeks to meet with a mastermind group interested in doing the same thing I was—improving our businesses, taking them to the next level and improving our personal lives with the skill of positive thinking. I was all for it.

For the first six weeks, I was enjoying the meetings and the DVD's were helping me. I was applying what I was learning and I was eager to learn more. I had no idea the Universe had already put into motion the actions that have changed me and my life forever. It was not until the eighth week that I started to understand how much this program had impacted me personally, specifically the seventh week's lesson, "Trample the Terror Barrier."

The Terror Barrier is a description used by Bob Proctor to describe a wall we hit or an adversity we face just as we feel brave enough to explore the vision, the dream or wish that we have held secret. We want to take a step beyond our comfort zone but we do not, or if we do, we often step back again because we are afraid of the unknown.

I'll never forget the day I walked out of the boardroom after watching "The Terror Barrier" DVD for the last time. I was a stark contrast to the woman who'd walked in, coffee in hand with a smile on her face, confident that she knew exactly where she was going.

We would watch the same DVD every day for a week. By the time the seventh week was over there was no question I had been affected by the information I had retained. When I stood up from my chair I knew right away something was different. I can only equate it to an image we have all seen in the movies. When someone dies, special effects show the soul leaving the body. I felt like I left myself sitting back in the chair and in retrospect I did. In one short week I had left my old self behind.

I looked at the other members of my mastermind group who had just watched the same thing I had but they didn't appear to be affected at all. They were talking normally but their voices sounded far away to me. I felt faint and knew I had to get out of there. As I was walking away, it was as if I could not keep up with myself. My mind was racing ahead of me, I could hardly breathe and my knees were weak. I wanted to run but my legs were leaden. I got into my vehicle to go to the office but I ended up at home and I don't remember driving there.

I stopped at the end of my driveway and looked around my yard. I drove down the driveway and parked my truck. I got out and starting wandering around my property. We were on the cusp of autumn and the leaves had just started to turn. This is my favourite time of year in the Maritimes but I knew it would not be long before the snow would be flying and I would be shovelling, so I told myself I could not entertain romantic thoughts about staying here just because it was a beautiful day. The "For Sale" sign at the end of the driveway quickly reminded me I had a plan, and I was glad because now even my own yard did not look the same to me. It used to provide a place of peace and security for me but on this day it provided neither peace nor security and it felt like a prison. I could not wait for the Sold sign to go up that would set me free.

Wandering around my yard I was thinking about my life and the changes I was making. The past week of watching the same DVD had helped me define my Terror Barrier. I had put a mental image to an obstacle and that has made it easier to see where I am and where I want to be. It is a clear picture in my head, like a photograph and I see it every day. To me, my Terror Barrier is a train tunnel high in a mountain pass that is filled solid with concrete many kilometres thick. I am the train chugging along with my life. As I crest the mountain, round the bend, there it is…my Terror Barrier and my dream life is on the other side.

At first, it looks impossible; I can never break through that! Therefore, I back down the mountain away from my dream and slip back into routine. Then my life becomes stifling again, I get restless and I start to dwell on my vision. I start to climb the mountain again. I round the bend only to arrive back at the tunnel. I stand and look at it for a while and give it a little kick. Ouch! That concrete is solid…and I retreat to the comfort zone of my life. I continued this trend of kicking and retreating until one day I kicked so hard the concrete cracked and I could not stop kicking.

Whether it is changing our career, moving to another city, selling all we own, moving to another country, ending a bad relationship or simply changing a daily routine or habit that has put us in a rut, it hurts to keep kicking at the concrete. Concrete, like life, is very unforgiving, but I had made the commitment to myself that I was going to do everything I had in me to break through because I wanted change.

I had no idea that making these changes was going to affect me as it has. I have read about people who pack up their families and travel around the world in a boat. If they can do that, then I should be able make a few changes until I feel comfortable with myself again. I had no idea where that comfortable feeling would come from or how I was going to get it, but I was not concerned with that. I just kept telling myself I had to keep the faith that everything would work out as it should if I just kept moving forward and kicking.

We all have thoughts at one time or another of changing the picture. When life burdens us with responsibility and debt, boring routine and no change or end in sight that is when we start to dwell upon another way of living. But first we must face our fears.

Manufacturing an idea of relief is fantastic, even romantic. Creating the scenario in our minds is fun, talking about it is fun, taking action to get results is not so much fun. It is then, at the point of action that we often allow fear and doubt to settle into our souls and take over. We are afraid to move forward. We become afraid to take steps to reach our goals because insecurities start whispering to us, telling us we cannot possibly do it.

Then we start talking ourselves out of our dream. "Who am I kidding; my husband/wife would never go for that! I am just about to get that promotion I have worked so hard to get. I have worked my whole life to get my pension; I couldn't possibly change jobs now. I could never sell my home and just drive away. Where would I go? I can't leave my kids and my grandchildren. What would my friends and family think? What will I do for income? What about all my stuff?"

All fair and reasonable questions and I recommend you ask yourself all of these and more before you make decisions you cannot reverse.

"We are allowed to be selfish as long as we do not cause pain or violate the rights of others." So think before you quit your life as it is today. Think long and hard about the trickle affect your decisions will have on those you care about.

The Terror Barrier is yours and yours alone. You come face to face with it when you realize you can no longer live as you were, and you find yourself taking steps to change. When the commitment you make to yourself feels so right and you cannot turn back on it, no matter how much you are vulnerable or weak moments tell you to, that is when you start to break through you own Terror Barrier and it becomes the scariest place you have ever been. But you are the only one who can conquer it.

I have spoken with friends and strangers along my trek about my journey and almost every one of them has a dream of changing something in their life and they face similar fears about taking the steps to live that dream. The difference between so many others and me? I am doing everything I can everyday to attain my dreams and conquer my fears. And the funny part about it? Because I collapsed my own dreams and goals into someone else's, I didn't know what my dreams were anymore; I just knew I wasn't living them.

I no longer want to walk around with the fear continuing to cloak me ... it's too dark, too heavy. I want so desperately to understand why I was not satisfied with my life as it was. I ask myself all the time, "Why can't I be like everyone else? Why do I feel so compelled to change my life so drastically? Why do I feel so disconnected to my life?"

Now that I have taken steps to change my thoughts and my life, my personality, my consciousness and all I have learned from the books, CDs and DVDs will not allow me to retreat back into the safety net of my comfort zone anymore. I have burned the ship by selling my home, making sure I have nothing to retreat too. I wish I could tell you it was easy to do.

Once I made the decision and committed to myself to take action to change my life, I felt a sense relief and fear at the same time and because I had already changed the picture in my head, written it down and spoken it out loud, i.e. that I was going to get into my truck and explore my confusion, I could not turn back and I did not want to. The very idea of not following through with the plan that was now in full swing was not an option,

The concept of packing it all in and starting again, and taking the steps to get it done, were etched in my mind. It all seemed fairly clear to me. Sell my home, pack up my truck and drive until I was finished driving. I was going to drive until I found a place I could sit and ponder what I was supposed to be doing with my life and there was nothing anyone could have said to change my mind … and some did try to talk me out of going but I wanted my new life and nothing and no one was going to influence me or interfere… except Jack. Because love dictates where we live and how we spend our time, that was first on my agenda, to find out if we were in love and then make decisions.

I have many skills I could draw upon when I got to wherever I was going, so providing for myself was never a concern. It certainly sounds simple enough and it is a simple concept, but it's just not easy to get started. But you have to continue moving in a forward direction until you find yourself so far into your vision, and so caught up in your dream that you cannot turn back. Today, I have purposefully put myself in the zone of the Terror Barrier and I am afraid all the time because I am in the middle of it and don't know from day to day where I'm going to end up. But I'm not concerned about that. I just keep moving forward and where I end up at the end of the day … is where I am.

The first and most important step I took after I made up my mind to change my life was to speak with my children and get their thoughts and feelings about my plan. They were apprehensive at first, thinking about their own lives and how not having me around would affect them. It was a shock to them at first and I knew they couldn't really understand.

They are young and can barely see beyond today let alone two or three months after I am gone. When they shared their fears and concerns we would talk them through until they were comfortable. It was when they felt safe with their own ability to look after themselves that they started to understand to the best of their ability why I had to sell the house and leave. It was only when I would hear them speaking with each other and their friends about my plans as an exciting adventure that I knew they were going to be okay.

It became important to me to show them that no matter how old you are it is never too late to follow your heart and do every thing to stay focused on your dreams. I have tried to teach them to follow their dreams but to do it with a logical well thought out plan. But when we are young and inexperienced, "old" people talking to us doesn't mean very much. What do old people know? When I was young, my mother tried to make me understand the repercussions of actions I was contemplating but it made little sense at the time.

Now I have shared my plan and given my word to the most important people in my life, that I will figure this part of my life out and come back to them. Now I am accountable to them and I have no choice but to follow through with what I said I would do. They have always trusted my word and I will not disillusion them now. Today the doubts and the fear still overwhelm me and I continue to question my decisions but as each day passes I grow stronger as I get closer to getting through my Terror Barrier and finding answers to the questions that are still there.

During the months of driving alone and putting thousands of kilometres behind me, and especially on the days I had been driving for 11-14 hours, heading for some remote outpost I just had to visit because I liked the name,

I thought long and hard about the purpose of my journey. I shut my music off to listen to my own thoughts. I allowed my mind to wander and then to be triggered, especially when I was going somewhere where I would know no one and be alone and anonymous. Driving into the unknown has become one of the triggers for me.

When thoughts entered my mind, the ones that made my stomach lurch and shake, like "Where am I going? What am I going to do when I get there? Where am I going to live? When will I see my children again? Are they really okay without me around? When am I going to find peace in my soul? Is the money I have enough to see me through until I am ready to go to work? What will I do if my truck breaks down on this lonely dark road in this remote place with no cell phone reception? Will I ever see that person who makes me feel incredible again? And if not, will I ever find anyone who does? Will the Universe really bring me all I truly desire if I just trust and keep the faith? And why is it so hard to trust and keep the faith?"

When these thoughts are racing through my mind and it feels like they are all coming at me at once, I slow my mind down and picture each question as if it is an inch of my Terror Barrier. I take one at a time, ask it to myself out loud, roll around all scenarios until I come to an answer that I can live with then I kick it out of my brain and move on to the next one. I know I have had success with this method of dealing with questions that bring me anxiety because now when they come to mind, I have the answers.

Thinking back to the time I first met Bob, after I read The Secret and a few other of his books, but several months before enrolling in his program and embarking on my journey, I realize I had no idea at the time that I would be going on this journey. Over dinner he and I had a great conversation that confirmed how small the world is and how the Universe works in mysterious ways. He and my father were on the same Navel base as young men, at the same time. We laughed when he said, "The Universe was working to bring us together long before you were born."

I said "The Universe conspired for us to meet here and have dinner together?"

"Yes Suzanne."

"Wow, how did the Universe make this happen?"

"Through a sequence of events you put in motion prior to this dinner. They all led you to this table. Somewhere in the past you made it a true desire to be right here, right now, perhaps it was when you were reading one of my books. Your subconscious believed you and started to put into motion the events required for you to be here."

As I sat there listening to him speak with others around the table he kept looking over at me. It was eerie. Even though our conversation had moved to others I thought to myself, "We are not finished." The energy that surrounded us was undeniable, and I knew that somehow we would be meeting again. I knew that this man had already impacted my life through his books and I knew he was somehow going to continue to have an impact on my life, I just didn't know how. He had not yet introduced me to my Terror Barrier.

At the end of the night he said to me, "Suzanne, you are just starting to understand how the Universe works for you in your life. So many revelations in the past few years about events that have come to fruition for you, confirm you are starting to understand the power you possess. Pay attention!" He said "Pay Attention!" so firmly I felt like I had just been disciplined. And then he walked away.

As I said good night to him, I walked away wondering, "What powers do I possess and what am I supposed to pay attention to?"

In my hotel room I start questioning myself. Am I being brainwashed? Am I being led on because he is famous? Am I following along because of the man who introduced me to Bob? No, was the answer to all my questions. Bob was right. I was just starting to understand the power of my mind and I did have to pay attention. I had to become aware that when things happened in my life I played a major role in making them happen even if I was not consciously aware of it.

As I fell asleep I tried to remember if I had ever had an aspiration to meet Bob and I couldn't remember. I just knew when I saw him on TV and after I read his book that he had deeply affected me and I felt a connection. I let it go and I lay there wondering, "Did the Universe really bring us together to have this conversation over dinner?" And "Am I really thinking this way?"

A few months later I found myself with so many doubts about the Universe bringing me what I "truly desired" because I would never have consciously put myself in such an insecure environment. I could hear my own words coming back to me ... "We are not finished." After I finished Bob's program and my life and my mind were completely turned upside down, I wanted to have another conversation with him. This one would not be so pleasant. Had I known then, sitting calmly around a dinner table, what I know now, I would have delved deeper into conversations about the process of what I was going to go through, stepping up to my Terror Barrier. I would have warned him in advance to expect calls from me, as this could not possibly be what I "Truly Desired."

CHAPTER THREE

Manifestation

I love the word manifestation and all the derivatives and meanings of this word.

Clear, distinct, unmistakable, patent, open, palpable, visible, conspicuous, reveal, disclose, evince, evidence, demonstrate, declare, and express.

The psychoanalytic use of it is my favourite meaning; pertaining to conscious feelings, ideas, and impulses that contain repressed psychic material: the manifest content of a dream as opposed to the latent content that it conceals.

When we create a manifest of desires in our minds, and then forget about it, the subconscious mind does not forget about it and it cannot differentiate between wishes and reality. It is the conscious mind that knows the difference and it is when we are thinking in a conscious state about what is on our subconscious manifest, that we are working the two states of mind together to bring whatever it is we are consciously thinking about to fruition, manifesting the idea into reality, something tangible. Confused? That's okay. I was too at first.

As we all have so many other things to think about everyday, our own dreams and desires are often not thought about until the subconscious decides we need to think about what developments have occurred since the last time we took the time to think about them.

It continues to amaze me that when an idea or desire just suddenly flashes back into my mind how much more information I have than I did the last time I thought about it. It makes no difference what it is, renovating our homes or changing our lives. When we are not thinking of what we desire, we need to understand that the subconscious mind is still at work on that desire creating the steps that are necessary to get the very best end results.

It has become so important for me to understand that *I have to stop thinking about HOW* I am going to make what ever it is I desire happen, because that is when I panic. Thinking about the steps I would have to take to attain what I really want can be so daunting that this is when I start sending indecision and doubt and fear signals to my subconscious and soon enough I slide back to the wishing and dreaming stages instead of believing in my idea. I have learned to keep the finished picture in my mind; I have come to trust in the power of my mind and try not to use the words, "I wish." I have also learned to be more specific of how the finished picture looks; I make sure I add detail, because far too often my vision is attained with missing parts.

Say the following words either out loud or to yourself, right now, "I *wish* I could do___ (fill in the blanks with a desire) or "I *wish* I could have ____." How did they make you feel? Passive? Now say these words out loud or to yourself. "I *can* do ____! I *can* have ____!" Which ones gave you a greater sense of power, a feeling of confidence, just by saying them?

When a wish or a dream becomes a concrete idea, and you suddenly find yourself taking action to attain your idea, everything in your world changes and you are probably not even aware of the transition your mind has made from taking your wish from your subconscious and forming it into a conscious idea. Now your subconscious mind is no longer working on a wish; it is working on an idea. You will notice a dramatic difference in your thoughts every time you bring your idea into the conscious state of thinking, because now all you can see is yourself starting to take physical action to bring whatever it is that has been brewing and stewing in the back of your mind to reality. This is what happens when you forget about the "how." You probably are not even aware of how you got to the physical action part; you only know you did, and you could not stop yourself.

When you said to your self, "I *can* do that," instead of, "I *wish* I could do that" I bet your demeanour changed and perhaps even your posture. Did your shoulders straighten up a bit? Mine always do. I stand a little taller when I am using words that are giving me confidence and the little word "can" is one of the best ones a person can use to instil confidence in themselves or in another person, especially children. "Of course you *can* do it. You *can* do anything; you *can* have anything you truly desire, you *can* be anything you desire to be."

Power of suggestion ... red car... did you picture one? When I changed my words from, "I wish I could drive around the country until I am ready to stop driving," to "I can and I am going to drive around the country until I am ready to stop driving," from that moment on, every time I thought of my journey a road map appeared in my head. That led to the purchase of the road atlas and the highlighting of places I would visit. I knew as soon as I put it on paper, as soon as I highlighted the road out of my home town, my journey had begun and I had not even sold my house yet. There was no question that just by changing my words and believing in them and my idea, I set in motion the unstoppable steps to get what I wanted—driving around the country until I was ready to stop. I suggest you try that for a day or two just to see how it works out. See if by changing your language you notice a difference in you attitude. You can do it!

Now … think about a goal you have attained and try to think of the time it was just a wish, just a fleeting thought. Can you remember when it started to change and form into a concrete idea? You may find you are not able to remember when it first came into your head. It may seem like it was always there or you may be like me. I can recall the moment my fleeting thought became a concrete idea, a desire. It was when I started seeing all the repairs and maintenance that were looming over my house and I was no longer interested in taking care of any of them. From that moment on, each time I brought my idea to a conscious state of thinking it came with so much more information as to how I was going to make my idea a reality and the very best part was that I don't recall putting in a great deal of time thinking about "*how*" I was going to make it happen.

The steps regarding how I was going to attain my idea and goal of driving away did not come fast and they did not come at once. I know now that I was the biggest obstacle to getting to it sooner. Pricing my home so unrealistically was my subconscious telling me I was not ready, even though I thought I was; I was not ready to move onto the next part of my life. There were a few hurdles I had to jump over, and all of them were mental ones, before I was ready to handle the "Freedom" I was seeking. I know now that if my home had sold any sooner than it did I would have been wreck on the road.

The idea was simple enough. In my head it was not supposed to be a long process to get to the end result … my freedom. But I knew it would take some time, because a major part of being able to do what I was contemplating was being dictated to by the selling of my home. There are logical steps to selling a house. You need a For Sale sign, an offer from a buyer, and then negotiate a deal that works for everyone. But I hadn't factored in the mental steps. I was not aware that I was being resistant because I was afraid to let go of my security. I was terrified to take my hands off the wheel and relinquish control. I did not trust or have faith in my decisions yet.

If you were to have spoken with me then I would have sounded very sure of my plans but on the inside I was still allowing the doubt and fear to control how I was thinking and these thoughts would send me into physical fits of anxiety that were painful to the point of physically debilitating me. I was unable to make tea let alone decisions concerning my future.

As I lay on my bed or sat for hours in my chair, I prayed for guidance to help me work through this debilitating state. And I wanted to do this without filling the prescription the doctor had given me because I refused to believe I was depressed. I told myself that whatever this transition was I wanted to feel every minute of it including the pain. I knew this had to be part of the process to get me to the other side of my Terror Barrier and I wanted to get through it without softening its reality.

I have continued to endure the painful moments of my life without masking or altering my state of reality with drugs or alcohol. I do this because I want to be able to recognize the symptoms and know without any doubt that should I ever go through something like this again I can get past the pain that curls my body by twisting my insides with shocks of pain I do not think I will survive. I want to know I have the power to overcome it by using my mind and I want that mind to be clear.

It was only by relaxing my mind and understanding the "Law of Conscious Detachment," that I was able to understand that it has been my resistance to "accepting what is" that has been causing my suffering. What is meant by suffering? It is everything that does not work in my life—relationship problems, loss of loved ones, loneliness, sickness, accidents, guilt, monetary hardship, unfulfilled desires and so on. When I started to accept, "what is" I started to accept the unalterable realities in my life without resisting them and I started to think more clearly. Some things are just fact. They exist, and no matter how much I resist them or want them to be different, there is nothing I can do about them. I can only change what I can and have the wisdom to accept the unalterable situations as they are, without wasting mental or physical energy attempting to change what I cannot change. This is not a new revelation to me or to you, but we all struggle with this.

Out of acceptance comes involved detachment. What I want to attain is the ability to enjoy all the positive aspects of my life while allowing the negative ones to flow through me without resistance and with out affecting me so much. As much as I wanted to be in control, I had to come to terms with the fact that I could not force anything or anyone to do what I wanted. I could not make anything happen sooner than it was supposed to, such as selling my home for the price I wanted when I wanted. Nor could I make anyone feel or do what I wanted even though the pictures in my head were perfect.

Putting the positive thoughts on my subconscious manifest, the "freedom thoughts," and allowing the time required for these positive thoughts to work through to my conscious state of thinking was not easy. I was ready for my new life and I wanted it right now! But the Universe was not in agreement and no matter how I tried, I could not sell my house any faster, I could not make my dream life, my great idea, materialize any sooner until I stopped resisting and then and only then did the very best end result start to happen. As soon as I let go of the emotional attachments, when my home became just a house, I got up and started to take control of the only thing I could control—me.

I prayed out loud to whatever gods may be, to bring me something to distract my mind and my hands. I wanted something to preoccupy me until the offer for my home showed up and I could actually start to make concrete plans to drive away. I received an answer quickly in a big way. Not only did it bring me something to preoccupy myself with, it brought out a passion that was so deeply buried in my subconscious I had forgotten about it. It brought me back to writing—not this book, a book I wrote for my children when they were little—and with it came the most brilliant idea. I suddenly saw myself writing an entire series of books and publishing them.

This positive action allowed my mind to rest from the constant negativity I had created by continuing to think about "why is everything so upside down?" This preoccupation was what I needed to start recovering from a period of time when fear and doubt had clouded my mind, making me mentally and physically weak, and unable to make decisions that made sense to anyone.

About a week into writing I was sitting in my chair, laptop open, staring at the words in front of me, when the first clear thought I had had in months came to me. For me to get on with my life, I had to start reducing the price of my home. As soon as I had removed the emotional attachment I had for this house and come to terms with the sale, I looked at the road map I had highlighted in my atlas laying open on my kitchen table and saw my self driving those roads.

We know ourselves better than anyone. We know we cannot function or think properly until we come to these concrete feelings and purging all the junk off the manifest is the first course of action before we can get to the right emotions and the right feelings, and move to the next step.

When I detached from the emotion I had had regarding my house I was unstoppable. I got out of the chair and started packing boxes. I started living like my home was already sold. I imagined a closing date and I saw myself driving down the highway. I was going to be ready. I *expected* it to happen and there is nothing like expectation.

Whenever I got stuck in a negative thought I would sit down, open my laptop and start writing again until I worked through the negativity. It is amazing how much happier I was and how creative I was when I stopped the resistance and focused on something that was productive. This sounds ridiculous even to me but rarely having had an idle moment in my life, always having something to do or someone to take care of, suddenly finding myself with so much time on my hands and forcing myself to be productive was not easy.

It is unrealistic to be thinking about our desires constantly; we do have other things to think about. But if you have an outline, a picture in your mind of what you want to have happen in your life, of how you picture your life being if it is not the way you want it be today, you can be assured that your subconscious is working to make it happen—so make sure it's a great picture with lots of detail!

We all carry around this subconscious manifest and every now and then we take something from the file, look at it, and see how it is progressing. Most of the time we don't even realize how it happened, but we have created something more concrete to think about. We have manifested something that only started as a wish, which became an idea and when the idea is complete we are thrilled that we kept the belief in our idea, because now we are standing with the realization that we *made* it happen and the pride we burst with is exhilarating.

When I realize I have attained one goal I get excited about the next step. I take all that I have learned, mostly relaxing my brain and allowing time to pass while continuing to be progressive and keeping my feet moving forward and not forcing my will. I keep my mind open to all possibilities and suggestions, and allow whatever my next desire is to manifest itself with confidence and expectation that it will happen.

Every day I take time to think about my desires. Some desires are simple and easily attainable. "I desire to see my children and grandchildren, I desire to be sitting on Neiser's Beach poking a fire with my sister Kathryn and Roslyn, and I desire to hear my father laugh at a program on TV." These are desires I can have without having to process anything except getting into my truck or hopping on a plane. It is when I've seen that the ideas and desires that seemed to be out of reach for me have become attainable that I'm most surprised. And when I realize that I have attained them through the process of the subconscious manifest I created, that is even more astounding.

This journey I am on is a prime example of this. It was only a wish that came out of my mouth when life was overwhelming me and all I wanted to do was run away. I am sure we have all said, "I wish I could run away, even for a day!" Well I said it out loud and my subconscious believed me, turned it into an idea and it started sending instructions on how to attain "running away" to my subconscious and it manifested into this incredible journey.

If I ever had any doubts about the Universe manifesting something I truly desired, those doubts have been dashed because I have attained something huge that I felt was out of reach. It started out as a wish, a fantasy, not an idea, but for some reason I could never let it go so it must have been a true desire.

The first year I moved to Nova Scotia, we would take Sunday drives to explore our new home. Nova Scotia is not big a province so a day trip can cover a lot of ground. One of my favourite drives was to a lake not too far from our house and not very far from the city. No matter what time of year it was we could always find something to do there. We would pack a picnic lunch, fishing rods, swim suits or skates and go to the lake and hang out for hours. In the summer I would sit life guarding my children and my eyes would drift down the lake to the opposite end and dream of a house there.

There was one little home that had been there for years and a few hunters' cabins. But I saw my house, my yard, me poking bon fires, playing hide and seek in the night with my children, the gardens I would plant … I saw it all. Then I saw what I believed sealed the deal with the Universe. I saw the kitchen and I saw myself cooking in that kitchen.

For 10 years I dreamed about living there, never once believing it would ever become a reality. Then things in my life started to change and I found myself able to think about selling my current home and buying something a little larger for my growing family. When it came to our attention that the property near this lake was for sale we took the steps to purchase 5 acres and soon I found myself standing looking at the forest in front of me, next to a man with a chain saw in his hands, and I was pointing out which trees were to come down to create the driveway. I was delirious with excitement but I did not put together for many years how it was that I came to live there.

Epiphanies—I love them!

We had been living in our home for over ten years and I was sitting beside the lake down the "Freaky Forest Road" with my grandson and we were fishing. I was staring at him, listening to him squeal with delight, "Fish on!" thinking about how quickly time flies. It didn't seem that it had been that long ago that I was swimming and fishing here with his mom and his uncles creating the fantasy that we lived right here. Then it hit me like I had to hit the fish he'd just caught … Oh My God! I made this happen and it started long before the property was even for sale. In fact I remember thinking this was so far out of my reach financially it would never happen. But because I said out loud so often "I want to live here!" my subconscious listened and put the process of living here, right here, into action. It did not matter "how" long it took or 'how" it was going to happen … the "how" took care of itself. I spit it out to the Universe over twenty years ago and kept the dream alive for ten of those years, and I can now say, "Wow, look what I made happen!"

As I sat there with Owen I started to recall other parts of the fantasy. I was amazed at how all the thoughts of how my life would be when I lived here had come to fruition. I had the house, the kitchen, the bonfire pit. I played hide and seek in the dark with my children. I looked at my grandson, who was only four at the time so would never understand why Nannie was laughing and having a little "Holy Smokes" moment. He said "It's not that big a fish Nan," and I laughed even harder. Wish, idea, thought, energy, passion, action … receive. Believe it!

After so many revelations over the years, I know I have

to be very careful about what I wish for, what I breathe life into, and what and *who* I get passionate about. I have to be especially careful about the negative thoughts, because bad things can happen this way too. We do not wish any of the horrible, sad, awful stuff to happen to us or anyone else. But this has to happen so we know the difference between good and bad. So much of what I have in my life has come from the concerted, continuous effort of thinking about an idea that has become so real in my mind that I cannot help but take action to attain it.

When something does not happen for me, when things do not turn out as I hope they will, of course there is disappointment and I get frustrated but I have come to understand there really is a reason for everything and I have to be patient waiting for the reason to present itself.

It is when something does not happen that I sometimes find myself thanking whatever gods may be for not bringing an idea or desire to fruition. One of the things I was not supposed to do became apparent when I wanted to parasail out over the ocean in Mexico. When it was my turn to get strapped into the harness, I heard the guy behind me say. "I hope we don't miss our bus." He and his wife were leaving the beach to go on an excursion to see Ancient Ruins. But I was not in a hurry so I gave them my spot. His wife and I chatted as we watched her husband being strapped into the harness.

It is amazing the energy that surrounds us when we are about to put our lives in the hands of a couple of cables, a sheet of fabric and then be dangled hundreds of feet in the air. It is strangely exciting. When the boat pulled away from the shore and pulled this man up into the air, stretching him to the full length of the cable, all heads on the beach automatically looked up to watch. Then the unthinkable happened. The cable that was attached to the boat let go and the man started to fall from full height, down towards the ocean and he was not over deep water. The screams that came from his wife beside me were horrific. We all watched helplessly as he fell from the skies and we saw his parachute starting to collapse. We could see him struggling to manoeuvre his body and amazingly enough he kept himself upright. His sail filled with air and he was now not plummeting towards the water but using the cords to guide himself down and he landed unharmed, into the ocean.

It was a miracle he kept his wits about him. I am not sure how I would have handled myself up there and I am so happy never to have found out. Have you every said, "I am so glad I did not do that or go there, or, thank goodness it did not happen to me." This was one of those moments. The Universe stepped in, and blocked me from receiving what I thought I wanted and protected me. Have you ever forgotten something at home and had to turn around to retrieve it and cursed yourself for being so forgetful? Then when you pass by the accident that happened minutes before you arrived and said, "Oh my god, that could have been us!" Be grateful next time the Universe protects you.

Like so many who have discovered this "secret power," I have received many things I thought were out of reach or have done things I never thought I would be able to do. We have all said, "That was only a dream, I never thought it would actually happen." It is only in my quiet moments when I am thinking about the thing or the event that I connect the situation to the manifestation process, Wish, idea, thought, energy, passion, action … receive. I wonder today what I could have done with this "secret power" had I known and understood it when I was a child.

Now that I am not a child, my passions and desires are quite grown up. I had three missions when my thoughts drifted to the time my children were finally living on their own. They were—increase my income as I would be free to work differently, find a smaller home to take care of with less grass to cut, and romance—not necessarily in that order.

I achieved two of those missions almost immediately after expressing these desires out loud. I had increased my income *before* my children moved out and a new man came into my life who breathed a promising life into my future. And my home was for sale so the smaller home was going to be a reality soon enough.

My sheer will, determination and curiosity to find out what I have been manifesting over long periods can get the best of me. When I know I have been thinking about something for a long time, I get impatient and I wonder why it hasn't materialized yet. Where is it? I want it now! I try to force things to happen and all I get is adversity and obstacles.

When my home was taking too long to sell I would get frustrated and wonder what it was that I was not doing right. Why has my home not sold yet? Why am I still pacing around and around getting nowhere, when I appear to be so ready to move forward?

I had to stop trying to figure it out because as I have learned, regardless of how ready I appear to be, everything happens when it is supposed to happen in the way it is supposed to happen. I have also learned I have very little control over it as much as I would like to have that control. Understanding this fact, that I have little control, that has been a battle, and it's one I still fight.

Finally I started understanding what I had been reading in all the books and grasping the concepts on those CD's.

More importantly, I started applying the techniques, and the words I would not want to hear from anyone myself, were starting to come out of my own mouth. I just told myself, "It will happen when it is supposed to happen." Life is so much simpler now that I have relinquished some of the control.

Now when I realize I have been visualizing the same picture for a long period, I trust and have faith. If it something I truly desire, it will show up. As the Universe has shown me, it rarely comes in the way I want it to. It comes out of left field all the time, and it often takes some time to recognize it. It rarely comes in packages tied up in bows; it generally comes with adversity and pain. That is why I know when it does not show up the way I want it too, like not selling my home in the middle of winter, when I thought I was ready. It is the Universe's way of protecting me from myself. Even though I was physically ready to move in February, and had packed up most of my stuff, when it came right down to it, my true desire was to move in the spring and as I had said out loud many times, "I hope my closing date does not come on the day of a blizzard." And ultimately that is exactly what happened. It was spring.

Now that the images and desires of being free of all of the ties that had bound me to the house—the maintenance, property tax, bills, and debt—and the beautiful picture of freedom—had become a reality I found myself questioning it and asking myself if it was really something I truly desired?

We all speak of what we would do if we suddenly had millions of dollars, how our lives and the lives of the ones we love would change. Although I do not have millions of dollars, it is easy to visualize what the freedom would feel like if I did. Think about it. If you did not have house payments or rent, bills, debt, and the pressure of maintaining the day to day life you are living, how would that feel? I wanted to find a way to experience that. And winning the lottery is not an option if you do not buy tickets. I should have known that with my history of manifesting what I dwell upon, this picture had no choice but to come to life.

I believed in coincidence all my life ... but not any more. Things happen because *I* make them happen. I send out thought energy about what I desire to do or have. I send out thought energy about a person, they receive it and they contact me. Have you ever said, "I was just thinking about you?" There is not a person on this earth who has not had that happen to them. That is not coincidence—it is thought energy. I find myself practicing this art of trying to have someone contact me. Sometimes it works, especially if I am talking about them, other times it does not. I put this down to not have truly desired to hear from them at that time or to them not being open to receiving my energy. But before long, I am either hearing from that person directly or I will be speaking with someone and they will bring that person up. I scare myself sometimes. Am I a freak of nature? Yes, I am. Just ask my children.

When I am thinking about what I have created, I wonder how I made all that good stuff happen. The increase in income, the man, my happy children (most of the time)— all the really good things I have thought about. How did I do that and how do I continue to make it happen? Most importantly, how do I manifest the positive, gloriously happy, blissful moments and keep them happening?

Thinking positively has become a survival tool for me and it is not easy to maintain this way of thinking. When I find myself staying too long in a negative energy or keeping sad negative thoughts, I open my books to a random page and read what is on that page or I start to replay the CD's and DVD's that have helped me change my thoughts. It has become part of my healing process and this allows me to work through the negativity faster in a calmer state of mind.

I am not one for quoting spiritual scripture and I am not a fan of hearing someone spieling off positive phases when I am in the middle of a negative moment. Although I appreciate the sentiment and that they are trying to help, all I want them to tell me is how to get rid of the ugly feelings I am having right in that moment. I do not want to hear that "tomorrow will be a better day." But I have grown to accept that if I apply the messages from what I read and hear, tomorrow really will be a better day and I have the ability to improve this day too.

So often I wanted to call up the guru who influenced me and get him to "fix" whatever it was I was having a hard time accepting a "part of the process I must go through" to get what I really want. I wanted to blame him for my changing life and the pain associated with it. But I knew he had only made me aware that I could change any part of my life I did not like or add to the good parts to make them great.

Look up from reading and look around yourself. What you see is something you yourself have manifested. Do you like it? It really does not matter what the answer is because we all have the power to change it whether it is to get rid of what we don't like or increase more of what we do like.

Understanding this and practicing concentrating on my vision has brought so many wonderful things into my life. Remember though that it has to be a true and honest desire, because if it is not, the Universal Laws of Attraction may still bring it forward and if it is not a true and honest happy desire it will become a sad case of "be careful what you wish for, you just might get it."

Today my visions are clearer and I make sure I am more concise, more detailed in what it is I want. More importantly I am more aware of what I *do not* want. Now I practice patience. It has taken years for some of my visions to show up, to manifest. Does all this mental awareness ever end? No is the answer, a resounding NO! Visualizing my desires and taking action to attain them is all I want to do. Be aware that taking action to attain your goals will be like giving birth and raising a child, painfully exhausting, but the rewards are so worth it.

Now I have started to create another vision, one that when I left home I could not see. I have started to create another manifest and am etching it onto my subconscious. In my quiet moments when I am dwelling about my new dream life, I feel an incredible peace that I had no idea I could feel as I have never had it before. I have also started to understand why I created the manifest of running away. There was nothing that gave me a feeling of expectation and I felt empty and devoid of gratification although I was grateful for all I had. I had no idea what I, as an individual, as a woman, wanted to do, what my purpose on this earth after raising children, was supposed to be. I did not know what I would miss in my life if I did not have it. I had no idea what was important to me. My children, grandchildren and friends were not included; I knew I would miss them but that was all I knew.

I have started to visualize myself unpacking my "important stuff" from storage. I see the space, the view from my windows, my children and grandchildren visiting, and parties with the friends I choose to be with. I see myself writing my children's books at my desk or out on the patio, a career I choose, knowing that I will love what I do and the money will come. I hear laughter and it is coming from me. I see a love affair that is spectacular and will last my lifetime, because on this journey, I have allowed myself to feel what being in love is like and losing that love has enlightened me to what I am capable of giving and has shown me what I have been missing. I do miss it but I have learned not to collapse myself completely into someone else's dreams, I will maintain my own. I am seeing a life I did not see before I embarked on this journey. I did not see it because I did not know what was important.

CHAPTER FOUR

The Last Morning

The morning I awoke in my home for the last time, I thought it was really early as the sun had not yet passed across my face. Then reality hit. I was not up high in my bed but in my sleeping bag on the floor. Without opening my eyes I reached out and pulled my fingers along the carpet. It was still my carpet. I did not want to open my eyes; I did not want to see the reality of my life on this day. I did not want to see what was not there—the nothingness, the empty spaces where the "stuff" of my life used to be.

I was lying on my side, trying to grip the fibres of the carpet, trying to grasp onto something that would hold me there. I squeezed my eyes tight, praying that when I did open them, this would have all turned out to have been a nightmare and I would be in my bed, clutching the duvet, pillows all around, and my clock with the big red numbers would be coaxing me to get up as usual. But the hard, cold floor that had been my mattress for the past two nights, like the hard cold facts of life, were real and I had to face them. My back, hips and neck were stiff, my head ached from thinking too much, and from the nightmares that had plagued me throughout the night, but I had to open my eyes. I had to get up.

The first thing I saw was my three suitcases lying open. My new life was folded, rolled and neatly tucked inside them. What I was going to wear on my last day, when I took my last shower, when I stood on the warm tile and dried my body, in that spot for the last time and looked into the mirror for the last time did not matter. I just laid there staring at the suitcases. Did I pack the right clothes? What did it matter? Do I have too much? What did it matter? It was too late now. Everything I owned and loved was gone. The "stuff" of my life was gone and I did not know when I would see it again. I didn't care. I was numb.

Staring at the suitcases, I wondered, how I had packed my life into a suitcase when I did not know what or where my life was going to be? Where am I going? I don't know. I am just going. How long will I be gone? It didn't matter … until I came back. "Be Brave Suzanne," I whispered to myself. "This is the adventure, the moment; you have been planning. Today is the day. Your life starts now. You must get up."

As I lay on my side I looked up to the window. If I was in my bed, the sun would now be on my back and I would be able to see the pine trees that grew tall and strong on the rock ridge lining my driveway. But I was on the floor and could only see their tops. They were not moving. No wind, not today, no storm, not today. Everything was like me, quiet and still.

Through that window, every morning before I got up, I would take a few minutes while stretching to watch those trees grow. Together we had survived so many storms and hurricanes. It is the middle of spring and as I blink the sleep away, I can still see their branches which only weeks before were laden with snow. The weak ones have broken and normally I would have collected them for firewood, but not this spring—or the next. I would never see these trees again. How did I become so attached to these trees? "Stop it Suzanne," I told myself, "They are just trees." But they were my trees.

I rolled onto my back, stared at the ceiling and the nails cracking through the paint. I had always wanted to fix those. I saw myself going into the garage to get the hammer, the putty, the paint; they were going to be perfect again, there would be no more cracks. But the garage is now empty. I rolled to my other side and stared at the wall. The cracks that were there were so small, but I saw them, I knew they were there. I know every crack in every wall and every creak and stain but I did not have to concern my self with any of these issues any more. At 12 o'clock noon, someone else was going to own it.

The only cracks I have to concern myself with now are the invisible ones, the ones no one sees. The cracks that have fractured my soul and my spirit so deeply, that all the joy I had every felt in this home or in my life has seeped out. At this moment it seems impossible that I will ever feel joy or have lust for life again and I do not know what it will take to fill these cracks. But I have to find out. I have to!

For two nights, after my furniture had been moved out, I lay there in the dark, listening to the sounds that would be no more. It is true what they say "The silence is deafening." The second night alone there, my last night in my home, I was on the cusp of being asleep. Off in the distance, I heard the front door slam shut. I bolted up, holding my breath, clutched the sleeping bag around my knees, and called out my children's names one by one. I thought, maybe they had come to be with me, to sleep here with me but I got no response ... it was only my imagination. Only the echo of my own voice came back at me, through the empty house. I knew they were safe in their own beds, in their own homes. I was still alone. I had told them I wanted to be alone, but right now, I wished for them all to be here.

Wide awake again, I started to pray to the "help me get through this night gods." Through the window I could see the stars, the same constellation I had come to know so well. I knew the time of night just by looking out my window and saw how the stars were aligned, the big dipper would slowly slide across the sky. At 9 pm, it was in the window pane on the left, now it was on the right so I new it was almost 11pm. I thought it ironic that I was ending my time here the same way I started, in a sleeping bag on the floor—the same sleeping bag, the same floor before the furniture arrived. I'm sure it will seem funny one day, when I am safe and in my own bed once more but not tonight. It was the loneliest feeling I had ever felt in my home.

Tears that I promised myself would not happen started to fall. I bit my lip trying to make them stop. I shook my head and told myself to stop. I pressed my face to the pillow, wanting to smother the pain. I could not. The cries that no one heard, but I will never forget, reverberated off the walls back to me and it sounded like there were many of us crying. The ghosts who have haunted me for so long in this house were wailing with me. It was horrible to hear and excruciating to feel. My stomach was so knotted, so twisted, so filled with fear that I pulled myself into the fetal position and held myself tight trying to make the pain go away. But it did not work. I stood up and paced the floors, wandered the empty rooms, my one towel in my hands, pressed to my face covering my mouth. The only thing I could do was let it out. Together, the ghosts and I cried, hollered at each other and cursed at the night. I let it all out. Finally, exhausted and drained I went back to my room and crawled inside my sleeping bag.

I closed my eyes and soon enough, there they were again,

the voices and the sounds. But this time I was asleep and could not open my eyes. As much as I tried to open them I could not. I heard my children running down the stairs the squeals of delight and joy on Christmas mornings, running for the school bus, laughing with their friends in their rooms. I could hear them coughing in the night, calling my name, having bad dreams, calling me to hold them, to sing to them, making them feel safe. I could smell the bacon seeping under my bedroom door the mornings they told me to stay in bed, Mother's Day. I hear them laughing, I hear them fighting, I hear the pots and pans banging around, the cracking of eggs. I hear the quiet when they are doing what they should not be. I try to get up but I cannot move. I am asleep. I want to wake up, run down the hall, cradle them, go down to my daughter's room and see her sleeping, I want to wake up but I cannot. All through the night, the voices continued to haunt my dreams and I wanted them to be real.

Now I have to be prepared to fight for my own life, my own future, all alone, without the protection of these walls. Again I am asking myself, am I as brave as everyone is telling me or am I being foolish thinking I can just drive away? Who does that? What does it matter now? The wheels are in motion and I have given all my faith over to the Universe to keep me safe and guide me with the right decisions, to make the right turns on the highway of my life.

Now on this morning, my last morning, I will myself off the floor. I walk into my bathroom. White and green tiles are warm on my feet. I walk to the window; feel the sun on my body, look out at the trees, out at the lake in the distance, to the deck below. Everything is still and quiet. I see my gardens, where life is starting to push up through the ground, the little green sprouts of life reaching for the sky. They are me, all of them. They are me. All winter long, I lay dormant in my life waiting for today, to break through the frozen ground and reach for the sun. I should feel some happiness, a sense of freedom but I cannot help but grieve for the life I have to let go of.

I have to remind myself constantly that these are the gardens I cursed just days before as the weeds had already started to take over. I have to remind myself these are the walls I no longer want to fix. I have to remind myself these are the carpets I no longer want to clean. "It is too big, too much, too many weeds, too many cracks. Let it go Suzanne, let it go!" The conflict that is going on in side me is overwhelming. I turn away from the window for the last time.

I open the shower door stare at the open space, step inside the stall. Two shower heads—that is a lonely site. This is another reason you are leaving Suzanne, I tell myself, there's no one to share the shower with. There I go again; talking out loud. "Stop it!" I pull the knob for the last time and the water flows the same way it did yesterday, steady and warm. I stare at the other shower head and turn it on too. I love the way the water hits me from all sides. I want to stand here forever. I want the water to wash away this pain that has become a part of me. I watch the water, and the bubbles from the soap swirl at my feel, circle the drain and disappear. I wish it had the power to wash me free of these feelings and thoughts; I want those to circle at my feet and then be gone too.

These thoughts I am having are ridiculous, I know that. But for some reason I feel the need to think them, keep them close, on the periphery of my mind. I continue the thoughts even though I know that leaving here is the right thing. But I am afraid if I let them go I will have no thoughts or feelings at all. I know if I stay in this house I will go crazy. The evidence is already starting to present itself. I don't want to become the crazy old lady who lives in the big house, talking to herself when she is alone, and letting stray cats come to stay.

Suddenly it dawns on me that I have created everything that is happening to me. At one time or another I planted the seeds of running away from all of this, and the seeds took root. Even when everyone was living here, when the children were home, I was planning for this day. I was always a realist; I knew they would grow up and move away, it is the natural evolution of North American life. I clearly remember, and it was not that long ago, that I wanted them to be gone, not before they were ready, but gone, happily living their own lives, and now they are. I remember the times, visualizing in my leisure moments, while listening to the chaos that happens when you have children, I remember thinking how wonderful it would be just to get into my vehicle and drive away, if only for a moment of peace. While I was doing this there was never a destination and I never saw myself returning because I never really thought it would happen.

At this moment, and it is a little too late, I knew I should have made my vision a lot more specific. Because in two days I was making that desire a reality and I had no destination although I told those who asked to avoid sounding like I was crazy and acting irrationally and going off without a plan that I was going to Alaska. I had heard that that was the place people went to when they ran away.

I was physically tired and emotionally drained of all it took to care for this life. I wanted the gardens to be concrete and the pool filled with rocks. Now I questioned all the things I had done. "Did I plant the wrong seeds? Did I put the wrong message out to the Universe and now the Universe has grown this garden of despair for me?" But is it despair or is it excitement that is making my insides shake and seize up with fear and my mind run rampant with maniacal thoughts?

Drying myself off, I twisted my hair up in my one towel and walked naked across the warm tiles to the carpet, making sure to notice every detail of the room, the window sills, the lights in the ceiling, the bathtub that sits in the corner, the glass bricks surrounding the shower that allowed in the light, the empty closet, the sounds as I walked, the look of my wet foot prints. I paused at every window trying to remember the image of what I saw even though it was already tattooed onto my brain. "I will never forget this. I was a fortunate woman to have been able to create this for my family, to live, grow and be safe here. But now it is time to let go Suzanne."

I hear the ghosts again; I wish I could see them as clearly as I hear them. I talk to them, thank them, ask them to keep the next family safe and happy in this home, then, I tell them goodbye. I laugh at myself, convinced I have really lost my mind now.

I zip up my bags, roll up my sleeping bag, and take my one towel and my pillow, but the feeling of forgetting something is nagging. There is no place to hide anything but I walk around my room, look in the closet, and open the drawers and look in the cabinet under the sink. There is nothing. I know I am just procrastinating; I do not want to walk through the bedroom door.

Dressed and ready to go, I am early, I still have some time. I walk out of my room and stand at the top of the stairs and set my bags down, but I am not ready to descend yet. I walk down the long hallway leading to the empty bedrooms, look in, walk in and open the closets. Nothing left.

I turn and walk into the games room with the big round window where I stood so many times watching my kids play hockey and basketball in the driveway, watching for them all to come home on the school bus, where I stood as they slept peacefully in their beds behind those walls, watching the snow fall in the night silently filling up the driveway, creating a magical wonderland my children would wake up to.

I turn and look at the pool table with the balls set up for the next game. I want to take one of the cues and smash the white ball so hard into the perfectly racked triangle of balls, breaking the silence. I want to crank up some music and dance once more in this room. I run my hand over the felt as I walk around the table, wishing for just one more game with my children, just one more game with my friends.

Back at the window I stand with my arms crossed tightly over my chest, as if I am preventing myself from exploding, my forehead pressed against the glass, trying desperately not to fall apart.

I see the fire pit that we sang and danced around so many times, wild and free. The gigantic pine tree that Hurricane Juan knocked over like a toothpick, the same tree my son fell out of and broke his arm, the same tree whose root system I spent weeks cleaning, creating a piece of art.

As I walk back down the hall towards the stairs, I slide my fingers along the walls, leaving a line of prints no one will see. I stop at the top of the stairs. My suitcases, sleeping bag and pillow are waiting for me. It will take two trips to get them down. I cannot look back. I talk to myself. "Do not look back Suzanne, pick up the bags and go. Do not go back into any room, do not, for if you do, you will be late and you will be having a breakdown in someone else's home."

Descending the curved staircase for the last time, I keep my head up. I look through the window above the front door and watch as the tree tops disappear below the sill with each step I take. I pause on the bottom stair, take a deep breath and step down.

I take my bags to my truck, stand there and look at them. All stacked neatly with room to sleep in the back should the need arise. Again I realize I manifested this. I told the Universe I wanted a smaller home but I should have been more specific. I close the hatch and turn to walk the brick walkway, back into my home to lock the door for the last time. As I do this, I notice the bricks shifting and lifting on the walkway, heaved from the ice in the ground. I remember cursing them while I shovelled the snow, coming to a dead stop as I was going full tilt pushing the snow, how the pain shot up through my arms. I swore I would not be shovelling snow off this walkway one more winter. I realized at that moment, I manifested this desire, I will not be shovelling snow off this walkway ever again.

I take my shoes off for the last time, wanting to feel the solid of the ceramic floor. Sliding my feet along I feel the rise and fall of each tile. I stand at the edge of the hardwood, not wanting to step on it, afraid I will fall down into the warmth of it and not get up. Why didn't I accept the invitations from the kids or my friends to be here when I did this? Because I wanted to be alone, I wanted to experience this by myself. I knew that by leaving this house I was going to suffer one of the most profound emotional experiences of my life and I did not want to have any witnesses who would create inhibitions that would interfere with this moment. I wanted to feel everything, every emotion that had been manifesting long before I put the for sale sign at the end of the driveway.

As I went from room to room on the main floor, I was happy, sad, delirious, angry, confused, conflicted, excited and afraid. I was full of doubt and fear. Talking out loud, raising my voice in the empty rooms just to hear the echo, I said "Goodbye, thank you … I'll miss you. Goodbye."

I walk past the kitchen, down the hall and hear the sounds of my grandson and I playing hockey in what we called, "the hockey hall of fame." I remembered his little voice screeching with delight as he slapped that foam hockey puck as hard as he could at me, the goalie. I would have to leap out of the way and he would yell, "I scored!" and jump up and down and do his victory dance. We would laugh and I would wrestle him to the floor. This hall also leads to my daughter's room, now his mother. I walk in and open the closet. Nothing.

"Hello?"

"Hi, I'm here, in Carly's room."

My friend Lee has shown up. I forgot that she was coming to pick up the shop vac that was in the garage.

"Hey coffee, thanks so much!"

"How ya doing"

"Great, just saying good bye to the ghosts who tormented me all night."

"Really?"

"Yes, my overactive imagination was working overtime and of course, you know me, I had to indulge it."

She is looking at me too closely, looking for signs that had become far too familiar to her—the knitted eyebrows, the quiver of the lower lip.

"I'm okay."

We talk for a bit, reflecting about our own good times here, and the not so good times, especially this past winter She rubs my shoulder and says, "We should get going, it's almost noon." We walk outside and I help her put the vacuum cleaner in her car.

"You coming over?"

"Yes, I'll be right behind you, just going to lock up."

Lee drives away and I turn and stare up at the house. I am so happy I do not have to stain that part way up there, where the ladder could not reach.

Back in the front hall, the door wide open, with my shoes back on, I look up the staircase one last time. I look into the dining room one last time. It is noon and I am now standing in someone else's home. I set the alarm for the last time. I pull the door closed and turn the key. That's it. Locked. Now all I have to do is walk to the truck, get in and drive away.

Okay, I have done it. I am in my truck. I put my seat belt on and it holds me down. I drive the long driveway away from this life. "Do not look back. Do not look in the rear view mirror."

I turn the corner out of the driveway and pull to the side of my road and turn off my truck. I cannot see the house through the trees of what was my property three minutes ago. I pick up my cell phone. I am shaking as I push the buttons. There is only one person on this planet that I feel the need to call, my cousin Roslyn. She is the only person who has walked this life with me, the only person who understands why this is so hard. She and I talk almost every day. She has been the most consistent person in my life. Although she lives in another city in another province, I know she is feeling for me right now, watching her clock, picturing what I am doing minute by minute this morning.

I hear the ring through the hands-free unit above my head. She picks it up on the second ring because she knows it is me and has been waiting for my call. The only word that comes out of my mouth is her name, "Ros…" I cannot say another word. She says to me "Suzanne, it's okay. Cry honey…cry. I wish I was there. I am so sorry you are going through this. I wish I could take the pain away. Cry, I'm here. I'm there." I cannot even find the words to describe the hysteria I am experiencing. Locked in my car, on the side of the road, sobbing so uncontrollably, I cannot breathe, gasping for breath, heaving so violently I feel as if I am breaking ribs with each gasp.

"Suzanne, Suzanne…can you hear me?"

"Yes. I'm sitting just outside the driveway."

"Listen to me, you must drive away. You have to get off of that street. You have done all you can do. Yes, you had a great life there, now you get to live the life *you* want, a life you deserve. Turn the truck back on and drive away. You can do it. Look at what you have done in your life. Look at all the hard times you have suffered alone, the years alone raising children, looking after that giant house and property. It sucked the life out of you and now you are free of it! Go…. you are now free! It may not seem so great today but it will be soon, I promise. How many people on this earth get to do what you are doing? How many people have the courage to do what you have done? Go now and don't look back. Do you have somewhere to go and be with someone?"

"Yes, Lee is expecting me."

"Oh good, drive to Lee's, she will make you tea, coffee or ply you with wine, whatever you need…just go there. Lee will allow you to be this way until you are ready to be this way no more."

"Okay. I will call you shortly. Thank you Roslyn." It was all I could sputter out. I dried my face, caught my breath and drove to Lee's. I did as Ros suggested, I did not look in the rear view mirror and I do not remember the drive to Lee's.

In Lee's driveway I sat there for a minute looking at her

gardens in front of me. Growing straight up and thriving I saw the plants we dug from the ground of my gardens the week before and they were loving their new home. I saw the garden ornaments and the wooden swing fitting in so well, like they had always been there. I smiled at them. It gave me hope that I will thrive and grow straight up when I am planted in my new life. I told her one day I will be back to dig these up and take my swing and ornaments back. But at that moment I couldn't picture it. I felt dehydrated and wilted. I wanted to dig a hole, lie down in the dirt and die. No energy to get out of the vehicle and walk into her home, no energy to talk about anything. No energy to get on with the new life I had plotted, planned and schemed about for so long.

Then there was Lee, standing on her porch, watching me.

"What are you doing? Come in."

Walking felt robotic, mechanical. Why did I feel so heavy? Why did it feel like my body was still sitting in the driver's seat? The words coming out of my mouth sounded delayed as they echoed in my head.

"Can I get you something? Are you hungry? Suzanne…"

"Pardon, I'm sorry, I'm listening, just not comprehending so well right now." I didn't want to talk; I didn't want to admit I had no home. I did not want to say the words … I have no home. I did not want to think my children had no home to go home to for Sunday dinners. I did not want to sit down, stand up or drive anywhere. I had no idea what to do, how to feel, what to say or where to go.

I picked a chair in her kitchen, sat in it and did nothing but breathe. She looked at me for what seemed like a long time, waiting for me to come back to earth. She could tell I had been crying and I told her I had been speaking with Roslyn. I told her again about the ghosts that kept waking me up. She made me tea and we sat there in silence letting the reality sink in.

"What are you going to do now? I know you are not leaving for a couple of days. Do you want to stay here?" Everyone knew I was leaving town in 2 days and I had choices of where I could stay but I declined them all.

"No, I am going to go downtown, check into a hotel with a big bed and sleep until I wake up. I am going to take my children out to dinner tomorrow night. Then the next morning … I'm going to drive away. But thanks."

As we sat there, Lee looking at me with her big dark eyes, wondering what to say to this woman who was sitting in her kitchen almost comatose, she started to tell me how fortunate I was to be doing what I was doing. I know she meant well but I thought if I heard this one more time, I was going to scream! She too thinks I am brave. She tells me how she wants to run away and start anew all the time, but wouldn't know where to begin. Too many ties to this place, to this town. The dream is a good one but there is no way she could do it and she has no desire to do it. She loves to go away but she loves coming back here. I feel envious of her knowing where she wants to be.

It's a funny thing when people say to me, and so many do, that they would like to do what I am doing but are too attached, too lazy, have too much commitment, or the biggest thing … are too afraid. I, on the other hand, feel no attachments to this town other than my children, and they have their own lives now. I really like this city and unless some life-changing event happens while I'm on this journey, I will come back to live here.

I am not lazy and have a huge desire to see what the Universe has to offer me and the truth was I was too afraid to stay. I was afraid that if I stayed I would be sucked back into the vortex of the daily routine that had suffocated me into making the drastic decisions I had made in the first place. If I stayed I was afraid my life was going to be a ritual of continually fixing something or someone and I would never know what was out there for me. I was afraid I would never find out why I was put on this earth, what my true purpose was after raising kids, what was around the next corner or over the next mountain. There would be no time, I would be too busy doing what everyone else wanted and expected me to do.

There was a stirring in my soul that for years I had to suppress because something had to be fixed or someone had to be cared for and I didn't mind any of it. It was my choice. I chose my life when I was young. It was a conscious decision I remember so clearly, to have children when I was young so when they were ready to move along with their lives I would still be young enough to explore my own life in whatever manner I chose. I have no regrets about this decision, not one. Besides, I had made a promise I intended to keep.

Sitting in Lee's kitchen I started to think about the promise that made little sense to me at the time I made it.

CHAPTER FIVE

The Promise

My mother would talk with me in the few minutes of the day she was able to talk in the days before she died. She would never have the opportunity to meet my boys, they were not born yet, but my daughter had been cuddled, rocked and loved by her. She said to me as she lay dying, "Suzanne, you will be surprised at how different life will be when your children are happy, healthy and have moved out on their own. You will have survived the hardest job in the world, being a mother. Do the very best you can everyday, because as you can see, the time for us to die comes far too soon. While I lay here, I have had lots of time to think and the only regret I have is that I did not listen to my heart after you all moved out. It spoke to me often but I was too afraid to really listen and now my life is ending. I have talked with your brothers and your sister and I have not said to them what I am saying to you. You are a lot like me, I saw myself in you and I do not want you to make the same mistake I made."

I could not say a word.

"I want you to make one promise to me."

I was sitting on the side of my old bed, holding her hand, in my old bedroom, in the home where I grew up, and I could not even comprehend that she was dying let alone make her a promise about a life I had yet to live.

"When the time comes and you have done the best you could with your children, promise me you will not allow the world you find yourself in to dictate the kind of life you should be living to you just because it is what everyone else is doing. Promise me that when you feel the pull and tug on your heart, a restlessness in your soul and it is telling you to do something different with your life, pay attention to it, do not sit still and ignore it because those around you tell you that it is a ridiculous or selfish idea; promise me you will explore that adventurous spirit you have always had."

I remember her words made no sense to me as I had always felt I was where I was supposed to be and did pretty much anything I wanted to do. But I was young and had not experienced enough of life to understand what she was saying about the restlessness and the pull and tug at my heart.

"If you find yourself restless, just follow your heart. It will be broken along the way, I promise you that, but it will rarely be wrong and you will be stronger because of those heartbreaks, trust in that. Use your logical mind to keep you financially secure, but never worry about the money, it will always be there for you when you need it. But most of all… Sannie Babe, (her nickname for me) … promise me you will love yourself, be kind to yourself and trust your instincts." My mother died three days later. She was only 47. I was 25.

I understand now, the restlessness in my soul, the pull and tug on my heart and I want to speak to my mother and tell her I am going to find out what my restless spirit is seeking. I want to tell her I have taken the risks; I have listened to my heart and *it is* broken today. I have kept my promise. I have left my children safe with all the tools to look after themselves I did the best I could. I taught them well and I am showing them it is okay to follow your heart even though it will break, as they know mine is broken today. I want to tell her I am so afraid today and have been for so long I cannot remember when I was not, but I am listening to my heart and trusting my instincts. I want to tell her I got into my truck and drove away from a life that was no longer fulfilling to me. I want to tell her I am terrified every waking moment and my nights are filled with restless sleep, nightmares and loneliness. I want to drive to her, have her hug me and hear her sing to me. I want to hear her voice telling me everything is going to be okay. But I cannot. I can only continue to keep my promise to her until this restlessness finds some peace, harmony and balance.

It would be so good to hear her voice as I know it would make the fear subside, something only mothers can do, even for a moment, to allow me to sleep through one night. I want to sit with her, have a cup of tea, laugh about all of this and have her tell me she is proud of me for doing what she was too afraid to do. But I cannot.

I want her to know that I am okay. I want to tell her the visions, the dreams and goals I have for myself. I want to tell her I am working hard at moving forward to attain them and I am getting closer every day and that I am getting stronger and happier too. But I cannot; I just have to trust that she knew I would keep my promise. Somewhere in my heart I know she knows I have kept my promise.

CHAPTER SIX

The Gypsy and the Warrior

It started with a pondering question to myself. In two years, when my youngest child will be graduating high school, what am *I* going to do then? Raising children for 30 years, 98% as a single parent and still single today by choice, what am I going to do after that? What is on the other side of that mountain and am I brave enough to find out?

I had travelled enough back roads, explored many coves and bays underwater diving with my daughter and friends, hiked lots of trails, and climbed many hills, (Nova Scotia doesn't really have mountains) to know I was done with Nova Scotia for a while. I was ready for new adventures but how was I going to this?

What would it take to be free to explore the other side of the mountain? Where would I live and what would I do for money? These words kept coming back to me, "Do what you love, and the money will come." That's all fine and well when you are young and if you know what you love to do. I am not old but I knew what I was dreaming about was going to take money. Although I enjoyed the many things I have done for income, I did not "love" anything I had worked at so far in my life. I only know these things: I love to travel and travelling requires money. I love to write but writing also takes money. What was I going to do? I knew I would find the answers.

Apparently, it is "normal" to dream about changing our lives but, "not normal" to actually do it. It is difficult to conceive that you would quit your job, resign from your career, sell your home and seek out a new life. It is even more, "less normal," for a mother to think about leaving her children behind, even if they are grown, and just drive away. At least many of my friends saw it that way. But I can tell you this. There are many, many mothers who dream about the day their children are living on their own and they see themselves driving away. And for a lot of them it cannot happen soon enough.

To many of the people I know it was only a dream not something anyone actually did. Were they afraid to let go, to step outside their safe houses without a plan? To me … it seemed perfectly natural. But then again, up until now, I always had a safe house to return too. So was it perfectly natural or was I just dreaming too? Did they know something I didn't know?

I must have sounded daft to them. But I couldn't stop the vision that continued to show up in my head when I thought about the next phase of my life. Then the fear started to creep in, little by little, without warning. Was it created by other people inflicting their own fears? Was I picking up their vibrations of doubt? Maybe, but I have never allowed this to affect decisions in the past. Why was I starting to doubt myself and my decisions now? Why was I allowing this fear to take over my thinking and most importantly how would I stop it? My answer is always the same; I stop it by doing exactly what I always do. I go to the source of the fear and in this case the source of the fear is the question, "Can I really get in my truck and drive away?"

I am not normal. This is not my description of myself; everything I do is normal…to me. Those that know me well have often said, "Suzanne, no one I know would do that, like that, or think like that, except you"…what ever *that* was. At the end of last Fall, when I told them I was driving Jack's car across the country for him, on the brink of a Canadian winter, it did not surprise them. Telling them I was doing it *alone* apparently confirmed I was not normal … at least to them. It did not even enter my head to be concerned. They, on the other hand had all kinds of reasons I should be concerned. They tried inflicting their own fears on me and giving me their reasons they would never do what I was going to do, especially the women. Their fears made no sense to me, they were mostly concerned about the amount of time I would be alone and that was the part I was looking forward to the most. I am a logical woman; I would take precautions to keep myself safe. Most people do not purposefully plan to put themselves in harm's way, and I would not either.

When I told my friends I'd resigned from my career, they thought I must have found another job, but I had not. When I told them I'd sold my home they assumed I was buying a smaller one in the same area. I was not. Therefore, you can imagine their reaction when I told them I was leaving town and I had no idea when or if I would be back here to live.

Their reactions were varied but basically the same.

"What do mean your leaving town?"

"Where are you going?"

"What about your kids?"

"You can't just leave."

I would look at them and say, "Whatever do you mean? Yes I can, I can do anything I want."

This is the attitude that has given me the nickname The Gypsy.

A Gypsy? Yes I am, but not the thieving kind, the good kind we conjure up in our minds—free spirited, transient, living with few ties, not much baggage and going on great adventures. I was always up for an adventure. Most often, I was the one creating the adventure.

For a restless spirit or a gypsy-like mind, sitting still can be difficult. We are the ones sitting with our backs to the wall scouting out all the exits to make the fast get away when the event is over. We want to be moving, exploring, investigating all there is outside our comfort zone. It is exciting to us. We thrive on the unknown. It is scary and exciting to us … ooooah, what's going to happen next? Let's just drive a bit further, let's see what is around the next corner. We are like children cranking the Jack-in-the-Box faster and faster because we love the thrill of the *POP!* We do not know when it is going to happen; we just know *it is* going to happen. That is how certain I was when I made the decisions that have changed my life forever and I can *never ever* go back to living how I was.

In the beginning I had no idea how or when I was going to achieve this vision, this dream. I have learned not to concern myself with the how … because "how" does not matter, but I knew the "when" was near when my last child came bounding down the stairs with his play station in hand, a suitcase with his clothes in it, and rummaged through my fridge and pantry, proudly proclaiming he was moving out.

I did not even know what my fears were; I just knew I was about to embark upon the scariest and the most exciting part of my life, and because I was feeling scared and insecure all the time at this point, I was looking forward to the exciting parts. As I have been heard to say, many times, "if it's not scary and exciting it's probably not worth doing." Not my saying but I like it.

I on the other hand, prefer to think of myself as a Warrior. A Warrior, in my mind, goes into battle with a winning attitude. They are not afraid of the fight. They are leaders, and lead themselves and their armies into battle without questioning the outcome. There can only be one outcome for a Warrior—victory. A Warrior has integrity and respect for their opponent. They understand there can only be one winner. I decided I was going to be the winner. I was going to win the battle I was embarking on. I was going to fight to achieve all the goals I set for myself and I was not going back until I did. Therefore, my goals had to be attainable and the reward had to be worth it.

I do not think my goals are unreasonable—peace in my mind, love in my life and money in the bank. The rewards are that I get to go back to see my children, grandchildren and my friends—victorious. Nevertheless, my opponents are worthy ones—fear and self doubt—and they often win many battles.

When I feel a change in the wind, and it sweeps warm over my skin, I shudder with excitement. I love that feeling. I know something in my life is changing. I believe this represents something I have thought about, is coming to life, I am just not sure what that something is, when this is happening.

I used to focus on those shudders and try to figure out what was on those winds of change. What did it mean? I used to talk about it, asking those around me, "did you feel that?" Now I do not mention it, I just embrace the feeling and let it go. I give it over to the universe and have faith it will present the reasons to me when the time is right. Once again, I find myself practicing patience.

Since receiving a copy of a book written by Napoleon Hill, "Think and Grow Rich" and enrolling in the 12-week Bob Proctor program "Thinking into Results," to increase my productivity in business and my personal life, I practice daily, to go where few minds dare to go. I often find myself slipping into my conscious un-comfort zone until I become so uncomfortable, I have to take action or I am going to go mad! I am literally transforming my mind into my most valuable asset just by thinking I *can*.

When I am sitting quietly thinking about my past life, I miss parts of it, of course, but I was being untruthful to myself in that life. It was "safe," and I know I can recreate the very best "safe" parts and make them better. Even when I left it behind and did not have a plan, I knew my uncertain future was going to better, I had made the decision it was going to be.

That life was all fine when I was raising children but now I have to raise me. And how do you raise yourself? I am trusting that the universe has a plan for me and my adventurous spirit. I am practising positive thinking and creating positive vibrations knowing it will bring me to exactly what I am supposed to do, where I am supposed to go and how I am supposed to be. I know that sounds flaky, but I can't help believing it. That does not mean I sit around and wait, I have to be proactive, keep positive thoughts and keep my feet moving forward.

We know ourselves well enough to know when we have had enough. When our stomachs are full we put the fork down and push away from the table. When we have had enough mentally we have to remove ourselves from the cause. I have had to remove myself from negative energy around me just to sit for a period of time, quietly creating positive thoughts. This is not easy to do because there is so much sadness and ungratefulness in the world and I am not immune to it.

If the people around me lived their lives in a negative way, had self defeatist attitudes towards life, spoke out loud too often about how their lives sucked and if I saw they were not actively seeking ways to improve them, I had to let them go. It sounds harsh but it was necessary. Although I would try to help them, listen to them, introduce them to the books I was reading, the CD's and DVD's I was using that have helped improve my own mind and attitude ultimately it was up to them. If they didn't want to take advantage of these tools after witnessing firsthand how effectively they had worked for me, I had to let them go. I pray everyday to the "whatever I can conceive and believe, I can achieve"* gods to help them. I believe with all my heart they will succeed if they take that first step of believing in themselves. It has to become so uncomfortable for them that they can no longer stand it before they take the first step toward their own Terror Barrier and give it a kick. Until they do that I have had to continue to love them from afar.

Was this difficult to do? Yes, very hard. But it's funny what the results of letting them go have been. Since being away from them, they too have taken steps to change their lives by facing their own fears. Some have moved to new homes, creating positive environments for themselves. Some have changed jobs even though it meant less money and they are happier now because they have more time for the important things they had no time to pay attention to before. Some have embarked upon new relationships when they were beginning to believe they were going to be alone forever. Some have left unhappy relationships they thought they were going to be in forever.

Why did this happen after I left? Why could they not make any of these changes while I was there? They talked about the changes they wanted to make with me, especially

* Napoleon Hill

when they were helping me pack up my home. I could see the anxiety in their faces when they spoke of how their lives as they were currently living them bored them. I could see the despair in their faces when they talked about the dead end jobs they'd been in for so long and the fear that would cross their faces when I suggested they find another one they liked. I can still see the tears as they talked about their loneliness and fear of being alone forever. I see the tears of those who feared being in loveless relationships that would probably see them die of unhappiness long before they should just to get out of the relationship.

I believe they found the courage to face their fears by watching me—the Gypsy with the Warrior attitude—take control of my life, step into the unknown void and just do it. If this is the case, and I did inspire my friends to change what they did not like about their lives, I am thrilled I had this affect. I want to believe it was because I inspired them to do their own self-analysis and they found what they truly desired and took action to achieve it. I cannot wait to get back with them and toast all our new lives.

When I speak with them on the phone I can hear it in their voices. Their attitudes have changed and they speak positively about their lives. They have new visions and goals. They went to war and I know it was not easy. I followed their transitions with regular updates over the phone and e-mail. I was not with them physically when they won their battles, but apparently it was better that I was not.

They became Warriors and they helped me achieve another goal I had no idea I had. I found a way to help my friends help themselves by showing them it is okay to step outside your comfort zone, believe in yourself and trust your instincts.

CHAPTER SEVEN

Driving Away

The morning I was leaving Nova Scotia there was nothing left for me to do except say goodbye to Nick. I had spent the past several weeks saying good bye to friends and I had said my good byes to Carly the night before after having dinner with all three of my kids. Nick came down to my hotel to have breakfast with me. Driving him back to his apartment we were trying so hard to be brave. "Nick, honey, you will be fine without me. I am only a plane ride away if you need me."

"I know."

I didn't want to look at him as I could tell the closer we got to his place, the more real to us that I am leaving became, and the harder it was for him to be strong. The tears came from me first and they were contagious. From the corner of my eye I saw his shoulders drop as he gave in to the emotion. The sobs that came out of Nick were heart wrenching. The dam had broken and the two of us were in North Street traffic crying our hearts out. Using our sleeves to try and dry our faces, we tried to calm each other down. I pulled up to the curb of his apartment and he reached over to hug me. I said, "Let's get out of the truck."

Standing on the sidewalk it seemed to me he had grown taller since last night. As he towered over me, he wrapped his big arms around me and I laid my head on his chest feeling the rise and fall with each breath he took.

"Baby Boy, promise me you will look after yourself, your brother, sister and your nephew. I need you to be the big strong man I see before me. I cannot be worried about you. Please promise me you will take care of yourself. Trust your instincts and trust you will be ok when things get tough, and I can promise you there will be a few rough days, especially the next few coming up. Gather your friends close and go to Carly's if you get too lonely for me."

"I will momma."

"I have to go."

I got in my truck and looked back at him standing there. He was no longer my dependant little boy, he is a man and I am proud of him. I smiled at him, wove and drove away.

My oldest son Marc was waiting for me at his home, because he was going to travel with me for the couple of days it would take to get to Ontario. He had some time off and I did not want to travel those first days on my own. I was afraid I would get to the border of New Brunswick and turn around, so I invited him to travel with me.

He was standing outside with a few friends when I arrived, and as he put his bags in my truck, he asked, "Can I drive?"

"No."

When we started to drive I told him it was important for me to drive this first leg. I wanted to take responsibility for driving myself away from everyone and everything.

He nodded his understanding but I wonder if he really did understand.

Long periods of time passed without either one of us speaking. I let the local radio station play until we were outside its reception area. I tried to take in every thing I passed as if I were seeing it for the first time instead of the last time. I am not sure why I was acting as if I would never return; maybe I was scrutinizing everything so I could make decisions in the future about whether I actually wanted to return.

As we got closer to crossing over the border from Nova Scotia into New Brunswick, every breath I took became a conscious effort. I would sigh then sigh again. I was trying to fill my lungs but I could not.

"You okay mom?"

"Yes sweetie, I'm just catching my breath."

I could not look at him. I could not look into his big brown eyes. I could feel them staring at me then he would look away, stare out the window.

I wanted to talk but I didn't know what to say.

I tried so hard not to transfer my anxious emotions, but I could tell this was not working. He started shifting in his seat.

When I did look over at him, he was staring ahead at the road, and I saw there were tears falling down his face but he made no sound.

I put my hand on his.

"It's going to be ok pal, I promise. We will get through this. You know I have to do this."

"I know. I was just thinking about not being able to drop in to see you whenever I want."

His voice is soft and full of love.

He is struggling to speak, "I don't like to think of you being alone. It freaks me out to think you have no destination and no one will be there when you get there."

"I know where I'm going."

"Where?

"Alaska." It came out of my mouth so easily, so naturally, "Alaska," as if I said it everyday.

"Why Alaska? I have heard you say that but it makes no sense to me, you don't know anyone there."

"I don't know why, something is pulling me in that direction. I won't know people in a lot of the places I am going."

I can tell he is picturing everything he ever knew or saw about Alaska.

I say to him, "Someone once said to me, Alaska is the place people go when they run away."

"Yes but it is so far away."

"I want to go somewhere where I do not know anyone and they won't know me. I want to be anonymous for a while."

He laughed, "You could never be anonymous."

"What do you mean? Yes I can."

"Really mom, look at you, cute little blonde, driving a little Mercedes SUV, out-of-town license plates. You don't know who will notice these things and I can see it now—you pull into some remote Alaskan diner, the parking lot filled with pickup trucks and rifle racks. You walk in. Do you think no one is going to look at you?"

"Maybe, but so what, they probably look at every one who walks through the door."

"I don't think you should go there by yourself. You will attract attention you don't need."

"I thought of that already. But I cannot allow that to stop me. I will stay aware of who is looking at me. I will try to sit in places where I can keep my eye on my truck too. I promise. Please try not to worry."

I chuckled to myself thinking about Marc worrying about me. His life was changing quickly too and he was soon going to find out what it was like to worry about a child of his own. The following autumn he was going to become a father.

When he came to me and told me, he was going to be a father, I was confused.

He was pacing around the deck as I was weeding one of the gardens. You can tell when one of your children is trying to find the words to tell you something they know is going to be a shock. So I did what I always do, I let them know I am aware they have something to say and tell them when they are ready to tell me I am ready to listen. Then he just spit it out.

"I'm going to be a father"

I stood up and looked him square in the face.

"What do mean you are going to be a father? You are just a kid yourself."

He was not a kid, just a young man.

"Sure, one day when you have all your ducks in a row, you and your wife will sit down, the two of you will have a discussion and blah, blah blah ..." His eyes glazed over listening to me.

"Haha, that's funny … now tell me why you are really here. Do you need money?"

Of course! They always need money. I wanted it to be money, it was the only time in my life I wanted my child to be standing there asking me for money. But I knew what he was telling me was a fact. I was going to be a grandmother again.

After talking with the mother of my future grandchild, my mind was at ease. She is a good little mom, and I knew my son would make a very loving, attentive father. I am so proud of him. Knowing the heartaches children inflict that I have been suffering from for 30 years, I sighed, hugged them and then realized I might not be here when this babe was born but would have to deal with that when the time came.

The time came. Did I go back? I did not. I was in a Northern British Columbian town on the look out for grizzly bears that were prowling the neighbourhood, trying to figure out where I would go from here. Alaska was just a few mountains away.

CHAPTER EIGHT

Men … Do They Suffer Too?

The rain had been holding off for us as we crossed the border into New Brunswick. We could see dark clouds ahead and we would wave our hand like Jedi Warriors and say, "Move away," and when they did we would laugh, mystified by our power. This opened the conversation to how we have the power to light our own way.

Marc was driving. I was staring off into the distance and every now and then I would look in the side view mirror to see what was behind us—what I was leaving behind. I could see the dark rain clouds that we had pushed away were now directly over the road we had just passed.

I said "Isn't funny how we did that to the clouds, made them stay off our path until we passed?" He nodded and I could tell he was thinking about other things. I asked him, "Marc, do you believe you have the ability to attain anything you want to have?"

"Sometimes."

"I believe I can have any thing I truly desire."

He shook his head. I could tell he was thinking …here she goes again with her "the universe will bring us all we truly desire" talk.

"Marc, have you ever had moments when you realized that something you thought about or, someone you thought about suddenly appeared and it freaked you out?"

"Yes, we all have had that happen to us."

"How about a song that comes on the radio that you haven't heard in a while but were just thinking about it. Isn't that the weirdest thing when that happens?"

"Yes, I have a song in my head right now that I have been thinking about for the last couple of hundred kilometres and I can't get it out of my head. I can't think of the name of the group either and it is bugging me."

"Sing a few lines, maybe I can help." We are a family of trivia, especially music. If I do not know the song, lyric or singer, it is almost guaranteed, one phone call and Carly will know.

"I will walk 500 miles and I will walk 500 more."

We start to sing the song and are laughing at how appropriate this song is for what we are doing. But for the life of us we cannot remember who the artists are.

We make our one phone call but get no response. Soon enough we have forgotten about the song.

"Marc, tell me what you think about what I am doing."

"What do you mean?"

"Oh, you know, just packing up and leaving, wanting to go to Alaska. Do you think I am crazy?"

"Well, not crazy, but everyone who knows you has always known you to be different."

"Different? We are all different but what do you mean?"

He is feeling uncomfortable now and his ears are turning red.

I turn in my seat and look at him.

"Tell me what you mean."

"Oh mom, you know what I mean. You do things very few people would actually do. Lots of people say they are going to do things when the time is right but when the time comes they don't. When you get an idea in your head there is no changing it. So when you said when the house sold and you were leaving town, we believed you."

"What do mean by that? I do things very few people actually do."

"Like right now, you said you were going to sell the house and leave, just go with no destination. Who does that? I knew when you told me, I could see it in your eyes; you were leaving and not coming back until you got better."

"Better?"

"Yes, better. Remember last Fall when I came in the house and you were sitting on the couch with your computer on the table in front of you. You had started writing The Lippy Cats and you were just sitting there, staring at the words in front of you. You looked up when I came in and I sat beside you. You were not my mother anymore."

"What? I will always be your mother."

"No that's not what I mean. Suddenly you were someone else to me. I had never seen this person before. I can't explain it."

Trying not to seem anxious about what he was trying to say, even though I was, I adjusted myself in my seat, so as not to stare so intensely at him while he was driving and talking, I watched the road in front of us. I wanted him to feel he could find the words to describe what and who he saw sitting there. I didn't want to appear eager so I bit my lip to stop blurting out suggestions. I wanted to hear in his own words without my influence, what he saw that day.

"You were broken, I never saw a broken person before. It all seemed to happen so fast and no one knew what to do. We didn't know what to do for you except make you tea. You looked different, Nick said you looked like a ghost when he was there one day, it scared him I think."

"I didn't know you talked with each other about me."

"We don't really but this was different, especially since last Fall."

"What do you think happened last Fall?"

"Everything changed. You were changing. It was like everyday you moved further and further away from everyone. You stopped going out, stopped working, stopped laughing, stop going to your book club, stopped playing Bonko with all your girlfriends. You just stopped. We didn't know what to think. We couldn't believe that your life was so affected by that man. We were surprised by how you allowed yourself to become so consumed with him and how you let it consume you. It wasn't like you. You always turfed any man who got to close; you barely let them come through the front door. If they did get past the front door, we knew you must be serious about them, but even then we knew they would soon be gone."

"What do you mean, turfed?" I knew exactly what he meant but I wanted to hear his views on this.

"Every man that has shown some interest in you over the last decade, every time they get a little comfortable, you would say you didn't like them anymore, they would start to curl up on the couch like the cat, and as soon as you saw that happening you'd turf them."

"I guess I didn't want them to get too comfortable. I wasn't comfortable with them being in my house curling up like the cat. That's not what I wanted."

"We couldn't figure out why this guy was so different. Why you have been so hell bent on continuing to allow yourself to be affected by this man. You have so many other choices."

"Instinct, Marc. It's is what I've always said to the three of you—follow your instincts and you will do the right thing.

I am following them now. I have to get closer to him, at least be in the same time zone to find out if my instincts are right. And if they are not I will be able to continue on with my journey without wondering about that part of my life. Being on the road without distraction from all of you will allow me to figure this out. His coming into my life when he did has huge significance but I'm not sure why. At times I think it was too show me I could feel love again. I'm not sure that this man is the "one" for me; we have not had enough time to be physically together. As you know we are rarely ever in the same time zone, but he has come back into my life for a reason. I do know that to find the answers, I have to go and see him, in his environment, around his friends and family, to see if he is the man I have pictured in my head or, if like so many things in life, when you get to see them up close and personal they are no longer what you had pictured. Does that make sense?

"Oh make no mistake, you are going to find out it is different. That he is different."

"How do you know that?"

"I don't know I just feel it. Being with you showed him another way of life, a good fun life and he wanted to be a part of it. What guy wouldn't want to be a part of that? You're fun and easy to be with. Then he became unsure of what he wanted and you paid for that. We watched how it has been since you met him, and especially since he went back to his life. You've lost your fun."

I smiled at this; my son thought I was fun.

"Do you believe I am doing the right thing?"

"I believe *you think* you are doing the right thing. I don't want you to be hurt again by what you find when you get there. I think he will continue to be the same way he has been."

"How has he been?"

"I am not sure what to say only that you always said you never know where you stood with him. He was there then he was not, that come here go away thing went on for too long and it still does. Look at all the contact you have and it never makes anything clearer for you."

"What? Why would you say that?

"Because that is the way it was and continues to be."

I find myself amazed at my young son's insight and then start justifying why I let this happen.

"You know Marc; he is in a place he has never been in his life too. For the first time he is free to make choices and decisions for himself that do not involve his children or obligations to a relationship. We did not plan on meeting each other and messing each other's lives up. I have disrupted his life too and it is confusing for both of us. I want to have a clear destination when it comes to him. I have been alone longer than he has and I am ready for commitment. He is just starting to figure out what being alone is all about. I think it is important that he goes through that transition but for some reason we cannot let that happen. We have tried several times to be alone and forget about each other but we keep coming back to each other and it is making us both crazy. He is important to me Marc."

"Does he do that for you? Make you feel important? Does he even want to do that for you? Look what you do for him. Look what you *are* doing for him—driving yourself across the country again to get closer to a man who won't even be there when you get there."

"I knew he wasn't going to be there. He will only be gone for a week but I didn't plan on seeing him until much later anyway. I'll visit with Bruce and wait for Lee to fly in. He and I will meet up after she flies home."

I could tell Marc was getting frustrated.

"You know Marc, he didn't ask me to do this. And he's also put a lot of time and energy into getting to me. Besides, you do realize he's only a part of the reason I am doing this? I'm doing this for myself. But to find out what is right for me, what is important in my life, I have to find out about him. I have to put myself in a position that we can get to each other when the timing is right for both of us and get to know each other on our own terms. I have to know Marc. I have to know if this man is genuine and that my feelings for him are too."

"Oh mom, there is no question your feelings are genuine."

We drove in silence for a while, my spidy senses tingling after our conversation. My body started to sweat and fear was creeping in. For the first time in a long time, I was starting to doubt my instincts. I wanted to turn around. I wanted to keep going. I started sending out thought energy to him, I wanted the phone to ring and have it be him telling me he couldn't wait for me to get there. He did not call. I started to pray to the gods of "help me make the right decision" but they must have been busy too.

I wondered about Marc's descriptions of the behaviour this man exhibited. I already knew that he was going through his own stuff so I justified his behaviour, but I was wondering if his behaviour was typical of men. I started to wonder about men in general, and in particular about the ones I knew.

Do men go through transitions in life like women do? Of course they do! Men are not exempt from feeling trapped in their lives. Men are not immune to being affected by adversities and obstacles. It is my own perception of men that has delayed my understanding that men can get off track as much or more than women can.

I have an antiquated image of men that tells me they are strong, reliable and steady in their emotions, like the image I have of my father. In my mind there is no way men go through what women go through. The rollercoaster of emotions, the "we never know who we are talking to from one moment to the next as the swing of moods has transformed the sane person I was just speaking with into a irrational, can't make a decision, making-no sense person." These are descriptions that have been used to describe me and I know when I am being that person, and now that I am thinking about it, I have encountered these same emotional traits in men. I never put it together that they might be undergoing some sort of personal transition because I did not want to believe they could be affected. I wanted them to be strong and steady but unfortunately I can now see that they are as susceptible to their emotions as I am.

So now that I understand that I am encountering a man I care about going through his own transition, I have to be sensitive to what comes out of my mouth and listen to him differently. I have to be aware that the two of us, together, swinging from tree to tree with our moods and emotions, could wind up being the death of us if we don't handle this dual transition with care.

I don't like having come to understand that men do suffer emotionally because I liked my perception of the big strong man that could handle anything, especially his emotions. On the other hand I do like it when men talk about their feelings. I believe it helps women understand why relationships start to break down and go sideways. When we hear about these things from our partners we at least know that something is going on with them and that it generally has nothing to do with us.

We need to be aware of these transitions so when we experience them we can say, "Honey, do you remember when you were in that valley, that place when you were all mixed up and didn't know what you wanted? Do you remember how hellish that was on us? Well now it's my turn and I need you to understand, even though I may react badly and respond in a nasty way with you, it won't last. It has nothing to do with you and I need you to support me by listening to me and trying to understand your role in my transition. Mostly it is just to stand by me until I come out of the valley. Remember, I did that for you, with you, that is how we got through your bad moments. Realizing it was going to pass, as hard as it was, I just had to be patient. Now it's my turn to be this way for a while and you need to understand. I won't always be this way."

As we all know, continuous poking and prodding, and asking questions like, "What's wrong?" can send a person who is already in a mood running in the opposite direction when this is not our intention at all. It is unfortunate these transitions by both men and women often come with casualties, usually the relationship. Again I find myself telling myself I need to practice patience.

The knowledge that he is going through his own, "figure out who I am and what I want," moment in his life has made me rethink things. It does not matter how much I want to be with him, it does not matter how "right" I think we are, it does not matter how beautiful the picture I have for us is, I cannot and will not force my will on him.

He has to come to see what I see on his own terms. If and when the time comes and we are on the same page, we will then be able to discuss what it is we really both desire and the expectations we have for each other. Until then I will watch him carefully from afar and up close, when we take the time to get to each other, to see how he handles his new-found freedom and how he handles me and my new-found freedom.

This is an important relationship to both of us and I believe that no matter what happens, we have brought an astounding amount of growth to each other in a short period of time and we will always be a part of each others lives, even if it is from afar. I just have to continue to convince my self I can do this. I can be patient and I have to accept what he wants for his own life just as much as he has to accept the decisions I have made and continue to make for my life.

Being patient when I think I want something so badly and I can make it work is not easy for me. Watching him in his transitional state is a Terror Barrier and I will get through this one too, but to do this I have to work through what happened last Fall. So while I am sitting in the passenger seat and we are crossing into Quebec, after having Marc tell me his perception of what last Fall was like, I start to think about what actually happened.

CHAPTER NINE

Last Fall … The Dream Seller

Everything was going so well. My career was keeping me busy, my children were happy, that day, and I was happy too. I was at the office sitting at my desk concentrating on the papers that were in front of me when a colleague walked up to me and asked me if I had a few minutes. I told him I was busy with some contracts but asked him what was up.

"I have a friend who is coming into town this weekend to present a business plan that will provide all those who are interested with a way to earn extra income."

I looked curiously at this man standing there holding a brochure and said, "What kind of business plan?" As he started to explain, I very quickly realized this was something I was not going to be interested in. I had been involved with this kind of income stream many years before and knew exactly the kind of commitment it was going to require so I shut him down before he got any more words out of his mouth.

"You know … I am so busy right now I do not have time to even entertain another job. Sorry." I knew the moment the words came out of my mouth and how they came out of my mouth were quick and rude. I turned back to my contracts and he walked away.

Feeling badly for my behaviour I finished reading over the contracts and walked down to his office, apologized for being so abrupt and asked him to show me what he had. I respected this man and told him so, "Look I am sorry for how quickly I shut you down. I should have realized if you were taking the time to investigate this plan I should have at least given you the opportunity to speak. Show me what you have there."

The moment I looked at the information I did see the opportunity and I knew myself well enough to know that if I did get involved I would make some extra income.

He asked me to come and listen to this friend of his who was going to be speaking on Saturday morning and to bring along anyone I felt could also benefit.

I was hesitant to commit but I said I would think about it.

Saturday morning arrived and I decided I would go. On the drive there I had decided not to get involved in the business but I would go to fill up a chair. When I arrived I took my seat and watched, unknowing my life had changed as soon as I entered the room.

As I sat and listened to the speaker I could tell right away he was polished. His delivery was flawless and very scripted. It was obvious he had been doing this a long time. As I sat there watching him I found my thoughts drifting. I was not listening to him anymore. I was thinking about him. I was critiquing him. He was not model handsome but I am rarely attracted to that kind of handsome; he was not articulate in his speech but he was charming and he made us laugh. He clearly stated he was not formally educated beyond the high school level, but of course I knew you do not have to be university-educated to be successful, I know plenty of successful people who did *not* finished high school. I shifted in my chair, and wondered why I was so intrigued by this man. He did not meet any of the criteria that had in the past been important to me. He was not a man I would have looked twice at but here I was staring at him wondering what it was about him that was making me uncomfortable.

After the presentation I spoke with him and told him I had previous experience in this kind of business and had had some success with it, I liked it and I was interested in hearing more. I knew he was meeting with our mutual friend for dinner and I invited myself to join them.

Sitting beside him at dinner, watching how he interacted with us, he and I were soon involved in a conversation that had nothing to do with business. We had not ignored our two other dinner companions, but I was lost in listening to him speak to me. Listening to stories about his adventures and where around the world his work had taken him. I had to force myself to tear my eyes away from him and involve the other two men sitting with us. I wondered if I was being obvious to my colleague. I saw him looking at me and hoped I didn't look like the school girl I was feeling like inside. I was fairly sure I wasn't acting the way I was feeling, but it was hard not to glow.

From that moment on I could not get this man out of my head. It did not take long for us to become friends. I became one of his contacts in our city, as I did join the business, and our conversations over the phone and in person soon became personal. We did not mean for it to happen. Neither one of us was looking for a relationship. I was open and available but he was not available—not married, just not available. I was not able to entertain any ideas about this man, because he was not free.

It was very strange being attracted to a man to whom I could not talk to about what I was thinking and I was also afraid of how I was feeling. I told myself this would pass. It was infatuation. I justified my denial. How could I possibly be thinking this was a man I wanted to spend time with? He didn't fit my criteria.

🍃

It was the most bizarre relationship from the start. We felt a connection that transcended across the country, he picked up my vibration and I his. And when we were together it was also being felt by everyone who walked within ten feet of us. It was the beginning of my understanding of just how powerful our personal energy force field was. Suddenly we were attracting advances, personally and for business from people all around us who wanted to be apart of our energy. It was the most glorious feeling I have every known.

While we were working together I learned a lot about him, or at least as much as he wanted me too know. He told me he had been working on how to change his "situation," for a long time. His life and who he was, and even though he still cared a great deal about the life he had co-created, he was changing and the life he was living personally had not been progressing, growing with him, for quite some time, long before I met him. But because of his work he had procrastinated and time just went by and he continued to live the same way.

But now he was taking steps to free himself and I followed his transition very closely. I had to stay grounded and not expect anything from him. I had to allow him the time and space to figure out how to free himself from his commitments without my influence.

It soon became apparent that we were unable to do this. We could not deny what was happening and I became the catalyst for him. We could not believe the universe brought us together. When we found out how parallel our lives were, it seemed to confirm for us how perfect we were for each other. We really liked our friendship. We both had been in love before, but I knew for sure I had never been *in* love like this. I had never allowed myself to love this way, and he said he was feeling the same. It was surreal to both of us.

Over the next few months we grew closer and there was barely an hour of any day that we were not in contact. The texting was constant when we could not talk on the phone, and the conversations on the phone went on for hours. When I knew he was coming to town we would count down the days and when I picked him up from the airport we were together from the moment he landed until he left.

Blip… "Plane has landed."

"Yeah! Always so happy when you are on the ground."

"Where are you?"

"I am here."

"I see you. You're beautiful."

"Thank you baby. I see you."

It was crazy! We were like love-struck teenagers addicted to texting. I know we all say this in the first trimester of our relationships but I can honestly say now, as I do have a few experiences in my life to compare this too…For the first time in my life, I found myself out of control with emotions I had no idea I could feel, nor did I know how to deal with them.

My endorphins were on fire. It was blissful and painful at the same time. I felt so vulnerable and so exposed as if he could read every thought and feel every emotion I was having whether he was on the phone, in the room or across the country. I was in unfamiliar territory and I loved it. I ached just to hear his voice, receive a text or be in the same room with him. How did every thought, every action, and every conversation, suddenly become about getting to each other? The energy we were sending back and forth, even when we were not in the same time zone, was received instantly and it was wildly exciting.

After taking the steps to change his life he moved to my city to work and be closer to me. I was over the moon. We allowed ourselves to be in love for a moment, perhaps for the first time in our lives. We shared the intimacies of a beautiful relationship, which up until we met, to me had only been folklore. We were both entering a phase of our lives we had never been in before; we were going to have freedom from so many obligations that had dominated every breathing moment of our lives for the past 30 years. We were not going to have children around. For the first time in my life, I was going to have a relationship without inhibitions and family responsibilities because our children were now adults.

He had rented an apartment in town and was working a lot. His business was expanding and it was an exciting time. His work continued to take him to other cities so it was still difficult to really find out who he was. We travelled together to different parts of the Atlantic Provinces for work, places we had never been before and it was exciting and new. But even so I was still unable to see him in his natural environment. I began to suspect this was where he is most comfortable, on the move, living out of a suitcase, rarely staying put for very long.

Although all the stars seemed to have aligned for us, several weeks into him being in my town I started to notice changes in our relationship. He had become distant and secretive. I became distant and cautious. He was becoming impatient and I was too. My life had changed so fast I no longer felt in control of my thinking. I was being swept away and I felt like I was free-falling.

A few days prior to leaving on one of our trips to Newfoundland my "spidy senses" were on overload, I had started to battle with myself about him. I wanted desperately to understand why I could not quite feel safe with this man. It was as if we were on the verge of either getting married or separating. There was no middle ground for me to relax in.

On the plane he reached across and gently laid the book I was reading down.

"Tell me what's going on."

"What do you mean?"

"Suzanne, I know there is something. Talk to me."

The words that came out of my mouth were not planned but came out as if I had been thinking about them for a while.

"This will be my last trip with you."

"What do you mean?"

"I don't know where to start, so I just will. I have made a lot of changes in my life, my home is up for sale, I resigned from my career to work in this business with you, you have moved to be closer to me and work here, but I think I am feeling like the changes, especially the ones involving us that have taken me off my course are starting to confuse me. And since you moved here I see changes in you too that make me uneasy. "

He was not saying anything, just watching me and listening to me very intently.

"I am conflicted about not continuing on with my goals and plans I had before I met you. I think I need to spend some time alone to think." It was weird how quickly the energy around us changed and I picked up a vibe from him that was not what I was expecting but it all makes sense now… I was giving him an out.

"Well if that is what you think, you need to do that."

I shot him a look that said… "Not the right answer!"

We went on to enjoy our time working and touring Newfoundland but when we got back home it did not take me long to sit him down and say, "Ok what is going on with you. I feel a sense of urgency and I do not like it."

He was having a hard time looking at me. I knew, instinctively, I knew exactly what was going to come out of his mouth. I could have spit the words out for him but I wanted him to say them.

"I am feeling guilty about how I left my life. I feel like something is missing, something unfinished. I need to go back to find out and make sure I have made the right decision. In addition, my business is suffering and so is yours because of the time we are spending together."

I could not believe my ears. It was as if he was reading from a script I wrote.

He went on to say, "For us to ever have a chance I have to go back and finish what I was committed to, both personally and professionally, until I am no longer committed."

"But what about your commitments here, you promised everyone here you were going to be working here for at least six months. You have barely been here two months."

"I can fly back and forth as I have been doing."

I could not believe what I was hearing but from that moment on, even though we were never the same, we still could not stay away from each other or find a way to sever the emotional ties.

That was it, he was going to leave and there was nothing I could do. As unreal as it sounded to me, as much as I wanted it not to be true, it was true and I understood everything he said.

He was not wrong, I agreed with him, we got so caught up in our emotions that we had both pushed our own goals and dreams away and obviously … the Universe did not like that because if it had, we would not be in this place of dis-ease.

There was nothing left for me to say. I had to wish

him well, and we let each other go. Was this hard? Yes it was. It was the hardest decision I ever made concerning a relationship, but it had to be made.

I was devastated. He was gone and I was lost. The damage that he left in his wake was unbelievable. I had made so many changes to my own life since he arrived in my life one year ago, believing in the fantasy we had created, not only was my emotional state of mind damaged but I had changed my career to work with him. I had resigned from a career that just a few months before, I believed I would do for the rest of my life. Now, I was so emotionally distraught and I knew I was never going to work with him again and because of those DVD's I could no longer even consider "going back," to doing what I was doing just a few short months earlier. I didn't know how to go backwards. My mind had developed skills to only move me forward. Furthermore, I couldn't even think about working. I could not think. My body and my mind were not working.

Marc was right. I was broken.

This was the beginning of a transition that first had to rip my world apart before I could start implementing the skills I had learned from the books, CD's and that one particular DVD on The Terror Barrier, and these skills had nothing to do with work.

It was over two months since he had left and I was still not functioning properly.

Early in the Fall, while pacing around my home, I receive a phone call, a phone call we all dread receiving. My father, who lives on the opposite side of the country, on the other coast, so far away, had suffered a stroke. Having lived the past 23 years of my life on opposite coasts, my father and I are amazingly close. During those years, we have been able to spend a great deal of time together with his visits to me and mine to him. When I started to spiral out of control with my emotions, I did not let him know. I did not want my father to worry. When I received the call from his wife that my father had had a stroke, my knees went weak. He had a heart attack five years earlier so I asked myself if he would survive this.

I sat down on my stairs and listened to the prognosis. Too early to tell. What do I do now? My mind immediately went to my bank account. It had had a stroke as well and was not recovering at all! My sister, brothers and I decided I would sit still for a few days to see how he progressed. They were closer and would keep me up to date. I started praying to "the stroke recovery gods'" to make my dad well. This added to my fear and confirmed that life is short. I had to find a way to get back to being me, to find some joy.

Joy? What a novel concept. Such a simple, beautiful word. I wanted some joy in my life. I sat on my stairs for a long time, staring up at the window above the front door. It was in need of cleaning and I started to cry. I became frustrated with my self. What is going on with me? Why did the idea of cleaning the window make me cry? It was not the chore, it was the fact that I had no energy to move off the stair, my father had had a stroke and I could not see my way to get to him unless it became a dire situation and *all* my windows needed cleaning. I did not see that the answer to this dilemma, of getting to my father, was parked in my driveway.

A few weeks after my dad's stroke and he was home recovering, I made a decision that I had to get out of my house and not just to the grocery store. I had to have a change of scenery. I could not stand pacing around my home one more day waiting for something different to happen, waiting for my house to sell. Being in the fetal position for the last several weeks, forcing myself everyday to get up, get dressed and be normal was not working. All I was doing was the hurry up and wait thing, day after day, waiting for the night to come so I could go back to bed and not sleep. I was standing looking out the window at the pending maritime storm that was looming, staring at a car that somehow had to get back to Alberta before the snow flew and the light bulb went on. I'll drive it myself. My life, my vision, my dream and goals had come crashing to the floor and I fell with them. What else did I have to do?

I understand I had created this scenario. I understand I took the actions that put me in this position. Of course, I had a plan when I set the plan in motion, a great plan. What I did not see coming, and a crystal ball would have been helpful here, was my reaction when the plan went terribly wrong. I had no idea I had so many deep-seeded fears that would decide to surface just as I was making major changes in my life. My Terror Barrier presented itself in a fierce way and I knew I had to face it before I could move along with any other plans I had been making.

I did not want to wait to find out the reason this was happening, I wanted to know the reason now! I wanted to know today what I'm supposed to be doing, what I am supposed to be thinking. Thinking? I was not thinking, I was reacting, reacting to whatever was happening at the moment. My mind had become so consumed with negative thoughts I was unable to think about the next five minutes let alone what I was going to do in five months if that was how long it was going to take my home to sell. My body was so racked with fear I was unable to leave home, until that moment I stood looking at the car. I picked up my phone and called Jack.

"Hi, have you figured out how to get your car back to Alberta?"

He has another car there so it was not a pressing issue but he did want this car to be there too.

"No, I was thinking of putting on the train."

"I want to get away for a while and I was thinking I would take a week or two and drive it out there for you."

Silence on the other end of the phone told me he just pictured the same moment I did, the moment we would have to meet.

"Well that would be great and I know you would like to get away. How are you doing?"

"I'm okay, but I think the drive would do me some good."

"Well if you want to do that, I'm okay with that."

"Thank you."

"Suzanne, you know I am trying very hard to do the right thing with my life here. I can't have you coming here under any pretence other than dropping the car off."

"I know that. I am not anticipating anything. I just want to get away for a while and while I was staring out the window this idea came to me."

"When do you want to leave?"

"Thursday."

"This Thursday? That's only two days away."

"I know but I'm ready to go."

"Ok, I will call you later. And Suzanne … I am looking forward to seeing you."

"Me too."

I called my daughter and told her I was going to drive to Alberta to drop the car off and fly home. I asked her if it was possible for her to take a few days and drive with me as far as Toronto. Timing could not have been better, and as I have said before, everything happens for a reason. There was a Christmas party in Brampton that some of my closest friends were having and I was not planning on going but now I could as stopping and staying with Roslyn was one of my stops en route to Alberta. Two days later we were on the road. Taking positive action instead of spending too much time thinking negative thoughts got me moving again.

The day we left Halifax it was late November and winter was setting in all across Canada. Even the most seasoned drivers would question this quest but I didn't think twice about it. I felt better being on the move. We arrived in Brampton the same day one of my friends was burying her husband. Could it get any more depressing? He had died unexpectedly the day I decided to drive the car to Alberta. As they did not know we were coming we did not go to the funeral. Carly and I decided it would be too much of a distraction for us to just show up.

The following night we showed up at the party and surprised all the ladies which was fun to do. Each one of them, throughout the night came up to me and commented on my weight loss. They knew I was going through a difficult time with the changes I had made and knew the loss of my relationship had had a terrible affect on me, but they had no idea there was so much more that was happening to me. How do you explain The Terror Barrier at a party? Even though I found myself surrounded by people who cared about me, I was looking at the exit and willing time to pass so I could be on the road again. I wanted to be alone.

The morning I put Carly on a plane back home, as we were hugging goodbye, she whispered in my ear, "Mom, trust your instincts and come home safe." That sent me into a flurry of tears. It is what I have always whispered into their ears when they are going on a trip without me and I am hugging them goodbye. I told her that was exactly what I was doing, trusting my instincts.

I left her, said good bye to Roslyn and two days later I was out of Ontario. I had my book, Think and Grow Rich, a biography of Abraham Lincoln on CD, and Bob Proctor on CD as well as my favourite music. I had been convincing myself I was doing the right thing the whole time I was driving. Leaving home and taking some time to be alone was good for me.

I was heading for the mountains. Isn't that the place everyone heads for when they are in need of clarification about issues that are giving them trouble? I've heard them say "I'm going up the mountain and I'm not coming down until I figure it out." Well if it worked for them, it surely has to have some magical power and it will work for me. I found myself seeking answers from a mountain. I felt ridiculous but I was thinking the mountain was a metaphor because I had no plans to actually go into the mountains. I always knew, to find the answers, I had to look inside myself. I pushed the play button on the CD player and there was Bob Proctor telling me I could have anything I wanted as long as I truly desired it. I didn't want to listen to Bob as it was one of Bob's programs I attended that put me here in the first place. I wanted to poke him in the eye. I changed the CD.

As the road passed behind me the unknown of what was ahead of me played through my mind. I was going to face the person that introduced me to another way of thinking. I was fine as far as I was concerned until he put that book into my hands. Think and Grow Rich by Napoleon Hill. I was fine until he said I should enrol in Bob Proctor's 12-week-Program, "Thinking into Results." I thought I was fine. The results of that program brought me to the realization I was not fine and I could not go *back* to being fine no matter how much I tried regain the moments of being blissfully ignorant. I was not fine.

Very few people around me were aware or understood that I *had* to get into that car and drive away. Even fewer knew that I had hit a wall and stepped up to my Terror Barrier and that I had to fight for my sanity every breathing, waking moment to break through this barrier. To them, I was always the woman who took care of every one and every thing and did it well. During this time, I would get up each day, smile when my children walked through the door so they would not worry. Although it was not long before I could no longer hide it from them, from anyone. I had lost nearly 20 lbs I could not afford to lose and I was not going to the gym. Now they were looking after me and I could stand it no longer. I had to get away.

I had been driving from the East Coast for five days. I was thinking about the changes I had made in the past few months. I had resigned from my career, put my house up for sale and the love of my life and I decided he needed to go back to a life he felt was unfinished and I had no income. The car I was driving was not my own, it was his and it belonged in Calgary, not in my driveway as a constant reminder. My mind was confused, my body ached and I had no interest in doing any of the things that just weeks before I would do without thinking.

I arrived in Alberta and checked into a hotel for the night. The next morning I was going to see him, the man who had broken my heart. I had no idea what to expect so I expected nothing. When he arrived we talked for a while then he left. He just left, saying he would call me later to make arrangement for me to fly home. I didn't know what to do. I knew this was the universe testing me and tests are designed to let us know what we do not know, what we need to work on and I was failing this test badly.

I was angry at the world for giving me this test. I was in a hotel parking lot in Red Deer, Alberta, sitting in his car, thinking I would do some sightseeing, when I realized it was not the world I was angry with, I was angry with me. I was responsible for driving here. I put myself in this car and drove myself thousands of kilometres away from home thinking I was going to find peace and some resolution when I got here. I did not. I found more loneliness and confusion than I had ever experienced before. I had to dig deep, gather all my strength, wipe my face and turn the key. But I couldn't. I was paralyzed. Then he called.

"Listen, why don't you just keep my car for a while and drive to B.C. and visit your family. You could use some time with them. Go visit your dad for a few days."

"Really, that would be fantastic. It is funny you should offer that as I was thinking the same thing before I left home, being so close I tried to figure out a way to get there."

"Okay, there ya go."

"I would like to see you again before I leave town."

"I'm sorry Suzanne, I can't do that. It is just too hard. But you go and don't worry about my car. I'm going to be away most of next week anyway and you will probably be back in Nova Scotia before I get back. Just let me know when you want to leave and I'll make the arrangements."

I hung up the phone thinking you have no idea what hard is.

I had to call someone, someone who would talk me down from the escalating hysteria that was sure to follow the heaving sobs that started coming out of me. I called my cousin in Princeton. I wanted to let him know I was going to drive through the Rockies today and to expect me at his pub for dinner. Funny how life works. He was not going to be there, he was leaving shortly to catch a plane to Calgary for the Grey Cup Game. He would be flying right over me.

He said, "Suzanne, are you okay?"

"No, I'm not. I am sitting in a hotel parking lot, the man I thought I was going to spend my life with is fifteen minutes up the road and he cannot come to see me. I thought he would help me, talk with me, but he can't."

"What do you mean he can't?"

"He says he cannot because he is afraid of his own weaknesses. He is following through with what he came back to finish and seeing me is just too much of a temptation."

As these words came out of my mouth, I felt a strange sense of strengthening in my respect for him and envy for what he was doing. I felt a weird sense of pride for him sticking to the commitment he had made to himself and his life here. I was proud of him for having the discipline to follow through; I just wanted it to be with me.

"He left me this morning knowing I was upset, but could do nothing that would have made a difference, so he just said to take the car, go over the Rockies, visit with family and drop the car off when I was done. He is fifteen minutes away and he is unwilling to be with me, hold me, and tell me everything is going to be okay."

"Suzanne, are you listening to me. Start the car and drive here. I will let Chris the bartender, know you are coming. You can have dinner here and you can stay at my place for the night or as long as you want. You are going to be fine."

He then proceeded to tell me about his break-up with

his wife. I knew it was a bad situation for him. I just had no idea how bad it was. He said it had taken him a long time to recover and he was still not 100 percent. I felt horrible for him and wondered how I could be so selfish. There is so much sorrow in the world. People hurt people, that is just the way it is. I had to turn the key. I had to drive away.

At that moment, I really disliked the saying, "you can run away from where you physically are, but you cannot run away from your self." I wanted to be so far away from where I was, from the realities of my life and how it was changing. I wanted to get so far away from myself, this new self, the one that made me get in this car and drive myself smack into a situation I knew was going to turn out this way. Even knowing that, I still came. I had to. I had to know for sure.

I started to drive and talk to myself. The sound of my own voice and my words sounded foreign to me. It was as if someone else was speaking. "What did you expect to find here? What made you think it was going to be different?" Answering myself aloud, I said, "I thought I would find closure, I thought I would find an understanding of the changes that took place over the past few months. I thought the wind, the music, the solitude and a different geographical picture would help me." I was wrong. The fear only increased.

This transition of tossing out the old and allowing in the new is supposed to be a good thing, or so all the experts keep telling me. But as this new woman I'm becoming is trying so desperately to emerge, the old self is trying just as hard to keep the new one stuffed inside. It's such a battle, that I want to throw the new woman out on the street, leave her behind. Nevertheless, I cannot get rid of her. She is here to stay and torture me until I can stand it no longer and I have to accept her.

I knew I had to start accepting things as they were, that I had become someone new, because I knew I could not go back—not to being my old self, not to being with him or living the life of the safe and familiar. I had to find a way to accept this new self who was now in the driver's seat and realize that the old self, had to be left at the curb.

My mind would not take a break. It was a continuous playing of Bob Proctor's voice telling me, I could have anything I truly desired. Really? Did I "truly desire this?" I did not think so.

Originally, I was going to drop the car off in Calgary and fly home, but now, I was not ready to go home. After talking with my cousin, and with Jack, I decided since I was so close to family in B.C., I *would* continue through the Rockies to see if visiting family would help shake this feeling of dis-ease that had crept into my soul like a plague.

CHAPTER TEN
Sliding Off the Edge of Sanity

The drive is incredibly beautiful, the mountains majestic. "Wow, look where I am!" The weather forecast called for light snow in the direction I was heading, West, and a storm was going to blow through from the East and I would be in it if I was to stay. I was prepared for light snow. My mind at this point was focused on how to rid myself of this feeling. How to heal from wounds that had only recently begun to surface and had been compounded by this heart ache. How to learn to love living in this moment? It is after all, the only sure thing in this world we have, this moment, and I was not loving it.

The wounds had become like open sores, seeping with infection. Although they could not be seen with the naked eye, they were painful. I felt as if I had been hit in the back of the head with something so hard, it knocked me down and I was carrying a weight so heavy on my chest, it made it hard to breathe. Now I had to get up and carry this weight around with me. I did not want to. It was too hard and too heavy. I knew how to do it, I really did, I knew how to pick myself up, I had done it many times in the past, but this time I was not ready. I knew I had to process this and everything else before I could heal.

Many mornings, after far too few hours of sleep, I would wake up, curse the light and say to myself, "Damn, I woke up." It was not that I did not want to live, I did, I really liked living, and I know how to do it well. I remember how it felt, not living in fear, not having to carry this weight. Was I so distracted by years of caring for everyone else, and what they needed, I tucked away my own issues? Yes I did.

I thought I was the one who embraced life and faced all the challenges head on. I just could not believe that now, I woke up feeling the same way day after day, sad. When was it going to change? Isn't it true what they say? "Sleep on it, all will be better tomorrow. The answers will come while you sleep." Maybe, if I could sleep and wake feeling rested, I would find out that it was true.

I already knew the only cure was in my mind. I knew the only one who was able to help me was me. I had to change my thinking back to the positive but I could only do that by accepting the changes that were happening to me, but acceptance is not always easy to achieve.

I should have been more focused on the road and the weather. It was one of those moments when you look in the rear-view mirror and realize and you don't remember driving those last few kilometres. In this case, it was the last few hundred kilometres. There were few cars coming from the other direction. 200km and very little traffic on this major road coming from Banff National Park, the direction I was heading, this should have been an indication to me that something was just not right.

The reason there was no traffic became apparent 65km from my destination … Road Closed due to an Avalanche. "Oh my god, Suzanne! How could you have missed the signs indicating road closure?" Again, I am talking out loud to myself. More importantly, the fuel gauge read 70km until empty. I knew I could make it if I could continue forward. Retracing back along the road in my mind, I didn't recall seeing any gas stations, hotels or services of any kind for the past 2 hours. "How could I have been so preoccupied?"

This is what happens when we allow our insecurities to distract us; I was so caught up in my thoughts of how I was feeling I stopped looking after myself. I stopped seeing and registering what the signs were saying. I knew I had to get it together or I was going to be spending the night in this car, with a Rocky Mountain snowstorm coming my way. This was not a cozy little Chalet with a big hot tub and fireplace and I couldn't recall seeing one along this route.

I had no choice. I turned the car around and started to pray to "the gas station gods" to help me get through this. There had been a storm predicted from the East, where I had just driven away from and now, heading East, all I could see was the wall of snow and I had no choice but to drive right into it. Although the car had good snow tires, it was still slippery, visibility was poor, I could not see the edge of the road and I was alone on this highway driving through a mountain range with zero cell phone reception. The signs to the nearest town read over 200km away.

The gas gauge was now registering empty. I really dislike the little gas pump picture flashing on the dashboard. Every flash was like a jab of reality, "Get it together Suzanne!" Over and over, flashing, flashing. It was making fun of me! I wanted to scream, but there was no point … who would hear me? I had had no cell phone reception for the last hour and half so calling for help was out of the question. I had no choice but to drive until I ran out of gas and wait for someone to come along.

The fuel gauge needle had settled down well beyond the empty line and it was not going to move anymore. I was praying out loud making promises I intended to keep, as we all do when we are in need of saving and answers. I could not see the road or, what was written on the signs I passed because the blowing snow was sticking to everything.

Just as the thought of the repercussions for the car if I run out of gas enter my head, I felt the car start to sputter. Through the blur of the tears that were just ready to spill over, ahead through the blizzard I saw lights. I didn't care what they were lighting up, I was stopping. As I turned down a sloping driveway I wondered if I would get back up, and there was the most beautiful site I have ever seen… GAS…OPEN. "Thank you, Thank you, Thank you!" I was gratefully choking out through the happy tears that were now falling. I started shaking my head at this miracle and swore that I had manifested this little gas stop. It appeared in the middle of nowhere like an oasis in the desert.

After filling the car, I walked into the tiny building. I smiled at the man behind the counter.

"Hi there, do you have any information on the road closures?"

"No English."

"Ok then, Thank you."

Sitting in the car consulting my road atlas I made the decision to head back to where I had come from. 220km back around the mountains to the nearest trunk road, cut across the province and I would be fine. With a full tank, bottled water and a bag of chips, I was feeling better. I actually believed at that moment I was going to be alright. I was wrong.

The roads were treacherous so there were not many vehicles, only the ones on serious missions and that was me. I was determined to put as many kilometres between me and Jack as I could. The speed I could travel was slow to almost stopped and when I reached the road that would take me across the province, I was only 50 kilometres from where I had started 6 hours earlier, 50 kilometres from where he was.

On the trunk road, I passed several motels and I should have stopped for the night when it got dark, but having already lost several hours I wanted to get a few more hours behind me. I would have stopped if a crystal ball had told me what lay ahead for me.

It was pitch black and the traffic looked heavy on a hill I was approaching. I had no idea why there were cars parked at the top and at the side of the road at the bottom. No one was stopping us from going so I followed the car in front of me. Half way up the hill, we all started sliding. This was a four-lane highway and the cars and trucks that were all around were suddenly sliding all over the place. I hit a patch of black ice and the car picked up speed, turned right around and started sliding backwards and sideways towards the guardrail that is only designed to show us where the side of the road ends and where the edge of the canyon begins, I took my hands off the wheel and the car came to a stop. I was completely sideways, the rear of the car facing the canyon, with only centimetres between me and end of the guardrail. I could not believe I didn't hit it. I stepped on the gas but that only moved me more sideways and closer to the edge where there was no guardrail.

Looking around in a panic, I called the closest person geographically to me, the owner of the car – Jack. I was hysterical. I had a hands-free phone unit above my head and all he could hear was me crying, screaming about the cars and semi tractor trailers that were smashing into each other and narrowly missing me. There was nothing he could do and I heard him starting to pray.

Then the situation with the other vehicles got really out of control and my panicked screams now became high pitched delirium.

"Oh My God! Oh My God! Giant headlights are coming right at me I have to get out of the car! He's going to hit me!"

"No don't get out of the car, stay in the car!"

I had no idea what was going to happen if this giant truck that was sliding right for me hit me. I would most likely go down the canyon backwards never to be seen again, I had to jump out. I had no coat on and cowboy boots on my feet and no grip. My boots hit the ice and I started skating down the hill towards the side of the road at the same time watching the truck that was sliding so fast, towards the front of the car. Then it stopped. I couldn't believe it just stopped. I was out of my mind at that point. All I could hear was the crashing of metal all around me and all I could see were headlights spinning in circles. And I could hear Jack through the open car door, calling my name.

The next thing I knew a man was standing in front of me. The driver had gotten out of his truck. I was freezing, it was −11 and I was crying again. He put his hand on my shoulder and asked me if I was alright.

I looked at him and his kind face and I blurted out, "Alright? No, I am not alright! I was nearly killed! I would have plunged to my death into that canyon and the road was closed. I nearly ran out of gas. I am thousands of kilometres from home, I'm hungry and I don't know where I am!" He calmed me down and walked me back to the car. I put my coat on and Jack, who was still on the phone, stopped praying.

My legs were rubber as I settled back into the car. I had to focus as the truck rolled back and drove in front of me, I put my foot on the gas and it was like there was no ice at all. I started thanking what ever gods may be for keeping me alive.

I was so exhausted, cold and emotionally drained I promised myself I'd stop at the first place that had a vacancy sign. As it turned out, it was a Chalet with a fireplace and a big hot tub.

The front desk person was startled when he looked at me. I thought it was because he could tell I was frazzled. I just looked back at him, gave him my credit card and asked if there was food available at this time of night. He pointed down the hall almost afraid to speak. When I looked in the mirror before heading down the hall for dinner, I understood why he was looking at me the way he was, I had trails of salt from my tears mixed with dirt and it was all over my face. I was a mess inside and out. I washed my face, brushed my hair and headed down the hall for dinner.

Where was I? I was in Canmore but I had not consulted my map since arriving and I was not going to until morning. I had no idea where Canmore was except it was in Alberta. I had no idea how far I had travelled or how far I had to go. I had no idea about anything as I climbed into bed. I turned out the light and left the fireplace burning. The glow from the flame was eerie and the shadows of the unfamiliar room made me lonely for home. There was no one to call, no one could come over, no one would understand. I laid there, numb, confused and fear was my bed partner. Tears were falling to my pillow. I flipped it over and that side was wet too. I told myself tomorrow was going to be a better day. It had to be.

The morning was beautiful. It was still quite dark but I could see the sun was rising above the Three Sisters Mountain Range and I was mesmerized by the shear beauty of it. I looked at the clock beside the bed again, because I was sure it said it was after 8 a.m. but why was it so dark? Of course, because of the mountains the sun takes a while to rise above them. I had forgotten this, living on the East coast for so many years, I had forgotten the setting sun comes early and the rising sun is late. I took my time. I wanted to be a part of that moment. Standing beside the car, taking pictures, I looked around this small town. I felt something there. I could live here. Perhaps when I sell my home I will explore this town for a while. This day was going to be better. I was feeling better. Consulting my map, although I had driven for10 hours, I had only travelled a little over 250km from where I had started yesterday morning. I had a long way to go.

Figuring out where I was and where I wanted to be, I made up my mind I was going to get to Honeymoon Bay on Vancouver Island that night, even though it was still a ferry ride and 1100 kilometres away. I figured if all went well today I could still stop at my cousin's pub in Princeton and catch the last ferry to the Island. I would arrive close to midnight but I was determined I was going to sleep in a familiar bed that night.

This was my first drive through the Rocky Mountain passes in the winter and this one was easy. The sun was shining, the roads were clear and dry but my mind was on overdrive. I was aware of my mood. I felt happier. The drive through the mountains did something for me. I felt a peace around me. How could I not feel happier when the pure awesomeness of the sun on the mountains put life on this day in perspective for me? I was leaving a life behind and a new day of new beginnings had begun. I also realized that I had had no intention of travelling into the mountains when

I first started on this trek, but because I spoke it out loud as something I thought I needed to do, I manifested this just by thinking I wanted to go and see my dad.

Over dinner in Princeton at The Brownbridge Pub I order Seafood chowder. I laughed with the bartender Chris as he pointed out to me I had come all the way from the East coast, the seafood capital of Canada to eat seafood here. It was funny but I think I chose it because it was comfort food, familiar and warm.

When I arrived in Honeymoon Bay, eight days after leaving Nova Scotia, I fell asleep almost immediately. It was as I knew it would be, warm and safe. I have been coming here, staying with my friend, Mr. Aswell for almost 30 years. In the morning, as I was lying in my bed, recalling the last several days, I could hear him in the kitchen talking on the phone. "Yeah, she showed up here last night around midnight…. No, I didn't know she was coming; she called yesterday to say she would be showing up late…. No, she drove from Nova Scotia…. Yes, Nova Scotia…. I know, but you know her…. No, I don't know what's up, she is still sleeping. I got the feeling she is not staying for long. She is driving a car with Alberta plates…. Yes I know, that drive through the mountain this time of year is risky."

I smelled the coffee and got up, and I walked into the kitchen with a blanket around me. I looked at him and he just stared at me. I hadn't seen him when I got in the night before as it was late and he was in bed.

"Want some breakfast?"

"No thanks, coffee is fine."

"How long have you been on the road?"

"Eight days."

"Did you drive straight through?"

"No I stopped in Ontario for two night and two nights in Alberta. If I had driven straight through it would have only taken five days"

"So…it took only 5 days of driving to get here?"

"Yes"

"Wow, alone?"

"Most of it. Carly drove to Ontario with me then flew home"

"Okay …dinner tonight?"

"I'm not sure. I'm going to see my dad and my sister is visiting with him too. I will call if I am not going to be here. I'll leave you a message."

"You okay?"

"Not really, but I will be."

Mr. Aswell left and I drank my coffee, while staring out at the lake that had once provided so much peace for me. Now standing in this kitchen that was so familiar to me, I found no solace. The anxiety, the emotions, the reality of what was happening to my life came crashing down on me. Unable to stand, I sat at the table and cried. I felt doomed to stay in this state of despair. I knew I had to give myself some time and I knew I had just arrived after a very long trek across the country and was worn out. But that had never mattered before. In the past, as soon as I walked through this door, I was better, even if I never needed to be better. "Oh my God…what the hell is going on with me?" I thought. Then it hit me … I am not the same woman. Someone else had walked through that door.

CHAPTER ELEVEN

The Caribou

A defining moment of strength

My father did not know I was coming. My sister knew I was on the road but did not know when I was going to show up and she did not tell my father I was coming. My father was surprised but not surprised when I just walked in. It is what we do to with each other, we just show up. He also knew something emotional was going on with me but I told him very little over the phone. I did not want him to worry. Now there was no hiding it. I hugged them and went into the room where my sister was, I didn't want to address any questions.

I went in the bedroom where Katie was just waking up. I stood there until she registered it was me she was looking at. We hugged and she said she was so glad I was there. "Wow" She said. "You look great! How was the drive? I didn't expect you so soon. You okay?" My sister knew I was not okay. My weight was down, dangerously low. I was pale and had dark circles under my eyes and hollows in my cheeks. But I thanked her for saying so.

Lack of nutrition can do damage to the brain and the body in a hurry, I know this, but I did not care. Food was the last thing on my mind when it should have been the first thing. Pacing, in her room, my clothes falling off me, not interested in eating, antsy, I wanted to keep moving. "Come on, come on, let's go for a drive, let's go get a coffee." She looked at me and said, "You just drove 7500 kilometres and you want to drive some more?" "Yes, yes, get dressed, get in the car."

I was afraid to sit still. I knew if I sat for too long, my mind would conjure up images that were not real, then compound and cover up the truth. I know this because over the last 7500 kilometres I had done just that, made stuff up and believed it.

I had to drive. I wanted to get back in the car so I did not have to face the questions that would bring reality to my life about what I was doing and what I had just done, by driving across the country. I knew eventually I would have to get real but right at that moment I wanted to get in the car so I could continue to avoid the truth.

While driving I could feel anything I wanted. I could feel all the emotions and let them out without anyone witnessing and I wanted to feel everything. I wanted to let it all out, get it all out, and then let it go. I wanted to be free of the torment I continued to have because of the thoughts I was having. Also while driving concentrating on staying safely on the road, keeping track of where I was going and my turnoffs had become my biggest distractions and I was not ready to let these distractions go.

I know the Island well; Katie and I took a few back roads and talked. As we drove, it helped to be able to try to explain out loud to someone who was objective, sympathetic and who cared about me, the changes and how they have affected me. I know I made little sense to her when I tried to explain what has happened. The words coming out of my mouth were scattered, so she knew my mind was scattered as well. She listened and tried to tell me what I was feeling was normal for what I was going through. Waiting for my home to sell, no income, children leaving home, love lost, baring my soul, exposing truths to myself about my life; of course it is going to have adverse affects.

Normal? No, no no! If this is what normal felt like I want abnormal and I wanted it now.

We drove to familiar places that had in the past made me happy and made me feel safe. This course of action seemed like it should work but it did not. Why was I looking to the past with its familiar faces and secure places to make me feel safe and normal? I was hoping it would take some of this fear away. Why did these places of former comfort and the people who I was always comfortable with, suddenly make me feel sadder and out of place? Why did I feel more afraid than ever? Because I was changing.

Stepping into my past showed me that if I did not accept and continue with this change, if I went back home and slipped back into life as it was, I would be in exactly the same place years from now too, only older. So, I continued kicking at my Terror Barrier. I had no choice because suddenly there was no place on this planet where I felt normal and safe.

I said to my sister, "I have to get out of here. I have to go somewhere new where nothing is familiar." She looked at me and said, "Suzanne, stop right now! You do not have to slow down but you do have to calm down." I looked at her dumbfounded and said, "Have you been listening to Bob Proctor Cds?"

"No, why?" she asked looking at me wondering why I would ask her that.

"Because, that is exactly what he said we all must do."

"Where do you think you want to go that will give you what you are looking for? You do know that everywhere but here winter is raging."

"Yes I know, but I can't sit still."

I wanted more than anything to be calm but I was neither able to calm down or slow down. I wanted my insides to stop shaking and my head to stop spinning. I wanted to get back in that car and continue driving. I told her I was going to leave the next day. When she realized I was going and she could not talk me out of it, and knowing I had no destination mapped out she and her friend decided they were going with me and made a plan for us. We were going North—directly into the stormy weather.

I know she knew I should not be left alone. She knew I did not have the motivation to feed myself other than bits of this and that if I were alone because I was already so far gone off the eating chart to understand the repercussions this was having on my body and my brain. I was not out to harm myself in anyway intentionally, I was not suicidal, I had just gone so long without proper nutrition and it was taking its toll and I was not thinking rationally. She was afraid for me.

After visiting with my father, convincing him I was going to be okay and seeing he was okay too, I told him I was going to leave the next day. I felt so much guilt at just showing up then leaving so soon, but he said he understood and I know he did. We watched the Grey Cup together then I left to go back to Honeymoon Bay for dinner.

The next day I was back in the driver's seat, well my body was back in the driver's seat.

I had received several texts over the past few days from Jack and I was confused. He was feeling badly about how I left, he said he wanted things to be different. A little late I thought. Now I would be heading North, not back to Alberta and even if I were he was going out of town, so what did it matter? I would not see him.

We drove along the Sea to Sky Highway through to

Whistler and continued on into the Caribou Mountain Range. It is a spectacular drive with the wildlife, the mountains, the twisty roads, the canyons, the quaint small towns. All of this was exactly what I was looking for, new geographical scenery. It was stunning and I was happy not to be alone experiencing the beauty Mother Nature was providing. It was snowing lightly almost all of the time but visibility was good and the roads allowed me to travel at speeds that kept me from feeling like I was crawling along. Every now and then one of my travel companions would say, "Okay, we need to eat, we are going to stop at the next place we come across and we *all* are going to eat." I was forced to comply.

For the next few days, we ventured to many parts of the region looking at properties they were contemplating buying and the distractions were wonderful. I was feeling stronger and my mind was not racing with so many questions. To have company not only kept the lonely feelings at bay and they kept saying, "See, all will be fine. You can still laugh." I began to feel stronger. Funny how a few good meals and being with people who care about you can make a dreary outlook appear not so dreary.

The texting continued.

Blip

"Where are you now?"

"Horsefly."

"Really, that's the name of the town?"

"Yes, Katie wanted to see what this property looked like in the snow."

"You okay?"

"Yes are you?"

"Not really."

"Why, what's up?"

"Things, but I don't want to talk about them texting."

"Well, I am not alone, so I will call you later."

"I won't be able to talk later."

"Well then it will have to wait."

"Seeing you has done something to me."

"Perhaps you just need some time and whatever that is will pass."

"Maybe."

"I have to go, we are going to be driving again."

Hearing him say anything to the affect that his mind was switching up made me feel better but I did not get my hopes up. I told myself he was probably tired and thinking too much, just like I was.

It was late in the afternoon when we pulled into a little town surrounded by mountains. It was picture perfect, snow all around, Christmas lights everywhere, shops decorated and the "everything on sale" signs enticing shoppers to come in. Not one thing about this town would have indicated to us that we should not stay here.

We checked into the local hotel. Not your run of the mill chain, it was locally owned and operated and looked like something out of the Old West. After settling our luggage in our room, we went down to the lounge that is attached to the hotel to have dinner. After we ate I was ready to go to our room. I wanted to be able to text without being rude, but it was early and they said, "Not yet, let's sit here for a while, have a drink and play some pool." So it went, I racked them up and we started to play against each other.

My sister does not play so she was cheering me on to beat her friend. We went back and forth. I won one and he won two. Soon enough a couple of local guys asked if we wanted to play against them and the competition was on. Into the third or fourth win on our part, these two strangers were getting noticeably annoyed. They decided to bring in another friend to see if that would change their luck. It did not. We continued to win every game. The drinks for them and my pool partner were showing up before the last ones were finished and I began to feel uneasy. I am not much of a drinker and I am aware what alcohol can do to a person especially when they are being embarrassed on their home table by strangers.

Soon, the bar which had previously been almost empty, was now filling up quickly with men. My sister told me later how she saw as each one came in, they would nonchalantly wander around us, stand and watch us for a while then get on their cell phones and more were showing up. In what appeared to be a very short time, the place was busy. Besides the woman behind the bar, my sister and I were the only women in the place. My spidy senses were on high alert. My pool partner had felt the threatening vibration in the room as well.

Katie and I decided it was time to pack it in for the night. "Okay," I said. "I will finish off this game and we will go." Then one of the opposing players gave me a challenge. He said, "If you make that shot I will give you $20 dollars and pay your bar tab." I laughed and said, "That is getting away easy as I am drinking soda water. Furthermore my shot is short and true on the eight ball, it's going into the corner pocket even if I make a bad shot, so why would you put money on that shot?" Since we had not lost a game all night, it made no sense to me, but I accepted his challenge. I looked around the room. Everyone was standing still, arms crossed, watching. For that many people it was eerily quiet.

I had never thought I should miss a shot or lose any game on purpose before, but at that moment that is exactly what I thought. I needed to miss this shot to diffuse this suddenly hostile air that was surrounding me. Then something came over me and these thoughts ran through my head. "No way! You people have no idea what I have been through to get here. You have no idea how much I have to fight with myself everyday to win at living let alone win this foolish game of pool. I am not going to allow your insecurities or the fact that you feel I threaten your masculinity after beating you repeatedly at a game of pool to make me lose this game. I am not going to allow any of that to make me miss this shot. I am not going to allow you to intimidate me with fear into failure! No way!" Sounds like a lot of thinking going on for the few seconds, but I took a breath, flicked my hair back, bent over the table, eyed up my shot and sunk it. The room was still quiet. It was not the time for whooping it up in the end zone. I looked at him and said, "My twenty dollars please."

The circling posse was closing in. I looked at my sister, her big dark eyes staring across the room at me. She said I looked like a gold fish in a tank of piranha. I looked them in the eyes as I walked past them. I did not need my pool partner to protect me but I knew he was watching closely and was ready to pounce should I have shown one moment of need or fear. He could have done a fantastic job of protecting me. He has every color of every belt that is possible to attain in the world of marital arts.

Then the accusations started. I heard someone say, "They're hustlers." I stopped dead in my tracks, looked this very tall, very big man right in the eyes and shot back "What? You've got to be kidding?" It was then that the pack mentality kicked in. We were surrounded and I knew my martial arts friend was not just rotating his shoulders to relieve tension, he was warming up. I couldn't hold back the words coming out of my mouth. "If you think we came into your town to beat you all at pool for twenty bucks, you are sadly mistaken; you are out of your mind!" Never would I have ever been so bold as to confront a bunch of strangers in this manner before but they messed with me at the wrong moment. Between the texting confusing me and the new woman screaming to get out they had no idea who they were dealing with and frankly neither did I.

My pool partner was around the table so fast I knew it was going to get ugly. I looked at him and I am sure he felt the daggers coming from my eyes. I said to him, "Don't you dare say a word. We are leaving." The crowd parted like the Red Sea, my insides were shaking and my knees were knocking together as I walked, but my partner was not going to let it go so easily.

It was all my sister and I could do to talk him down quietly. I felt like I was in an old western movie. At any moment, my protector who thought he was Clint Eastwood was going to take them all out, and it would not have surprised me to hear him say, "Do you feel lucky punk? Well do ya?" or as Wyatt Earp would say, "I may not be able to get all of you but the first ones to advance are going down." The energy in the room was violent; I felt it and I wanted to get away from it. Negative, violent energy. This is what true fear feels like. If we had not been able to diffuse it, it would not have been pretty. We quickly walked him out of there and up to our room.

"What was that all about?" Katie asked

"I am not really sure but what I do know is somewhere

in that confusion I found some clarity and strength. I felt an overwhelming presence come over me just before I sunk the eight ball, an energy I have not felt in a while, a good strong energy and I was not going to back down when in the past I would have done everything to make the situation calm. I would have lost the game." It was not much but it was a start. I was beginning to feel like I could go home.

The texting continued.

We left for Calgary in the morning as I had to drop the car off and they did not want me driving anywhere alone, especially through the Rocky Mountains as the weather had turned nasty. As it turned out, because I detoured to the Caribou, Jack was going to be back in Alberta when I was there. After all the texting that had gone on the past few days, I was sure he would make time to see me before I left Alberta. He did not. It set me back when I was feeling some hope. He dashed that hope and my heart sank again. I left the car at the airport and my sister and her friend flew West and I flew East. I was not completely ready to go home, I was afraid to go back to the same waiting and wondering game, but I had no choice and no car.

On the plane I had lots of time to think. I was starting to make new plans for my life. At least I had experienced moments on this trek that gave me strength and that gave me hope. We had listened to Bob Proctor on CD and read enough Napoleon Hill that we started quoting them to each other, it was fun. We listened to the biography of Abraham Lincoln three times and I had talked positively to myself so much, everyday, that I had convinced myself I would be able to carry on with the missions I had long before I met Jack—to increase my income, continue to sell my home, get a smaller place of my own and find a new romance.

These were the ideas I had long ago. It was just now, breaking through adversity and facing some of my fear that I realized I had let them go when I found the romance. I became so involved with someone else's dreams and desires that I forgot my own.

The quest for the answer to the many questions I had for myself when I set out on this venture had been answered. "Could I change the way I think? Could I change the way I feel? Could I manifest a better way of life with peace, love and wealth by changing the way I think and react? Yes, I could. This Quest for these few answers had ended, now it was time to take action. I was away for three weeks and when I walked through the door of my home that was still for sale, I felt ready for it to sell. I was ready to move. The use of the car, The Caribou, and seeing my sister and her friend had helped motivate me and I was grateful to all of them.

I knew the maintaining of this mindset, now that I had set the image to positive, was not going to be easy. Life has a way of sucking us back into the fold of insecurity and fear, and sure enough, it did it with a slow vengeance. At this time I did not know I would be making the trip again, and the next time there would be no going back until the new woman inside stopped screaming and there would be no house to go back to.

As Marc and I started seeing signs leading us into Bowmanville, Ontario, I shook my head and said to Marc, "You know, the last time I drove through here six months ago, I was pretty much on the same mission, I cannot believe it! How can that be?"

Quick as a whip he flipped back to me, "Because mom, you have not let go."

"Let go of what?"

"Believing in him and he has never let go of you. Look at all the texting you two do."

"I know, I really like it. I think I am addicted to the texting."

"I think you are addicted to him."

We were laughing as our GPS was talking to us telling us to "turn right, turn right."

CHAPTER TWELVE

First Stop

Two days after leaving Nova Scotia Marc and I arrived in Bowmanville, Ontario. Sandi and Colin had been waiting for us. Although you could never tell by looking at me, my brain was now in a complete state of turmoil and confusion. It was all I could do to open my mouth and make a coherent sentence come out.

I was excited and scared.

I felt every as if nerve ending was exposed and yet I was numb.

I was happy and sad.

I was energized and exhausted.

I felt safe and terrified.

I wanted to live and I wanted to sleep forever.

And I was sick and tired of feeling sick and tired.

It was late in the afternoon, but the sun was still high in the sky, it was hot and humid, and we were sticky, smelly and tired. The humidity was unbearable to Marc and me and as soon as we got out of the truck it made me weak and I needed to sit down. Sandi came flying out her front door and when she greeted us the first thing out of her mouth, "Jesus Christ Suzanne, what the hell happened to you?" She had some idea about what I had been going through over the last several months but when she saw me she gasped. "You're a skeleton, I feel as if I will break you if I squeeze to hard. You told me you had lost weight but this is scary, this is ridiculous. We need to feed you."

"I'm alright, I just need to shower and get a cold drink."

She hugged Marc and we went inside.

I should have been excited. This first stop represented the start of a journey I had envisioned so long ago and it was now actually happening. I was excited to see Sandi and Colin, which was all I knew.

Standing in my room, the air conditioning cooling my skin, I looked at my luggage thinking that my life was in those bags. The sum total of what I thought was important was in those bags.

I just stood there, my arms hanging at my sides still feeling the weight of my bags which I just dropped at my feet. Without moving my head I scanned the room. Sandi loves horses. I looked at the horse shoes tacked to the walls, facing up so the luck wouldn't run out. I smiled at the irony because I don't believe in luck so much as I do fate, but standing there I found myself hoping the folklore and superstitions were true, feeling I could use all the luck I could get no matter how it was presented to me.

The comforter on the bed was snow white and I knew if I put my hand on it, it would feel cool to the touch. I wanted to lie down and sleep but why would this bed be any different? I would not be able to sleep here either.

I looked at the computer on the desk against the wall, its icon flashing its invitation to check e-mail but right then I didn't want to see who was thinking about me and who was not.

My eyes fell down to my bags, I knew I had to unzip a bag to get out clean clothes but I didn't want to. I felt that once I unzipped the bag I also unzipped my new life and I did not want to see what was in that bag. I barely remembered packing it. I do not remember a lot of things at that moment and I am afraid once I open the bag, everything is going to spill out all over Sandi's antique pine board floors and I will not be able to stuff it all back in. My new life will be all over Sandi's floor and I will not be able to pick it up.

The Chatter in my head starts like bickering old ladies.

"Wow, Look where I am!"

"Yes, I should feel grateful."

"I should feel something. I feel nothing."

"What have I done? Can I undo this? Do I want to undo this?"

"No I need to do this. I can not undo this. This is my life now. Some one else owns my home. I can't go back."

"Why have I done this?"

"Because I must if I want to find out what is out there for me, and I want to find out what is important to me."

"Stop thinking!"

"I wish I could stop thinking."

"Where am I going?"

"What does it matter? I just wanted to be away, I needed to be away. Now I am here and where I go tomorrow… makes no difference today."

"Smile, Suzanne. You are so good at covering up, smile just a while longer."

It takes all my concentration to pay attention when someone is speaking to me. I know it is the lack of nutrition and lack of sleep that is contributing to my inability to concentrate. Sandi was going to make sure I got both of those over the next few days.

I hear Marc's voice and it brings me back to earth. He introduces me to the two biggest German Shepherds I have ever seen and in his hands are the keys to Sandi's brand new Camero. He is going to take Colin out for a spin around the block. He is laughing and excited. I am so grateful he is with me. I smile at him, and try not to think about this time next week when he will not be with me

I knew from how I felt last Fall I was going to be afraid to stop driving; I was not ready to stop. I was amazed how quickly the days were passing and soon, Marc was going to be gone.

I keep seeing the moment I turn from him as he walks through security at the airport and I get in my vehicle and drive away from him. I know that day is looming but I must put this out of my head. I must smile while he is with me. I do not want his memory of this trip to be of me looking and acting sad and afraid. He needs to see the strong woman he grew up with doing something so extraordinary that he will burst with pride when he recounts this adventure to his children about their grandmother.

I had to continuously push away the images of the moment I hug my son goodbye. I had to stop feeling his arms around me, hearing him say, "Everything is going to be alright." I wanted to stop rehearsing in my mind what I will say to him before he boards the plane. Suddenly every second became important and I wanted to etch everything he said and did permanently in my brain—the way he moved, the way he laughed, the way he looked at me. I wanted my son to stay with me everywhere I went, but this was not the plan. He had his own life to live and where I was going no one could go with me. After I watched him drive away in Sandi's car, a smile as wide as the sky on his face I walked back to my room and unzipped my new life.

Sitting in the backyard, feeling refreshed from my shower I was finally able to relax and enjoy the cool drinks and snacks Sandi made for us. Marc was entertaining the dogs and I had a few minutes alone while Sandi was in the house.

As I was watching Marc trying to wrestle a ball on the end of a rope out of one of the dogs locked jaws, the thoughts and images of my other children and Marc leaving on the plane surfaced again. The wave of emotion that grips me makes my head start to spin and I break out in a sweat that is so hot, I start looking around for a towel or a cool shady spot to stand in, a puddle, a hose, anything to cool me and stop the flow that is now dripping down my back from my scalp. My body was rushing with anxiety, anticipation and fear. Sandi came back out and looked at me.

"What's wrong? You okay Sally?" (another nickname for me)

"Yes, I'm just having a hot flash."

"Really?"

"No, maybe, I don't know. The doctor said I am not, but I am wondering if the shock of last Fall hasn't sent me into premature menopause. That would certainly explain a lot of my anxiety, the hot sweaty moments of wanting to rip my clothes off, stick my head out the window of the truck like dogs do to cool off."

"What are you thinking about when this happens?"

"Well right now I was thinking about the day Marc leaves and the talks he and I had on the drive up here. I am so conflicted with what I don't want to happen and yet with what I can't wait to happen. He and I had some great talks along the way. We talked a lot about his fear of me being gone, being alone and not knowing when I will be back. He is concerned for my safety on the roads especially since that incident last winter. He pictures me getting tired and driving off the edge of a canyon. He is concerned I will get "there" and find that "there" has moved and "there" is going to disappointment me more than it did when I was home. He thinks I am making a mistake going to see Jack and that I will spiral out of control and no one will be there to help me get up and make me tea. I told him not to worry about me, I will be alright. I told him he is the man of my life, of our family and he needs to look after our family while I am gone. Oh Sandi, it was heart wrenching, watching him through his tears telling me he will do his best to look after his sister, brother and himself."

Our time with Sandi and Colin allowed me to be far enough away from home to be able to come to terms with the past few weeks of my life and it was close enough should I have come to realize I did not want to go any further and drive back. I was hoping I could find some excitement in thinking about the unknown that lay ahead. I was hoping the Gypsy with the Warrior attitude in me would take over but it did not. All I knew was that I could not go back with these feelings of being unfinished.

CHAPTER THIRTEEN

Death and Wonderland

After leaving Bowmanville, Marc and I drove the few hours to Roslyn and Gary's home in Brampton, Ontario. Even though it seemed to take forever to me, I could not believe we were sitting in their driveway already. Didn't we just leave Nova Scotia, I barely remembered the drive. Time had become a test of patience for me. Tick, tick, tick … so slow. I wanted it to pass quickly and at the same time I wanted it to stand still. I would stare at the clock on the dashboard as Marc was driving and watch the second hand tick away the minutes of my new life, I wanted to stick my hand inside that clock and rip its guts out. It was going so slowly yet here we were, on the last leg of our journey together and I wanted to turn the hands of that clock back, but to which time?

Staying with Sandi and Colin for those few days allowed me to get some rest and fuel my body. I was feeling rested and at ease for the first time in so long I could not remember the last time had I felt this way. But I did remember. It was when I was cradled in Jack's arms. So when I arrived at Roslyn's I had a new energy and it felt good.

Ros and I are first cousins. My father and her mother are brother and sister. Being with Roslyn has always made me feel at peace. She has the best life, the only solid, still scxy marriagc I admire. They have great kids and she has always been the voice of reason and logic for me especially in the moments in my life when I wanted to take my kids and hang them up on the wall like wall paper and keep them there until they turned 18. I did the same for her, listened and walked her through moments when life had thrown her curve balls and she was having moments of losing her mind.

Sitting in her driveway, I knew I was in the very best place and with the only person on this earth that would be able to keep me together and allow me to fall apart, when I put Marc on the plane in three days.

When my father told me we had cousins in Ontario it made no impact on me. I was twelve. Eleven years later, my mother told me our cousin, whom I had never met was coming to visit for a while and was going to stay in my old room. Roslyn showed up on our doorstep proudly proclaiming she had taken a year off university to travel around the West Coast to discover her family roots and had no idea how long she was going to stay. I thought she was crazy. Don't those actions sound oddly familiar? Travelling around until whenever? She is a Gypsy too! It must be in our blood. The moment we met, it was instant friendship. She was 21 and I was 23, and since that day, 26 years ago I don't know what I would do without her. We speak just about every day and have been able to spend an amazing amount of time together considering we have always lived several provinces apart.

The Universe has a mysterious way of placing us just where we are supposed to be. Sitting in her backyard that first night, it was a beautiful warm, late spring evening. We were giddy, laughing at nothing, talking about nothing, watching her children, watching my child, enjoying the moment. Marc and I would look at each other and just smile. He knows how much Ros and I mean to each other and he could tell I was happy to be sitting there not having to do anything but breathe.

Making plans on the drive about everything there is to do in and around Toronto we had finally narrowed down the only thing we both agreed upon, well Marc really, I could have cared less about doing anything, but I was going to make the effort for him. He wanted to go to Canada's Wonderland. I am not big fan of roller coasters but that is what he wanted to do so the plans were set. The next morning we would spend the day together scaring the daylights out of ourselves.

The morning started with coffee in the kitchen. Marc and I stood back and watched the routine of getting kids off to school. The sights and the sounds still so familiar to me, it felt like yesterday I had been doing the very same thing.

"Do you have your homework in your back pack? Do you have your lunch? Jason your lunch is right there on the counter, how can it be in your backpack? Lindsay, I will pick you up after your volleyball practise, please don't make me wait today. Gary, don't forget we have a lunch meeting with a clients." I laughed at all of this.

"What's so funny?" Ros was looking at me.

"A big part of me is so glad I don't have to do this any more." But deep down inside, a pang and a yearning for life as it was, shivered up my spine. Would life ever be this simple again? "I did not think I would miss this but right now I do."

"Oh god, get over that feeling right now. You're going to Wonderland."

Everyone was gone and the house was quiet while Marc and I showered and dressed for rollercoaster heaven. When I got out of the shower I heard him talking on the phone with a friend back home and he was excited. Hearing him say he would see them in two days, I was determined to make this day one of our best times together. His excitement was a great energy for me to be around. We got into the truck, set the GPS for Wonderland and laughed at that, that we could set our lives to go to "Wonderland."

Parking was easy, there was lots of space. School had not let out for the summer so that meant the line-ups for the rides should be short. As we rounded a corner, that thought flew right out the window. There, across the parking lot must have been 200 school buses, empty. Oh well.

Both Marc and I decided that since we were going to need our hands to hang on while being thrilled from the rides, our phones and bags should stay in the car. I was not unhappy about leaving my phone behind for the day. My phone had become the only connection to a relationship that was inconsistent and waiting for the ring and the blip of a text message that was not so regular anymore, was making me insane. I heard them in my sleep. I was glad for the reprieve of it not being with me.

The humidity was not so thick and we were grateful for the cloud cover. It had rained earlier that morning and was still threatening overhead but we had never allowed the weather to dictate to us in the past and today was going to be no different.

Marc and I paid the fee to get in and I had to step up my gait to keep up with him. This was our first time here but we had heard so many fun things from Carly and others who love these theme parks. Ros and her family have season passes, so I was looking forward to seeing what the big deal was all about.

We walked through the gate, and people were everywhere. Little kids, high school kids, strollers, families, couples, old, young … they were all here. "Wow, Marc, Look where we are!"

"I know…it's crazy!" He had a grin on his face like all the other little kids.

"What are you grinning at?"

"Listen, do you hear that? Come on, come this way."

I had no idea what he was telling me to listen to. The people, the sounds of the rides, the music ... oh my god the music ... he was telling me to listen to the music.

We rounded a corner and there it was ... the song ... "I will walk 500 miles and I will walk 500 more." He looked at me and I looked back at him. He shouted over the music, "The Proclaimers! It's the Proclaimers!" Marc looked at me, his eyes wide and he was clearly freaked out! I laughed so hard I had to cross my legs. He was laughing and shaking his head, he couldn't stand still. He kept saying over and over, "You're a freak! You are a freak of nature! I can't believe this is happening. What is that all about?!"

At that moment, I knew he got it. I witnessed an epiphany of such magnitude it shook us both up. This was a defining moment in my son's life. He was finally understanding what I have been talking about for so many years, The Universal Laws and how we have to trust even when there appears to be no logical reason why something is happening to us or around us; even in the little things we feel mean nothing to us at the time, like the name of the singers we couldn't remember back in New Brunswick, we have to trust that the Universe will provide all the answers we need to every question that needs an answer.

Sometimes the answers come quickly, other answers can take years. This one came quickly, it only took four days. The Proclaimers will forever be etched in his mind as the band that brought him to a higher level of awareness, although he will not realize that or say that out loud until he is older. He doesn't want to sound like a "Freak of Nature" to his friends.

Whenever he hears that song, and I know he will hear it when he needs to hear it the most throughout his life, he will automatically come right back to this moment. Whenever he is having doubts I will be able to say to him, "Marc, remember the Proclaimers." It truly was Wonderland for me, a magical moment. From this day forward Marc will never doubt me when I say, "Trust in the Universe, it will provide." I will no longer sound like a flakey "Freak of Nature," because he has become one too!

The day was getting long for me and the rides were doing exactly what they always do. I had fun, I laughed, I screamed, I prayed and eventually I got on one that ended it for me. It made me feel seasick and I wanted to throw up and I couldn't ride anymore. Fortunately for us I did not throw up. We walked for a while, waiting for my nausea to settle down. Sitting on a bench drinking water, we watched as people were being hoisted up 156 feet in the air, then released as they glided through the air like a pendulum. "That's almost 16 stories high." I said to Marc.

"Yeah." He says. "I want to do that."

"Are they pulling a rip cord themselves? It looks like they do. Oh no way, they have to pull that and release it themselves? No way! That's crazy!" I looked over at Marc.

"Yeah, let's go do that."

I love swings, the slow easy glide, I can swing all day, but this was different. It was so high.

He was looking at me but I couldn't look at him.

"Really Marc, really? You want to do that?"

"Yes we will make it our last ride of the day. Come on, there is a not much of a line up."

"Why do you suppose that is, the line is not so long?"

"Because you have to pay extra for this ride."

"Really? It has nothing to do with the level of fear it instils? I cannot believe we have to pay extra to completely scare the life out of us. That's great, I can hardly wait."

It is our turn and Marc looks over at me. "You alright mom, you don't look so well."

"I'll be fine, still feeling a little weak from the last ride." Not true, I was not alright. Something was telling me this ride was going to change my life. Overanalyzing my intuition has become something I promised myself I would discipline myself not to do so much, but right now, I have to pay attention to it.

I ask myself, "is it the ride or is it something else?"

As he and I were standing in line, watching, I felt at peace with what I was about to do, swing 16 stories attached to a cable, piece of cake. At the same time my spidy senses were tingling out of control about something else. Nerves—I put it down to nerves. Who wouldn't be nervous? But I just knew it was not the ride that was making me feel this way.

I watched as the thrill seekers in front of us pulled the rip cord. It did not lurch or drop straight down, it swung smoothly like a giant pendulum. I told myself they were only screaming because it's what you are supposed to do when your body is flying through the air dangling by a wire.

We are bound from our necks to our ankles, only our arms are free. There is no way we are going to fall out of this suit. The cables and hooks are snapped into place on our backs and they tell us to lay forward. We are now horizontal, face down two feet off the ground. A slight tug and we are on our way up, but not before they ask us, "Which one of you is going to pull the rip cord?"

Without hesitation, I say "I am."

Marc looks at me and he can tell there is no debating this.

If we are going to plunge to our deaths after paying extra to do it, I am going to be the one who is responsible.

As we rise, we are locked at the elbows, my left arm through his right arm, with our hands crossing our chest. "How appropriate," I think to myself, "I am already in the eternal resting position," as we start to rise above Wonderland. It becomes quieter as we rise. It is so peaceful at the top and the view is fantastic. I want to stay here, in this peace, in Wonderland, but I am soon reminded I have a job to do. I turn and look at Marc, the smile on his face is again, as wide as the sky. Then breaking my spiritual moment is a voice booming out to us, "Pull the cord. Pull the cord!"

Without a moment of doubt or hesitation, I pull the cord. We are looking forward and the earth is coming up fast. As we are soaring through the air I am trying, once again, to ingrain deeply in my memory and my body the feelings and thoughts I am having at this moment. "I am loving this! I am free! I am flying and I am free!"

As we sailed through the air, neither one of us made a sound. Not a scream, not a gasp, nothing. We spread our arms, like we were going to catch someone who was running to hug us, wide and welcoming—we have wings. Still no sound from either one of us. We did not make a deal or a pact of any kind before going up. We never said, "I'm not going to scream, are you going to scream?" We just didn't make a sound.

I didn't want it to stop but of course far too soon we were lowered back to earth, unclamped, untied and our feet firmly planted on the ground. We headed to the booth where we could watch the video and of course we had to buy it.

"Great," I say. We can watch the scariest moment of my life anytime we want. Proof I am not without adventure."

We were done. Heading back to the truck Marc was pensive and so was I. It is a strange feeling to know something is happening but you can't quite put your finger on it. I was feeling his uneasy energy and he was feeling mine. We were not so happy anymore but neither one of us said anything at the time. He was getting used to feeling my moods swing like the ride. I was up, then I was down, but I was not used to feeling his energy swing as dramatically as I did on the walk back to the truck.

Of course the first thing we do after settling into the truck is check our phones. He turns his on and the sounds of messages came pouring in. I turn my on and it is the same thing—blip, blip, blip. We look at each other, he is already reading the text, mine have not finished coming in.

"Blake has been in a car accident."

"What, oh no … do they say what his condition is? Who was with him? Is anybody else hurt? Where is Nick?"

I read my own text as he listens to the voice mail.

"He is in critical condition."

I listen to my own voice mail.

Nick, my youngest son, and Blake share an apartment and he is one of Marc's best friends. They all have been friends for years. Blake had been a staple in our home for so long he started to look like us. Nick has left me messages so I know he is okay. He was at work when it happened. I call him. He is at the hospital with the rest of their friends that have started to gather. Blake's mom, Gail, is in with Blake, but they can't go in.

"Nick, honey, I want you to listen to me. Blake is going to be alright." I believed this with all my heart as the words were coming out of my mouth.

I am picturing Blake. Four days ago I hugged him

goodbye, he lifted me off the floor and he kissed the top of my head and said, "I am going to miss you sooo much! Come home soon!"

I couldn't believe this was happening. I can still feel my arms around him, my head on his chest and patting his heart, telling him to take care of this gang for me until I got back.

This could not be the Blake I would ground from being in my home and would show up the next day, and laugh when I reminded him he was grounded from being here and head up the stairs, mocking me, telling me, "You still love me, you can't ground me, I'm your third son."

He was right, I couldn't ground him for long, and they were all like my third sons. I loved them all.

"Nick, honey, you need to believe your buddy is going to pull through this. He is young and strong and has so much life left to live; he is going to be fine."

I closed my eyes and I could see him. I could see the emergency area of the hospital he was standing in. I could see all the kids that were gathering in the waiting room.

"Nick, I am going to call you back."

I called Carly.

She didn't even say hello, "Already on my way."

"Oh I am so glad. Call me when you get there."

Marc and I pulled out of Wonderland and into a world that would never be the same for any of us. It was Wonderland no more. It was a land of fear, fragility and death.

When we arrived back at Ros's, Marc went downstairs and I went up. I told Gary and Ros what was happening back in Halifax. They didn't know what to say. What can you say? It is the most unbelievable thing to hear when someone you know has been in an accident and the outcome is still unknown.

My phone rings and it's Nick. Carly is with him and he tells me the waiting room is full with Blake's friends. Blake's mom, Gail, had just come out to tell them they have more tests to do before they could determine the extent of his injuries and that he is still unconscious.

I hang up the phone. I look over at Marc and he is visibly shaking.

"Do you want to go home? I think you should go home."

"I don't know what to do. I don't want to leave you but I want to be there too."

"I understand that, but what do you want to do? I will be alright."

"Let's wait for the update and make our decision then."

"Ok, you're right, we'll wait."

Again I find myself wanting time to fly by, turn it back and stop at the same time.

Waiting and picturing all that is going on back home, is almost more than we can stand.

But what can you do?

How do you react, respond, and behave when you are so far away?

All you can do is feel helpless and wait.

Hours go by and the sound of the phone ringing in our quiet room makes us both jump.

"It's Nick." I push the button to hear my son's voice. He is crying.

"Mom … Gail just came flying out of Blake's room hysterical. She is screaming they can't stop the bleeding, they can't stop the bleeding!"

I am looking at Marc; his eyes are wide, frightened and filling up with tears.

"Nick, honey, Nick … listen to me. Something terrible is

happening to your friend. Something we cannot control. Oh sweetie I wish I was there. Is Carly there?"

"Yes."

"Let me speak with her."

Carly will be the oldest one there. She is 27 when the rest of them are only 17-21. She has watched them all grow up and knows them well.

"Carly, how are you holding up?"

"I am fine but Mom, it's so sad, all these guys crying and holding each other and the girls are out of control. It's the saddest thing I have ever seen. Their parents are showing up to take them home. It's awful. Nick latched onto me when I walked in and broke down sobbing. They all saw Gail crying and hysterical and that sent the whole room into hysterics. I am going to try to take Nick home but I think he wants to stay here. What should I do?"

"I think you need to let him do what he needs to do. If he wants to stay then he should stay."

"I don't want him to be alone. I will stay with him if he is going to stay."

"Thank you darlin', I am so relieved you are there with him, with all of them. Marc will want to go home tomorrow. I am going to see if we can change his ticket and if we can't I'll just get another flight for him. Call me later."

I get off the phone and tell Marc the prognosis is not good. "They don't know if he is going to make it through the night."

How do you tell your son one of his best buddies is going to die?

How do you prepare them for something no one, no matter how old we are, is ever prepared for. A child is going to die.

I have to keep busy. I have to keep him busy. I get on the phone. He gets on the computer.

"Check the airlines. See what flights are out first thing in the morning."

I speak with the airline that he is already booked with; they have nothing available at all for tomorrow.

"You're kidding right? Nothing? How can that be? What is happening in Nova Scotia that there are no seats available? Can we get on a waiting list? No?"

"Marc what have you found?"

"Nothing, everything is booked."

"You're kidding? Ok, it's late, let's try to get some sleep and try again in the morning."

I lay there, hearing Nick and Carly's voices over and over in my head. Seeing them, feeling their pain. Then it hits me. What am I going to do?

I am only four days away from home, four days into my new life and a tragedy has struck and my children are about to go through one of the most devastating times they will ever experience and I am not there.

I look over at Marc who is just staring off into space.

"Marc, what do you think I should do? Should I go back with you?"

"I don't know Mom. I don't know anything right now."

"What time did this happen?"

"Nick said around 2:30."

"Do you know what we were doing at 2:30?"

"Yes, we were flying."

"Yes we were. When the car Blake was a passenger in was being hit, we were flying through the air. Do you find that bizarre? When we were being pulled up, I knew something was happening. I thought it was because of what I was doing but it was because everyone was trying to get in touch with us. Did you feel it too?"

"Yes but I thought it was just because you were scared."

"Do you see what happened; do you understand the energy that was being sent across the country by everyone who tried to contact us? How we both changed when we walked out of the park, the ominous feeling that had come over us. We knew something was happening. Marc, promise me this is something you will pay attention too. The feelings and instincts we had were real."

He is just staring at me but I can not help it, I want to talk about this.

"Ask your sister what she thinks about this; it happens to her all the time. Over the years I have trusted my instincts and I have rarely been wrong. When I feel what I call, 'the winds of change,' and you have heard me say many times, my spidy senses are tingling, I know something is about to happen or is happening. I never know what it is at the moment but I put myself on alert to watch for it. I try not to dwell on it because I am aware of my own energy and what dwelling on an idea can do."

He is drifting off now. My talk has bored him but I know he understands it.

In the blackness of our room my phone lights up as it rings, and wakes Marc. It's Nick.

"Hi honey. How are you now?"

"I'm ok. I came home. I don't want to be here. I shut Blake's door. I don't want to see his stuff but his stuff is all around me."

"Are you alone?"

"No Emily is with me."

"Mom … what if Blake dies?"

He is starting to cry and so am I. We just cry quietly on the phone with each other. His heart is breaking. His world is changing and I am not there to hold him.

"Nick, do you want me to come home?"

"I don't know. I will call you tomorrow. I am going to go to bed now."

"Ok, honey. I love you."

"I love you too Momma. Good night."

Marc finally was able to fall back to sleep, I was not. For hours I laid there praying to the "make this all a horrible dream" gods.

I laid there, in the dark, listening to my son, across the room, tossing, turning, hearing the mournful sighs that would follow the long moments of him holding his breath, grinding his teeth, clenching his jaw. I could not and did not want to imagine what demons were haunting his dreams while the nightmare of what was happening to one of his best friends was unfolding back in our home town. It was one of the longest nights of my life.

As I lay awake I started praying once again, "Please protect our little friend Blake. Please don't take this child away from his mother. Please don't take this friend away. Please let us all hear him laugh at life again … Please, Please, and Please."

Why is this happening? What kind of test is this, for my kids, for us all? This is cruel.

When my phone rang, it was black in our room, the glow from my cell phone the only light illuminating the name of who was calling. Sitting up in my bed, I said the name of the caller out loud—"Nick." I did not want to answer the phone yet I could not answer it fast enough. Across the room I heard Marc stirring. He was now sitting up too and had turned on the small lamp that is on the table beside his head. His eyes were wide and terrified. He was watching for a reaction from me.

I could hardly make out Nick's words. The sounds I heard were not familiar yet I knew this was my son. The words I was trying so desperately to grasp and comprehend were echoing through the phone and into my brain. They ripped my guts wide open, spilling out every parent's worst nightmare. The hot searing knife that was his words sliced a gash through my soul, tearing away the very fabric of all that is right, safe, sane and just in our world.

"He died Mom ! … He diiied Mom! Blake died."

"What? Oh my god Nick, Nick, honey … no, no, no … What?"

"He died mom … Blake died!"

I was frozen where I sat. My eyes had not left Marc's face. I am listening to Nick and watching Marc.

Marc looks puzzled. His head is slightly turned to the side, the light appears to be casting a ghostly shadow across his face but I know it is not a shadow, I just watched the blood drain from his face. His tanned face is now translucent, his mouth is slightly open as if he just finished saying something, but he has said nothing. His eyebrows are knit as if waiting for an answer to a question he just asked. I watch him move, everything is now in slow motion. He wraps his arms around himself, trying to keep the answer that just slammed into his body, to a question he did not have to ask … trying to keep that answer from running up his body and into his brain.

I have not taken my eyes off of him.

Marc did not need to hear the words to know what was being said.

He slumps face first into his pillow and the low guttural

sound of agony coming from my son rips the silence of this room apart.

I have one son on the phone; and the other is across the room. The moans of sorrow, of grief so out of control are horrific, unbearable to me. What I hear coming through the phone line will haunt me for the rest of my life. Nick is unable to speak, his buddy, his roommate, his friend, his "bro" has just died.

What I see in front of me, across the room, will remain an image I will see for the rest of my life. I am staring at Marc, the reality of what has happened registers without me saying a word. I move to sit beside him, I put my free hand on his back. His body is shaking violently, uncontrollably. He starts to curl into the fetal position. "NO! NO! NO! Not Blake, Not Blake …"

The sounds I hear through the phone, coming from my child, grip my heart and squeeze my lungs. Marc can hear Nick and it escalates his cries. They are inconsolable and I say the only words I can say, "I am here Nick, honey … I am here. We are there."

I watch Marc helplessly as the wretchedness of his pain makes his body twist and contort so grotesquely, I can't stand it! He curls up then stretches out, then curls again. He is trying to stop the pain, as he gasps to catch his breath.

I am in shock, this has to be shock. I am sitting still, in a calm, stunned state, just listening, my free hand resting on Marc's back. I am helpless, there is nothing I can do but hold one and listen to the other.

Somewhere in this insanity I hear a voice,

"What happened? What is going on?"

It is Roslyn. She heard my phone ring. I look up, I know she is speaking, I just don't know what she is saying.

"Oh my god, Suzanne, what happened?" She knew before the words came out of her mouth. She sits beside me. Her eyes filling up with tears. I look at her. I can't say the words I have not yet said out loud to Marc.

"I need to call Carly, but I can't hang up this phone."

Roslyn hands me the house phone. My fingers are shaking as I push the buttons.

I hear her sleepy voice, "Hello?" I can tell she knows. Then … there they are … and I say them out loud.

"Carly, honey … Blake died."

"Oh Mom, no!"

"I need you to go to Nick. I am on my cell phone with him and he needs you."

"I am on my way. I will call you from his place. What's that noise? Is that Marc? Oh my god Mom …oh my god!"

"Nick, honey listen to me, Carly will be there shortly. She is on her way."

He says, "Okay, I have to go; I need to make some calls."

"Carly said she will call me when she gets there. Nick, there are no words, I have no words. I love you my baby boy. Marc will be home soon."

Hanging up the phone I am now free to use both arms to hold Marc safe to me. More than anything I want to absorb the pain he is feeling. He cries and cries, his body rising and falling, heaving with each sob.

"I want to go home."

"I know you do, we will check the airlines again but for right now let's just cry for our friend."

He and I sit holding each other, letting this unbelievably sad moment sink in. My mind is racing with images of what is going on back home. I think of Blake's mom. She had come to see me just days before I left, eight days before Blake died.

Standing in my front hall saying goodbye, Gail is shaking her head. "Wow I can't believe you are going."

"Me either."

"Too bad we never got the dinner the boys promised to make for us after they settled in."

"Yes we should have taken them up on that. But we would have had to make it and take it to them. I wanted to go, just to wear my muddy shoes on their carpet, leave dishes on the counter and then leave."

We laughed our heads off.

"You can't leave me here with them!" She says in a wavering sarcastic voice.

"Yes I can … they will be alright. I am only a phone call away if you think there is anything I should know."

"I won't need to call, at least not about them."

"No Gail, I don't think you will. We did a good job and they are going to be fine."

She hugged me and told me to stay safe. Gail and I became friends through our boys. We shared many moments of frustration and anxiety while raising these boys as single moms. I remember a specific moment when we laughed at how we would laugh one day at the antics these boys put us through. I was grateful we were there for each other during those times. Now there was nothing I could do for her, for any of us. Her son was gone.

I had no idea what to do. I could not call her on this day and tell her everything was going to be alright. I could not tell her Blake is a good kid and will come through this as I had many days when it was all we could do to get them through high school. I could not call her, I had no words. We would not laugh.

We were unable to get a flight for Marc. We couldn't

believe it; this had to be the Universe again, forcing us to sit still. I told him so too. "It was so we could process this together; allow you time to grieve with me so you can be strong for all those who are going to look to you for strength." I was not unhappy about this as I was able to spend this time listening to him, keeping an eye on him, holding him.

He spent hours on the phone with his friends and when he hung up from each call he would update me on what was going on. Everyone was rallying at Nick and Blake's apartment, supporting each other. I was proud of all of them.

When life shrouds us in darkness, we have to believe in miracles; we have to believe that the light will find the cracks and allow a healing to take place even though it does not feel possible.

This was a miracle I had prayed for months to happen.

Frankie had been a friend of Marc and Nick's for a long time, but Nick and Frankie did not always see eye to eye. Their rift had reached a boiling point some time ago and they had not been friends for a while. It tormented Nick daily and I could tell he was sad that their friendship had deteriorated to the degree it had, even though he would never admit it. Their pride was getting in the way. They even went as far as leaving if the other showed up at a party. Nick would not allow Frankie to visit with Blake, at their apartment, if he was going to be home, but I knew he really did not feel this way. I knew he missed his friend.

My phone rings and it's Carly. "Mom, you are not going to believe what just happened."

"Okay, tell me."

"There was a knock on the door and Nick answered it. Frankie was standing there. They looked at each other and

Nick fell apart. They hugged each other for the longest time and cried. Through their tears they kept telling each other how sorry they were. It was so sad and so happy at the same time, we all broke down again. There must be twenty people here crying."

"Oh Carly that is wonderful … I am so happy for them."

"They kept saying how happy Blake would be if he was here to see this."

"Yes he would be."

The rest of the day Marc and I stayed close to each other. We still had not decided if I would fly home or not. I could not make that decision right now. I just wanted to concentrate on getting him home.

The next morning, at the airport, I stood looking at my son. I was so proud of him. His compassion, his kind heart and soul had become more evident to me over the past two days. Listening to him on the phone consoling his friends, telling them he would be home soon and he would take care of them, made my heart swell. I knew Marc was going home a better man, a stronger man.

Everything I had been rehearsing about this moment, about Marc's departure seemed so trivial now. We were standing out side my truck near the departure doors at the airport and I looked up into his eyes.

"Marc, the world you left five days ago has changed. It may seem like nothing will ever be the same again, and it won't be, not without Blake. But I promise you this, one day the pain you feel today will start to subside. It may not feel like it will ever go away but it will. Your brother is going to need you in a way we could never begin to conceive before I left. Your sister and your friends and Gail will need you too, but please promise me, you will not give yourself to everyone, as I know you will want to. Make sure you take time for yourself to grieve. Talk to Carly and Nick, talk with your friends and Marc… Please my son, please, continue to trust your instincts. I love you. Call me when you get to Nick's."

As he is hugging me, holding me so close, his big arms encompassing me so completely, holding me tight, I think to myself, "These are not the arms of a my child, these are the arms of a my son, a man." I start to cry.

He kissed the top of my head. My face snuggled against him, feeling the warmth of his body on my cheek as I closed my eyes. I feel his heart beating so hard under my hand as I lay it on his chest, the same way I had hugged our little buddy Blake.

He looked down at me and asked me not to come in to airport with him. He wanted some time alone, to compose himself, before he got on the plane. I kissed him good bye, turned and walked away. When I looked back, he was gone.

Back at Roslyn's, and after Marc had called to tell me he was at Nick's and assured me they were alright. I was still feeling so conflicted as to what to do.

She and I sat together talking.

"How does life get so sad?"

"I don't know Ros, it just does, from one breath to the next. It just does."

"What are you going to do?"

"Not sure, I am afraid if I go back I will not leave."

"The kids will get through this without you, you know that. They are together, and all their friends are suffering too. There is safety in numbers. I think you should continue West, for yourself, continue with your plan. If it turns out you need to be back there, you can fly from wherever you are at that time."

"I wasn't even thinking that way. Of course I could. I'll sleep on it; I will know what I am supposed to do when I get in my truck in the morning."

"I think it is important for them to see you stay strong and determined in the face of adversity."

"Yes I thought of that too. I also need to know they can work their way through adversities without me around. What if something was to happen to me, while I am on the road? This is a test for them and for me. There is a reason this happened early in my journey. So many tests these days for all of us. I am tired of being tested and I know … this is only the beginning."

I was in the very best place. I thought about what I was thinking when I pulled in her driveway three days ago, how fragile I was feeling for myself, thinking I was going to fall apart, so unsure about everything I was doing. But right now, the level of grief I was feeling for everyone back home far outweighed what ever I was suffering and at that moment, I was able to forget why and who I was suffering from.

Blip…

"You there?"

"Yes, Marc is gone."

"What are you going to do?"

"Not sure. Going to make the decision in the morning."

As I tried to sleep I ran the original plan for myself through my head. The following morning I was to leave and start my journey West, alone. Now I had no idea which way to turn, West into the unknown or East, back to my children. Throughout the night I prayed for guidance. The texting during the night with Jack did not help me make any decisions either. I am not sure why, but I figured it was because I was looking for support and guidance from him. It was my time of need, but of course, how could he give it to me if he was unable to guide himself.

When morning arrived, did I get in my truck and drive back to Nova Scotia to be with my children? No I did not. I got into my truck and drove further away.

Was it the right decision? Today I can say absolutely, without a doubt, YES! I was so proud of how they carried themselves with grace and dignity during the next few days. Carly, followed by Marc, followed by Nick, led a procession of cars to the funeral and Marc read the eulogy at the funeral.

I knew I made the right decision, as hard as it was. My children grew so much, I grew so much. Now it was time to see how brave I really was.

CHAPTER FOURTEEN

Serious Transition

I heard a quote sometime ago, and it made me think of my friend Andrea.

"We all wear masks and the time comes when we cannot remove them without removing our own skin."
— *Andre Berthiaume*

Driving out of Ontario took me two days. Now, I was flying down the highway crossing the border into Manitoba. The sun was shining and right about now, Marc would be reading the eulogy at Blake's funeral.

I knew I was well over the speed limit but I did not care. The sun was shining and I had the windows down, my music on and I was singing loudly. Both the truck and my mind were in cruise control. I was on a mission; I was going to see my girlfriend Andrea in less than an hour and I was excited about seeing her.

Passing vehicles like they were standing still, I was feeling free. The highway is so flat and straight, with few obstructions so I figured I would see any radar traps. I was wrong.

The police officer was very nice.

"Welcome to Manitoba."

"I know you were going a lot faster when I first spotted you, but I am only going to give you a ticket for just over the limit."

"Well that is nice of you, thank you."

"You are a long way from home. Where are you heading in such a hurry?"

"Lunch, with a girlfriend in Winnipeg."

He chuckled, "Long way to come for lunch." After taking the pertinent information from me he went back to his car to write out my first speeding ticket since I was 18.

I took advantage of my unexpected stop and got out to stretch and take a few pictures. The cars I passed were now passing me. I was sure they were laughing at me, thanking me for finding this radar trap hidden behind the only stand of trees around. One even honked his horn. I waved.

The officer got out of his cruiser and we stood at my open trunk chitchatting for a while. He was holding the ticket and waving it around while using his hands to talk. I wanted him to give me the ticket so I could get on my way.

When he handed it to me, I looked at it. "No way! This cannot be the fine. That must be wrong. Oh my god how much would it have been if you had given me the next fine up?"

"Twice that amount, but like I said, when I saw you, I could tell you were going much faster than what I clocked you at. I am sure if I had been able to pick you up … I would have had to impound your vehicle."

"Well on that note, it was nice speaking with you. You have a great day."

I arrived at Andrea's home. She used to live in Nova Scotia and I know she misses it, so seeing someone from home was exciting for her.

She answered the door and she grabbed me, hugging me so tight.

"I missed you so much! Get in here!"

Standing in her kitchen we just stare at each other,

smiling. She is making me tea. I am so happy to be there. She is looking at me funny, "You have lost weight, you look great."

"Thanks."

"How did you do it?"

"Less food, more anxiety, I don't recommend it."

Andrea and I have a special relationship. She and I became friends many years ago. I was receiving treatment at a clinic where she worked. She is a critical care nurse and was working part-time in this clinic. She was walking out of the clinic at the same time I was. We could not help but walk side by side so it was only natural to start talking.

After introducing our selves she asked me, "Are you walking from here?"

"No I have a car and I am parked right here."

"I see you come in regularly, you must be just about finished."

"Yes I am. Are you walking somewhere?"

"Yes, home, I don't live far, five blocks."

"Would you like a drive?"

"Sure."

That was the beginning of one of the most treasured relationships I have in my life.

Our schedules allowed us to spend time together during the day when my children were in school.

I loved being at her apartment. It was in a heritage house in the South End of Halifax with high ceilings and lots of wood. From the moment I walked in I felt so comfortable, like I was home.

I was living with a man and the relationship was ending badly. I took every opportunity to get away from him and Andrea provided the escape I was looking for.

She was kind, caring and wanted nothing from me.

Now sitting in her home, so far from those days, I found myself yearning for her apartment again and the healing it provided.

"I needed you so much back then."

"I needed you too. I am so glad you came today. I think you need me now."

"Yes I do and it is not much different from then, unfortunately."

"I am sorry to hear that. Last summer when I was home you were in love. What happened?"

"I think I still am but it has changed. I am afraid he is not who I think he is portraying himself to be. He is one way on the phone and when we are together he is different, or I am different. I am not sure what to think. I changed every thing in my life, not for him, I had to change for me. I was afraid I was going to be stuck like so many people around me. I couldn't stand it. Now I am driving towards him and I feel sick to my stomach to think he might be someone different once we get in the same time zone for a while, that it will all have been an illusion created via telephone and texting. But it is not just him. Actually I know it is not just him, he has been a big support for me on so many levels but lately he has his own stuff to deal with. I believe that I am having an identity crisis" We laugh.

"Not you?"

"Yes me. I know it sounds ridiculous to me too. I always thought I was very well put together mentally, well most of the time. Now I can't find a place that makes me feel comfortable. All I can think about is getting to Alaska. I don't know why but something is telling me my answers will come to me when I get there, and in the next thought all I want to do is get to him. It's such a struggle as the two are so far apart. It's making me crazy. I want to get to him but at the same time I want to drive as far away as possible."

"Oh Sooz, I'm sorry you have to go through all of this. But look at the amazing trip you are on."

"Oh yes, it is a trip for sure."

Her husband had taken the children to daycare and then he went to work, so we had the house to ourselves. We are sitting on her couch, and I tell her about what is happening with my children back home, that how writing my children's books saved my sanity, I try to bring her up to date on what else has happened since I last saw her and the purpose behind my journey.

She says to me, "Why are you trivializing what is happening to you?"

"What, I don't think I am."

"Yes you are, you are trying to make it sound like you should not be experiencing any anxiety but look what you have done, just selling your home and leaving your life and your kids is enough to make most people crumble let alone fire into the mix the heartache and feeling the need to explore past pains. Don't ever say you wish you could just be like other people. Other people would not have the guts to do what you're doing. Look what I went through to get here. I didn't think for a minute it would have caused the anxiety it did. Remember the physical pain I went through? It was gross!"

There is a small framed photo mixed in with several others, sitting on the table beside me, the two of us smiling, I pick it up. We start to reminisce about those days in her apartment. She would make me tea. We would talk for hours. We would spend long moments not talking just breathing.

She asks me, "Do you remember that day I told you about Chris?"

"Yes."

"Do you remember how hard it was for me to change my way of thinking? How suddenly my entire belief system broke me down and I could not function for weeks? I felt like my skin was being shed. I was turning inside out and it created such a conflict I thought I was losing my mind. I had no idea who I was supposed to be."

"Yes I remember. It was painful to watch."

Like it was yesterday I see us in her apartment, sitting across from each other, I could tell she wanted to talk about something that was making her uncomfortable. She was pensive and unsure of herself, rubbing her arms like she was cold. I sat there watching her until she was ready to speak. I had come to know her so well by this point that I knew I was witnessing a transformation but I would never have guessed what she was about to tell me.

"There is a man asking me out all most every day now."

She had never been with a man.

This man who was asking her out, a doctor at the clinic, did not know she had never been with a man, and she thought she might go. She found herself thinking about him, children and a home. It was so strange for her to think this way. All her adult life, she had only been in love once, with a woman who left her for a man. She was heartbroken. But now she found herself in the same situation, thinking about a man and it was confusing to her.

"Your jumping the gun a bit here aren't you. You haven't gone out with him and you see yourself with him, and with children. Does he know you are gay?"

"No he doesn't and yes I want children but I just don't know if I could do it with a man."

"Do it? Do what?"

"Fall in love."

"Being in love, it does not matter who it is with, a man or a woman, it is the same feelings. All you can think about is getting to them, being with them. Their touch, their voice, everything about them, you just want to be a part of it. And unfortunately we can't help who we fall in love with, it just happens, and there are many different kinds of love, but the one you're seeking, is the one we all seek, it is the ultimate love."

She says so matter of factly, "Yes look at us. How do you explain this kind of love to anyone?"

"I don't explain it to anyone, so many would turn it ugly, make it scandalous." As the words came out of my mouth I could see the images in people's minds.

"I think I want this with him, but more."

"Women would understand this kind of love, maybe a few men."

I think about the women in my life, my friends, yes they would understand this and on another level, not as deep as Andrea's and my relationship unexpectedly grew to be; we do love each other this way. It's a loyalty that is hard to explain, that even though it can go through its own growing pains, women have an innate ability to love each other and stick together.

And she agrees with me ... there maybe a few men in our lives we feel this way about too.

Just to be held by her, without expectation; to allow myself to feel loved by her without expectation; to close my eyes and feel hands upon my body which was dis-eased, caressing me for the pure simple act of healing, was beautiful to me. I had never felt so loved in my whole life. Our words to each other, the way we listened to each other, we opened each others hearts and allowed in a love that made us feel whole that we had not experienced with anyone. It was what I always imagined love would feel like, the beautiful pictures of bliss when I was old enough to create those magical images of my relationship, watching fairytales of love, when I was young and had not been disillusioned by life. It is what I wanted from a man but had never found until I met Jack. He is the male version of Andrea and I want to love him like I do her, only with all the other perks … at least I think I do.

Trying to explain this kind of love, without sex, without obligation, without commitment is not easy, so we haven't tried to explain it, it was never anyone's business. Before now, only two people knew about how close she and I are, the two people we trusted not to make it ugly or scandalous. We knew they would understand it, and share the beauty of it, her husband Chris and Jack. It was selfless and nurturing, and it healed us both and showed us both the kind of love we wanted. And now we both want it with men.

We agreed the Universe brought me to her so she could explore her feelings of the transition she was making without the temptation or the chance of it becoming a sexual relationship. I was someone she could trust; someone who would listen to her fears and doubts without judgement. She came into my life when I needed love and compassion, to be held in a physical way that was not sexual, by someone who loved me.

"Just go out with him, give him a chance. Give yourself a chance. It will be wonderful. When the time is right, you will know when to tell him you have never been with a man. If he is someone meant to be with you he will accept that. Andie, when you allow yourself to be in love with a man, and you share yourself with him, when you connect on a higher level, when you are one, there is no better feeling in the world. Not that I am an expert on the topic, my track record is not great." She laughs at me. "I just know there have been moments in my life when I never wanted those moments to end. I thought I was in love, and I suppose I was at the time. I think you should go out with him. At the very least, go and experience it. How will you know if you don't take the risk?"

Andrea did go out with him and they did fall in love.

They moved to Winnipeg within the year. I was lonely for my friend, but now I had a level, a gauge, a bar, to which I could measure my feelings when I allowed love to enter my heart and the bar was high. I promised myself I would never sacrifice or settle for anything less.

Now many years later, I am sitting in their home. I smile at her and she moves closer to me.

She touches my face and holds her hand there, on my cheek.

Tears start to fall down my face.

"Andie I am so afraid. I have left my kids. I have left everything and everyone I know. I have a few stops to make along the way but after that … I have no idea where I am going, other than Alaska. I have given my faith over to the Universe and pray everyday I am doing the right thing. He made me feel things; I know he felt it too. I let my guard down and he unknowingly took advantage of that."

"Don't worry about anything Suzanne. You are a strong woman. Look at what you went through to get here. It took you years to recover. There were times when you didn't think you would make it through those days. This is nothing compared to that. He has no idea who you are. And if he does not take the time to find out, he is a fool."

She always had a way with words that made every thing sound so simple.

"This is a brand new life for you. You have only been living this life for a week. You have to give yourself time and trust your instincts as I know you always do. You are the only woman I know that would do this … and do it well. I am proud of you for taking the steps to change your life. I always knew you would do something extraordinary when the time was yours. Now look at you. I can tell you think you are weak and it seems like you are throwing yourself into the fire head first, but you're not. You are worn out. Please promise me you will feed yourself and sleep."

"Yup … eat and sleep. I will endeavour to do those two things everyday."

"Are you making fun of me?"

"No, I am serious. I will do those two things everyday."

We talk and laugh for a while longer but she can tell I am ready to leave. My eyes have been darting back and forth between her and the door.

"I am so happy for you Andie. Chris is a wonderful man. I am so glad I talked you into going out with him." We laugh. We hug goodbye. She holds me close and tells me to be careful and to slow down. I get back into my truck and drive away.

When I left her that day, I knew exactly how I wanted to think and feel when I was in love. It was honest and uninhibited and I know I will be unable to accept anything less. The few relationships I have had since meeting Andrea have been measured against that love, but only one has come close, and I am driving towards it.

Blip.. "Where are you now?"

"Just leaving Winnipeg."

"Did you see your friend?"

"Yes I did."

"How was that?'

"Fine."

"Tell me more."

"I got my first speeding ticket since I was 18."

"That's not good but that's not what I want to know about. Tell me more about your visit with Andrea."

"She is beautiful, happy and I wish you could meet her. Maybe someday you will."

"Maybe, someday."

"Are you packed and ready to leave town tomorrow?"

"Yes, it is strange to think you will be here and I will not be."

"Yes and after my time there last Fall I told myself, the next time I visit there I will be feeling different."

"Are you feeling different?"

"Not really."

"Well I hope to change that for you when I see you next."

"Wow, now I really am I looking forward to seeing you."

"When do you suppose that will be?"

"After I drop Lee off in Vancouver to fly home. Three weeks from now."

"Okay, well you drive safe."

"I will. And you enjoy your time away."

There it was, the turning point, he wanted to change something for me and regardless of what it was, I was just happy we were able to be talking calmly, because I really like the way we just talk.

CHAPTER FIFTEEN

Lee and I

I arrived in Alberta with a couple of days to spare before Lee arrived. I stay with my friend Bruce in the North West part of Calgary. I have known Bruce since I was 18. I met him the same time I met Mr. Aswell, and as he and Mr. Aswell have been friends most of their lives, Bruce has been able to follow my life and this journey via Mr. Aswell. It has been a long drive to get here. Leaving Andrea in Manitoba I make one stop in Regina then drive until I get here. Bruce opens the door and it is like no time has passed. He opens his home to me as if I am family and I was just here yesterday.

I was excited that Lee was flying in. Prior to my leaving Halifax May 29th, she and I had spent almost every day together since I showed up at her place late one September evening in a state of shock and despair looking for a glass of wine and an ear to bend. Lee is single, clever, and attractive and one of the most dedicated friends I have. When I hit the worst part of my demise, Lee sat with me and made me laugh. She has been a positive influence and I don't know what I would have done with out her. When my home was taking too long to sell, she, also my realtor, would work with me to help me keep the faith that had almost completely disappeared. It was a long cold blistering winter and Lee made it bearable.

I asked her to fly out West so we could spend some time together that didn't include drama or work. I wanted her to see where I would be spending some of my time. I wanted her to fly into Calgary so we could travel the Rocky Mountains, and then go on to Vancouver Island. Lee had never been this far West before and I am so familiar with it that I wanted to be her tour guide, especially on the Island. Two days of travel from Calgary including the ferry across to the Island and we arrived in Honeymoon Bay close to midnight. Mr. Aswell was already sleeping. I was elated to be there and have Lee with me. She has heard about my private retreat for as long as she has known me.

In the morning we get up to coffee that has been perked for us before Mr. Aswell goes to work. He does this for me every morning I am there. Lee is watching me dance to Legends of the 70's. I am in my element being here. I feel at home and I feel free. I am happy I feel comfortable here again.

Over the next few days Mr. Aswell takes us up the mountains, cooks for us, goes fishing and brings home fresh salmon and crabs. We sit on his beach and he brings out the salmon baked then sprinkled with maple syrup and the crab is seasoned with secret spices and baked and we are giddy sitting on the beach as each dish is brought out to us. Lee and I just sit in awe of our host. She looks at me and smiles. She instantly falls in love with Mr. Aswell, for the same reasons I have loved him for over 30 years. He is so giving and asks for nothing in return. He treats us as if we are precious, but as I have come to know this is how he is all the time. He fishes often, and has cooked the most incredible meals for himself his whole life. I know this but Lee has never seen a man present the meals that he does. One evening my cousin Roslyn calls just to find out what we are eating and when I tell her "Chicken Cordon Bleu" that he has made from scratch and I did not even see it happen, that it just appeared on plates, she swoons and we laugh. Mr. Aswell has been the most consistent man in my life and Lee knows that I do not share this space easily. Roslyn is the only other woman I have shared this with. They both know when I am here, it is to rest, rejuvenate, eat, sleep and then go back to my life. This time it is different, I have no home to go back to and I am so happy Lee is here to help me settle in to my new found freedom.

After taking Lee back to Vancouver to fly back to Nova Scotia, I meet with Jack, who is in Vancouver for a few days to work. When I say good bye to him, I say, "I don't know when I will see you again." Being aware that this constant reiteration of negative language can only do one thing—continue to fuel an already fragile relationship. We should be saying, "I'll see you soon."

Being back on Vancouver Island in the middle of the summer can make anyone forget their troubles. It is so beautiful and it is like stepping back in time as very little has changed. I spend July poking fires on Mr. Aswell's beach, reading, sleeping, fishing and trying to wrap my head around my new life.

Visiting with friends and family again has settled me down a bit. This time I am free from all responsibilities except myself and I have communication with Jack on a whole other level. I am no longer restricted, I am free to travel where I want and he is seeing me and my life in a whole new way. He had no idea I had this other life on the opposite coast from where he met me and I think he finds it a little unsettling, especially because I am staying with a man.

By the end July, it is time to move along. I have been away from home for two months heading into my third. I drive up the Island to stay with friends just South of Campbell River, I wake up to the sounds of Oyster River rushing by and I want to stay here. I have been here for four days and even though I am welcome to stay as long as I wish with my friend, Ketchy,

I want to find a place where I can unpack, be alone to think and not feel like I am imposing. I am feeling the need to look at my life, how it has changed since I left home and I have not taken a moment to reflect as the urge to continue driving and filling my time with distractions has been easy to do.

Sitting on the deck drinking cool summer concoctions I say to Ketchy, "I want to stay here for a while."

"You can stay as long as you want."

"I know that and thank you for making me feel so welcome but I am going to look around to see if I can find a little place on a river or the ocean that rents by the month."

"This time of year can be expensive, just stay here."

Leslie and Keith show up. I have known Leslie since she was 15 and I was 17. Once again I am amazed at how the Universe has brought me so far off the main road to this beautiful riverside property to meet up with Leslie. I have not seen her in twenty years. We did keep in touch periodically over the years but finding out my friend Ketchy had bought a home up the road from her blew my mind. What are the chances? Again the Universe sits us down exactly where we should be and who we are supposed to be with.

We are sitting, reminiscing about our wild teenage years and the years seem to melt away as we are doing almost exactly the same things we did way back then ... laughing, listening to music of the 70's, and the guys are just sitting back, watching and shaking their heads. Some things never change and I am grateful for the feelings of belonging.

I tell Leslie I am going to look for a cottage to rent for a month or two. I tell her I am going to inquire about a little home that is for sale down the road, fully furnished and my research told me it has been on the market for a long time, maybe the owner would be interested in renting it. I had already made the phone call and was waiting for the call back. It was perfect, right on the river, just up the road from all of them. It was just what I imagined when I was travelling through the Prairie Provinces and I thought the Universe had once again answered one of my requests.

Leslie says to me, "You don't want to live there."

"I don't? Why not?"

Ketchy and Keith now are busy in the greenhouse marvelling at how big the tomatoes are getting so they are not privy to this conversation.

"You want to live in the little guest house next door."

"Tell me about it."

"Well, they are two retired psychologists and they have a beautiful little guest house that is empty right now. I don't know if they would be interested in renting it but it would not hurt to inquire."

"What…right next door?"

"Yes, right through those trees."

We laugh at the prospects of me living right next door, what fun we would have!

The next morning, during my morning walk around Ketchy's property with my coffee I casually strolled along the fence separating the properties, scouting out the guest home to see if it was somewhere I could hang out for a month or so. I liked it.

That afternoon, Ketchy and I are doing one of my favourite activities, fishing in the river behind his house. We are also moving rocks, creating swimming holes as the water level has lowered creating large pools where we could lounge and let the river flow over us. As we are moving rocks I feel the time is right and I say to him, "I'll be back in a few minutes," and I head up to the house. I change out of my bathing suit into a long bohemian style skirt, put on a summer top and sandals and walk out the front door. Within 15 minutes I am back in my bathing suit, in the river, fishing rod in hand, having secured my accommodations for the next month. I am thinking about how to tell Ketchy I am not going to stay as he had been so adamant I stay, that I would not be intruding.

I procrastinate for a few hours and as we are barbecuing, I just blurt it out, "I'm moving out."

"What do you mean?"

"I found a place to stay for the next month."

"Really, where?"

"Next door."

"Next door?"

"Yes … over there."

"What? Pat and Wills'?"

He is dumbfounded and can't quite wrap his head around it.

"They have a guest house that is empty."

"Really? I did not know that. How did you know that?"

"Leslie told me about it last night."

"When did you do that, you have not been out of my sight since you arrived."

"This afternoon when we were in the river, remember I left for a few minutes?"

"Yes but I thought you just went to the bathroom, you were back so quick."

"Well I made up my mind to find a place and I made it happen."

"Did I do something to hurt your feelings or make you want to leave?"

I knew he would think this way.

"No Ketchy, I need some space to unpack everything out of my truck and be alone for while."

"You could do that here."

"No I couldn't, you don't know how much I really have. I would really feel like I was imposing and don't you think it is funny I will be living right next door?"

"When are you leaving?"

"Tomorrow."

"You don't mess around do you?"

"You know it's funny, when I was driving through the prairies I envisioned the kind of place I wanted to stay in. It spooked me when I walked into their guest home; it was like I had been there before."

"Well you are a weirdo that way. Remember last week when you called and my phone did not even ring because I picked it up and was calling you…that was weird."

I liked that he called me a weirdo, I like being a weirdo.

The next morning I moved into my new home. It was even more perfect than I imagined. Fully furnished, wood stove to warm the cool nights, large private acreage completely fenced, gardens to fulfill my need to dig in the dirt and the river ran behind the house with fish for me to catch. I had friends close by so I was not always alone and family a few hours away so I could visit.

I had peace to think and privacy to be myself. At first the couple that own this little piece of paradise were wary of this stranger. They thought perhaps they had acted too hastily in allowing this woman who just showed up on their doorstep to move in. They thought I was a woman who was in trouble, down on her luck, destitute and had nowhere else to go. They thought I needed a safe place to stay for a while until I got myself straightened out. They were not wrong except for the part about having nowhere else to go and the destitute part. I did need a safe place to stay to get my head straight. I continue to be amazed at how long I have been feeling disconnected with myself—the shakiness, the lack of desire to eat or interact with people, the desire to sleep but inability to do so for more than a few hours. All of this continued to fuel the anxiety I was feeling and I just wanted it to go away.

If I am not already convinced that I bring into my life exactly what and who I need, I am more convinced and find it more that just a little ironic when I find out Pat and Will's professional practice they retired from was specializing in Women's Issues and Relationships. I think to myself, they will need more than a month to figure me out, but, "Wow look where I am! And did I land on the right doorstep."

It took a while for them to get used to me being there, but they soon came to realize I was really in need of the quiet and privacy their lifestyle provided and we started to work around each other very well. We rarely saw each other and when we did we discussed the most perfect therapy for me, which garden I could rip apart and restructure or just pull some weeds from and it was perfect therapy for me. It kept my hands occupied and my mind free to wander.

I have rarely met two people who emanate dignity and grace as Will and Pat do. We did not discuss my state of mind, we did not have to, they were very in tune with the insecure vibration I was emitting and they knew I was in a place that was scary and new to me. They understood the transitions that were happening in my life and the actions I have taken to change my life and how these changes were deeply affecting me. Pat said to me one morning when she came upon me sitting outside with tears running down my cheeks, "Suzanne, this will pass. You have done the right thing breaking free of a life you no longer wanted, and try not to worry about your children. Of course you miss them but they will be fine. So many people would have stayed still and fought the desire to change their life and continued to be miserable. At least you are taking steps to find answers for yourself. The answers will come and they will come from places you least expect them. Give yourself some time to adjust and be patient."

"Pat, how do you learn to enjoy the moment? I look around at everything that is so visually beautiful, I know I should be grateful just for waking up and I don't understand why I still feel so unfulfilled. It is agonizing and frustrating to feel as if I want to be somewhere else all the time and when I get somewhere new I want to leave again."

"Well, you may have to keep moving until you find that place. And you will eventually find that. At least you have the opportunity to do that. Most people in this world have no choices. You would be surprised at how many people wake up each day, get in their cars and want to drive into a brick wall just to stop the madness in their lives."

"I get that."

"Many people, when they are going about their daily routine just want to turn left, get on a highway and never go back."

"I know! I had a conversation the other day with Leslie. She told me she has been praying for something different to happen in her life. Just something to stir it up a bit that is not dramatic or sad. Then I show up and she became inspired by my journey, by my courage to break the ties that bound me so tightly I could not breathe. I just looked at her and was confused because yet again here is another woman who appears to have it all together, great children, a man who loves her, and a career that she has chosen yet she feels like she wants to run away all the time. I can't get over how many people, especially women are suffocated by their lives and want to pack it all in. I know this woman back in Halifax who daily, on her way to work wants to drive into the concrete median just to stop the madness of her life. She is tired of being everything for every one. As she is nearing the concrete median she starts to plan how to do it. But then guilt and logic kick in and of course she does not drive into it, instead she says she starts to cry and she cries all the way to work. I couldn't live like that."

"That's why you have done what you have done. Even though you had everything in your life that would appear to fulfill anyone's life, it was not the right "everything" for you. The Universe combined with your desire and adventurous spirit conspired and gave you the strength to make decisions that at times made very little sense to you or to those around you. Now you have to trust and try to regain the faith you feel you have lost, and believe you have done the right thing and allow this painful transition that comes with adversity, insecurity, self-doubts and fears you cannot even describe. You have to allow those emotions to move through your body and your mind. It will take time. When you say it feels like a death has occurred, in some respects it has and you are the one responsible for the death. You walked away from all you believed, all you have ever known, the safe conventional life you were brought up to believe you must live, watching everyone around you struggle with their own lives believing this is what we all must do and you made the decision you were not going to be like everyone else but right now you doubt yourself and your decisions and you just don't know how to feel secure in this life yet. In time you will get comfortable with your nomadic life, a life that you have taken charge of and chosen. If in time you find it is not right for you, you will make another decision. At least you will know you gave yourself the chance, you broke free."

All the time Pat is speaking I am trying desperately to stop crying, to feel strong, and to see that she is right and logically I know she is. It is just so hard to believe.

Being grounded for a time, I invited Jack to come and visit me and he accepted. I wanted him to experience the Island from my view. We had only been able to see each other a few times since I left home so I was excited to bring him here and spend time when neither one of us had to be anywhere.

We walk up to the creek that has carved it's way through sandstone creating large deep pools... potholes, that flow down into Oyster River. There are waterfalls that I lay under cooling my skin. Ever since Leslie showed me this place that took my breath away when I first saw it, I wanted so badly to share it with everyone I know. It is magical, it is as if I am in a far away magical land and the waterfalls and potholes harbour healing powers, and when I am there alone, soaking in the sun rays dangling my feet in the deep pools I feel the energy of the water, and the serenity it provides and I want to stay there forever. But when Jack and I get there, I can tell he does not get the same energy from this place as I do and I feel like I have brought an intruder into my serenity and I quickly turn us away from there because suddenly my instincts are on overload about Jack again, I feel he is not the person I want to share this place with and at the same time I do not understand my feeling because for so long I have envisioned us in places like this. I cannot shake the feeling that Jack is hiding something from me, that he is not who I think he is and when he leaves I am more confused than ever. So I tell myself I am just insecure, I am imagining it, I have too much time on my hands, but as the month rolls on and because I want so much to believe his words of a future together, I doubt myself some more.

When the end of August was approaching I started to get antsy, wanting to get on the road again. I told Pat and Will I would be leaving to start my trek north. Pat was apprehensive about me wanting to go to Alaska alone. She was the first person to tell me about the "Highway of Tears", a stretch of road where many woman and young girls have gone missing and been found murdered over several years and the killer has never been found, but she is not the first person to tell me they were uneasy with my desire to go to Alaska alone. But like most things I am determined to do, I take the information and ultimately decide what to do when the time is upon me. At that moment I was going to Alaska and the "Highway of Tears" was not enough to deter me.

It is amazing how we connect with certain people in our lives and with Pat and Will, I know there is a connection that will last our lifetime. The morning I left, they packed me a little snack for the road and told me I could come back anytime. When I left I had no idea if I would be back, but I was grateful for the invitation and felt humbled that they felt that way about me.

Jack had called me a few days before I was leaving the Island and invited me to Calgary for a few days before I headed North. We both knew that when I left to go North it could mean months before I got back to anywhere close to where he would be. I accepted this invitation and I was looking forward to spending time with him as it would be the first time that I spent more than a day or two with him in his environment and it is what I have been wanting since I left home.

The first day I drove as far as Grand Forks, British Columbia, where my Uncle Allan and Aunt Flo live. To get to Grand Forks you have to drive the Hope-Princeton Highway and that is one of my favourite drives through the Rocky Mountains. It is windy with hairpin corners and canyons that frighten the daylights out of passengers if they look down.

For several nights earlier in the summer I stayed in Grand Forks to attend the celebration of my Aunt and Uncle renewing their wedding vows. My sister, her friend and I pitched tents in a canyon so dark I could not see my hand in front of my face. It was desert hot during the day and the nights were not much better. There were mountain goats navigating the cliffs and ledges as comfortably as we do sidewalks. Listening to coyotes howl, as if they were mocking me, daring me to step outside my comfort zone, I was convinced they were all probably circling my tent and I would have slept outside if it were not for the cries being so close. In addition, I had heard someone say earlier in the day that they had spotted a cougar sitting on a cliff, looking down at them and scanning them like entrees on a menu, I had not seen it with my own eyes so I do not know if it was a fact but I was not going to take any chances. This made me yearn for the comfort of my own bed and four walls that were not canvas.

In the mornings, I would wander about with my coffee gazing at the canyon walls. Being a rock freak this was an amazing place to be. Looking at the layers and thinking about the years it took to expose them, I wished I had paid more attention to grade five geology. I felt insignificant, tiny, a grain of sand, if that big. I wondered, again, what I was doing here, standing in this place. Why has the Universe surrounded me on three sides with this massive wall, so solid, with only one way out? I laughed to myself and the analogy I came up with.

This is a Terror Barrier but the Universe is still showing me a way out. As I was standing staring up at cliffs, far away in my thoughts, this solid intimidating wall, gave me a sign. It let go of a piece of itself, a large rock, not quite a boulder, but large, broke away and tumbled down. I heard the crack, turned in time to see it fall and watched as the dust settled on top of a pile that would have taken many decades to get so high. This was the Terror Barrier telling me, "I may be solid, I may scare you but I too can crumble, and rock by rock, bit by bit I will come down. Do not allow the size of me fool you; do not allow the size of your adversities to intimidate you. Do not give up. I will come down, rock by rock, just like your adversities will crumble away if you keep moving forward. But beware of the falling rocks along the way, they can crush you." Shivers went down my spine. The winds of change swept warmly over my skin. I looked around to see if anyone had witnessed this, but I was alone. I changed at that moment. I felt less fear, if only for a moment. The reprieve was wonderful.

I walked back to my tent to compose the speech I was going to give at the reception. Technology is wonderful, from the back of my truck I flashed up my computer, stuck my internet stick in and logged on to the internet in the middle of this canyon, took out my portable printer and printed off the Invictus' Poem. I felt this was appropriate for my Aunt and Uncle as they have been invictus, meaning unconquerable, in their 40 years of marriage. It is also the poem that, many years ago when I first received it, this poem taught me to pray to "whatever gods may be," and it also describes how I see myself. That no matter what has happened, is happening or will happen, it reminds me of who I really am.

Invictus

BY: *WILLIAM ERNEST HENLEY* *(1849–1902 / GLOUCESTER / ENGLAND)*

Out of the night that covers me,
Black as the pit from pole to pole,
I thank whatever gods may be
For my unconquerable soul.

In the fell clutch of circumstance
I have not winced nor cried aloud.
Under the bludgeonings of chance
My head is bloody, but unbowed.

Beyond this place of wrath and tears
Looms but the Horror of the shade,
And yet the menace of the years
Finds and shall find me unafraid.

It matters not how strait the gate,
How charged with punishments the scroll,
I am the master of my fate:
I am the captain of my soul.

When I leave Grand Forks it is the first of September and I am heading for Calgary. My apprehension about where I am going grows with each passing kilometre. I feel as the time is finally approaching that I will get some answers about this man that I have listened to for almost two years telling me all the wonderful things we will do in life. I finally feel I am going to see if my instincts are right or wrong.

CHAPTER SIXTEEN

When the Universe Speaks and My Instincts Are Screaming at Me ... I Should Listen

Blip... "You left awfully quickly."

"Well I have a long way to go."

"I have never seen you pack up so fast."

"I know, but you have lots to do to get yourself ready to leave town tomorrow."

"You okay?"

"Yes, I will text you when I get to Williams Lake."

That was the text conversation that has continued to come back to me time and again. Why was I ready to go? Why did I pack my stuff up so quickly and leave when all I had wanted for so long was to be there, I could have stayed another day and in the past I would have stayed until the very last second.

After spending a week with him at his home, relaxing, talking, laughing, walking, thinking, why was I so ready to go? Where I was going would be always be there, I did not have to go that day. I could have stayed one more day.

Here I was exactly where I had wanted to be for months, sitting quietly with him, in his home, doing nothing but just enjoying each other. For several thousand kilometres I pictured this exact scenario. I had convinced myself I wanted this so badly and now that I was here I wondered if it was a case of "be careful what you wish for."

While I was there I was not feeling anxious but I was feeling unsettled about us and I had to get answers to my question … where are we going with this relationship? This is the emotional obstacle that has been standing in my way for two years, the obstacle that I could not remove because we were rarely in the same time zone and I could not make a decisive decision one way or the other about him.

We had tried to end this relationship while I was living on the East Coast, more than once. We realized we were both making changes to our lives and figured we needed to be free of all relationship ties to really find out what we wanted as individuals. But no matter how hard we both tried to get on with our own lives, we kept finding our way back to each other. Both of us, flying in and out of different cities, me driving to where he would be working, him staying extra days just so we could be together, and the text messaging and phone calls kept us in such close contact it was like we were never apart, we were never free.

Living this way had become an obstacle for both of us; it was preoccupying, frustrating, never-ending and always surreal. When we were together, we knew we would be leaving each other again, me going back to where I lived and now, my seeming to always be going on some great adventure to some unknown region or he moving on to the next town to work, so in the moments we had together we rarely spoke of the future. It just did not seem to matter—we were happy in the moment.

Now that I am free, free to do whatever I want, to be anywhere I want, one of the first things on my agenda was to know if all these fantastic thoughts I was having about him, the images of a life we created in our minds, could be realized. I had to see him in his environment, how he relaxed, how he responded to me in his home. I had made up my mind to have a conversation, face to face, about the expectations we had for each other.

It is so easy to be with each other. The way we talk, the topics we discuss, the way we move around each other is so comfortable. When we are walking together, he is not ahead, he is not behind. We walk side by side. Early in our relationship and I will never forget when he said this to me because it was the first time we were together after he was free, he said, "This is the first time in my life I felt a woman walk beside me like we were equals. You are not ahead and you are not behind, we are side by side. I like it." I understood what he was saying and I liked it too. I liked it a lot.

Now two years since I met him and three months after I left home, we finally found some time to meet at his home. I am sitting in his living room and I watch him. I listen to him. I get to see what is important to him. I get to watch how he takes care of his life. Up until now I have only seen how he lives out of a suitcase.

He knows I am watching.

"What are you doing? I feel you watching every move I make."

"Yes I am. You fascinate me. I can't take my eyes off of you,"

He laughs, knowing I am making fun of him.

"Really, tell me what you see."

"Well, I am not ready to tell you what I see, it's too early in my visit, but you're right, I am watching you."

"Really?"

"Yes I am, but I can tell you I what I feel."

"Ok, tell me."

"For the first in a very long time, even before I left home, I feel at peace. I feel as if I am not running."

"Do you know why that is?"

"No, why?"

"Because I am at peace with you here."

I smiled at him. He has told me many times how he feels, he loves me, he adores me, he respects me, how he can't wait to see me. I have always liked it when he tells me and he said it often, "You scare me and excite me at the same time." His words from the past are the reason I am here. I want to know if his words and actions are the same.

I shift my position on the couch to face him. I look closely at him and I say, "I am happy you feel that way, at peace." But I did not expect the reaction I had inside me and I can not tell him so. I don't believe that the reason I feel at peace with myself is because he feels at peace with me there. I know it is because I finally have time to face one of my fears, and maybe, with this visit I will be able to shed the doubts that have plagued me about him since I met him. One way or the other, after two years of wondering, I was going to finally put things to rest. Either I loved him and we would continue to get closer or I don't and we won't.

It is impossible to make life decisions when you do not have all the facts. Having a relationship via technology was not my idea of getting to know someone. Being on the other end of a telephone, it is easy to say most anything and then hang up. It is safe.

When a life changing decision rests on knowing the facts you have to do everything you can to be able to make an informed decision. He knew everything about my life. He met my family, stayed in my home, met my colleagues and met my friends; yet even after this long I still knew very little about him.

I looked at this as I do most things in life, do the research then make the final decision.

But I could not Google him, I could not ask his family

and friends about him, I had never met them. The only time I saw him was when he was working and that was not who he was. So based upon the information I did have, watching him work, interacting with his colleagues, and during our personal time alone in hotel rooms or when he flew to wherever I was, that was not enough to make a final decision. Throughout the week of watching and listening I tried to stop myself from critiquing everything he said and did, but it was not easy. After all this was someone I was considering spending my life with.

I wondered if he was doing the same with me although he already had so much information about me from spending time in my life back home. He could make an informed decision and he had told me many times … "I am no longer looking, I have found everything I ever wanted in a woman." But knowing he had not spent much time not being a relationship I wondered how he knew that for sure and I wondered if he was watching me, critiquing me as well.

The moments I allowed the critiquing to stop, he was perfect. I didn't care about the clothes on the floor even though the laundry basket was right there, I didn't care about the dishes left in the living room or on the counter set right above the dishwasher. I didn't care about the wet towel thrown on the bed, or the toilet seat left up even when my hairbrush was knocked into it. I could have cared less about his jacket hung up on the back of the chair next to the closet where mine was hanging. I didn't care about the sticky stuff on his car seats I had to pick off before I sat down. I didn't notice how he stuffed his clean clothes I had washed, dried, folded and set on top of his dresser in any drawer, I didn't care that I had to go around and shut off all the lights and turn off the T.V. when I realized he was going to leave them all on when we were going out. I didn't care about any of it because I was watching to see how he was with me.

He treated me with kindness, he was attentive, loving and I melted when I was in his arms. I was weak in the knees with vulnerability when he held me and his voice was soft in my ear. In those moments I would have followed him anywhere. I had never allowed myself to be so taken in my whole life. There were no inhibitions, no doubts and no fears, from either one of us. It was bliss. At any given moment, when I was away from him, I could shut my eyes and be right back in his arms. I was in love with those moments.

Then ... too soon, here they were, those creepy feelings of doubt and fear seeping in again, something would happen and memories of last Fall would surface and my spidy senses would start to tingle.

I was reading my book, he was on the phone. I could not help but hear his one side of the conversation. It wasn't anything he was saying and I couldn't put my finger on it but my instincts were telling me to be wary, and I found myself *not* watching him but listening to him. It was his tone more so than his words and it gave me an uneasy feeling reminiscent of another time. I was not afraid, I was leery. I had heard this tone before. He had used it with me last Fall. He was telling whoever was on the phone that he did not appreciate the way they were doing business and he would no longer do business with them and if he changed his mind ... he would call them, but until then he did not want to hear from that person. There was no negotiating, no compromise, no more talking, that was that. It was the same tone he used with me when he said he had to go back to his life. I felt sorry for the person on the phone because I knew he meant it and there was no changing his mind, even though I could tell the person on the

phone had tried. Sitting there listening to him, I told myself
to be cautious because when I opened the conversation with
him I might hear that tone again.

For the next few days we had a great time with each other,
going out to dinner, staying in cooking, watching movies, we
even met one of his sons and his daughter for cheesecake,
and he got to met one of my brothers who was in town for
a few days. I was thrilled with the events that took place that
week. But I could not shake the feeling of doubt. I wanted it
to go away, I wanted to ignore it but I could not. I had already
made up my mind I was not leaving here until I addressed
these thoughts I was having and I would do this Saturday
night after dinner. I was going to ask him straight out, "What
are you thinking for us? What do you see for our future? Do
you think we have one?" I was confused about the in between
living, I did not know if I was free to date others or if he
wanted too, I did not know what to think and we both knew
we were too far gone, this was not a casual relationship. We
were at the point we were all in or all out.

I was concerned about what I would hear from him
because for the first time in his life he too was without
responsibilities, no small children to care for, and he had
only been single for a short period of time compared to
me. Early in his freedom we did talk about his new found
freedom and I said, "Perhaps you should have time on your
own, look around, see what's out there now that you are free
to look." That is not what I wanted but at the same time I
thought it was important for him to experience his new life
without feeling obligation or guilt if he did ask someone else
out for dinner, if that was what he wanted. As we had not
clearly defined our relationship I had to be prepared to hear
that this was what he might want to do, that this may be the

reason we had not defined things and he was afraid to tell me, but what he did say made me feel better, "Suzanne, I do not want to date." I was hoping that after the conversation I was preparing, I would hear the same thing.

Saturday morning I woke early, got up on one elbow and was staring at him, watching him sleep. As I watched him, I was not thinking about him. I was thinking about my next adventure, if I should get my truck tuned up before I left, and when would be a good time to leave. I was heading to Northern British Columbia to visit friends in the city of Mackenzie, explore that region for a while, then on to Alaska from there. I knew it was going to be some time before I saw him again and here I was thinking about … Alaska.

In my head I was packing up my suitcase and I was back in my truck, when he stirred and opened his eyes. Neither one of us said anything. We just looked at each other for a long time and I knew he could tell I was pensive and in deep thought. He told me later he knew something was different about me that morning. He felt a distance about me that he had never felt before and he was right. I was different, the phone call I listened to had built a wall of protection around me and I felt I was detaching from him.

When I woke up that morning, I had no intention of leaving that day or the next but something was happening, the winds of change were sweeping over me and I was suddenly restless to get on the move. Monday was when he was leaving town for work so I had planned on staying until then, or at least when I first arrived, that was the plan, but the Universe must have felt the shift in me and decided to make decisions for me.

Early Saturday evening we were sitting and talking, the mood was relaxed and we were looking forward to spending this evening doing a bunch of nothing and I was determined to have the conversation I had rehearsed so many times in my head. I was ready for whatever the outcome was going to be. We were just finished dinner and I was just about to say, "I have something I want to talk about," when my phone rang. I recognized the phone number and said out loud, "Oh, it's Mr. Aswell."

He knew who this man was, he was no secret, Jack knew this man on the phone has been a friend of mine for almost 32 years. I have stayed in his home so many times while visiting Honeymoon Bay on Vancouver Island we have lost count. I have never had an intimate relationship with this man and he was never a threat to any relationship I ever had as I was never a threat to any of his relationships. Most of the time neither one of knew what each other's relationship status was, it never mattered, and when we did know, it still did not matter. He always opened his home to me and I could go and stay there anytime I was on the Island. Mr. Aswell did not even have to be there for me to go there. It has become my home away from home. Lee and I had just been there for a week in June and I had spent a couple of more weeks there after she left, poking fires on his beach, thinking and making plans for my future, so hearing from him was not a surprise to me.

"Hello there! How are you?

Jack could only hear my side of the conversation.

"Yes, of course I want too! When are you going? Wait— let me get some paper and a pen."

My voice had elevated slightly with excitement and I was scurrying around looking for paper.

I was leaning on the counter writing furiously and out of the corner of my eye I could see him watching me but not watching me. I tried to tone my excitement down because I could feel the air had suddenly gotten thick.

"Ok go ahead … Yip, yes, say that again, turn where? … Do not go over Elkin Creek Bridge! Can you spell that? … Ok got it. Yes your timing could not have been better; I was going to Cheryl and Kenny's in Mackenzie then to Alaska…. Yes, I am still going, but I can go there when I leave you."

It was obvious I was taking down directions and there was no question I was going to be detoured from my current plan to head for Alaska.

"Okay, I will call you from Williams Lake when I arrive there. What's the satellite phone number for the cabin?"

Jotting down the directions in two minutes I wanted to make sure I got them right. I read them back to him, twice.

"Oh my god Mr. Aswell, if there is no cell phone reception what if I get lost? It sounds like the roads are trails and there are questionable land marks for someone who has never been there."

I was listening and getting more details when I remembered I have a road side assistant kit with a flare.

"Here is what I am going to do. If at any point I feel I am lost, I will stop driving. What time does it get dark? …. Okay, I will stop and set up camp around 7:00. At 9:00 p.m. if I have not arrived, I want you to go out side and I will shoot my flare to let you know I am okay and where I am. You can decide to come and get me then or I will sleep in my truck until morning and wait for you or search and rescue to arrive."

A big sigh came from across the room. I looked over and saw that he was staring off into space.

"No really I will be fine. I will have lots of supplies with me and I am always prepared to sleep in my truck if I have too. ….No, I have not had to but it is no big deal, really I will be fine."

Mr. Aswell was laughing and so was I. He knows me well. I would be fine.

"Today? I am in Calgary....Okay, great, I will see you Monday."

I hung up the phone and looked across the room.

"Well sounds like you are on another adventure."

"Oh boy," I thought to myself, how do I handle this? If the shoe were on the other foot how would I feel?

This was not the first time I have spent time with Mr. Aswell since Jack and I have known each other, as a matter of fact it will be the fourth or fifth time .... It never appeared to be a problem in the past as he knew this was a close friend and always will be.

"When are you leaving?"

"Tomorrow"

"Sunday."

"Yip, Sunday."

"I don't leave until Monday."

"Yes I know. They are only going to be there until the following Sunday and it is going to take me two days to get there."

"Where is it you are going? It sounded like it will be very remote."

"Yes it will be. I am going to his cabins in the Chilcotin Mountains."

"Where is that exactly?"

"The Chilcotin Mountains are in the Coastal Mountain Range, but first I have to get to Williams Lake Sunday night."

"That's a fourteen hour drive at least from here."

"Yes, well maybe not that long but it is another five or so from there depending on the driving conditions along the trails."

"Trails?"

"That's what he said, trails. Isn't it funny how this came about?"

"Funny?"

"Well not funny haha funny but funny in the sense that I was going that way to get to Cheryl and Kenny's in Mackenzie and now instead of turning right in Williams Lake I turn left. I find that curiously odd that Mr. Aswell would call and it all works out like this. The Universe sure works in mysterious ways. I have always wanted to go there but the timing just never seemed to work out."

"Well the timing is working now."

"You okay?"

"Sure, why wouldn't I be?

I knew he was just being gracious. I knew he was reacting inside but would never tell me and right then all I wanted to hear was ... "Don't go. I don't want you to go."

I watched him for a sign, any sign, sure my eyes were pleading for him to do something, say something ... please ... say something.

He did nothing. He did not say a word.

The rest of the evening was spent in uncomfortable moments of forced conversation and I was definitely not going to open up a conversation about us.

Sleep did not come easily for either one of us. We were still and quiet.

Sunday morning, because neither one of us slept very well, we dozed on and off well past the usual hour of rising. I was not looking forward to getting up and at the same time I could not wait to leave. As I lay there I realized I still had no closure. We did not have the conversation. I still felt uneasy about him and that really should have been enough for me to end it there but for some reason it was not. I knew it was because I was not sure if the doubts were about being with him or being without him … Oh my god! I wanted to leave here knowing something different, feeling something different.

"Want some coffee?"

"Sure."

I was looking at my suitcases on the floor. I had not brought all my cases up from my truck but enough to know it was going to take two trips.

It was awkward as I moved about his home collecting my things. I did not have too much spread around but packing up my computer and everything attached to it took a few minutes and he just sat there and watched me. Again I found myself looking at him, wanting him to read my mind … "Just ask me not to go, tell me you want me to stay … and I will." Not a word.

I felt a twinge of anger at that moment. I wanted to tell him what I was thinking, I wanted to ask him what he was thinking, but there was no way in hell I was going to do that. I knew it had to come freely from him.

He did not move from the couch until I came out pulling my cases to the front door.

"Here let me help you with those."

"No, no … I'm good. I can do this on my own. I will take this out to my truck then come back for the rest."

"What else is new Suzanne, you want to do everything on your own."

I shot back in defence … "No I don't, I just want to do this on my own. I have to rearrange a few things in the back of my truck, and then I will be back for the rest."

Walking to my truck to put my things in I thought

to myself, "What did he mean by that? That was the first time I had ever heard him say anything in that way. Was he critiquing me too? Oh no! How could I be leaving here this way? It wasn't supposed to be this way. It was supposed to get us both to a place of understanding.

Standing at the front door, not knowing what to say, wanting to hold him and never leave and run away at the same time. I can tell he is feeling the same way, wanting to hold me and wanting me to be gone.

"So, I don't know when I will see you again. Thank you for looking after me this week. I love your place, I really felt good here."

He told me to drive safe, hugged me tight and then that was it, I was gone and I still had no idea what to think or feel.

A few hours into my drive I had the overwhelming feeling of a weight being lifted off my shoulders. I felt a strange sense of relief not being there with him. I thought to myself the Universe has done it again. It put Mr. Aswell's call directly in front of the conversation I wanted to have. Was I not supposed to have it? Was this the Universe telling me I did not need to have it, that the answers were as plain as day. Shouldn't the fact that I felt relief not being there and did not need to hear the reasons spoken aloud be enough? That a phone call changed my plans to get me out of there earlier so I did not have to hear the responses to my questions, wasn't that enough? Why was this happening? Why was the Universe continuing to keep us from having closure, why was it continuing to keep us apart? Why does it continue to bring us together?

I think about him constantly, looking at my cell phone, willing it to ring and it does but it is not him. With the Rocky Mountain Range far behind, and in the dying daylight hours,

I see the peaks of the Coastal Mountain Range. I have been on the road for eight hours and I have at least three more hours to go before I get to Williams Lake.

My day turns into night and I watch the sun drop behind the mountains. It gets dark early when you live here. I am now driving a highway I have never driven before and I am getting tired. Narrow roads, few street lights, pitch black night and it has started to rain. The oncoming traffic headlights hurt my eyes. My GPS pipes up, making me jump in my seat, telling me, "You are still on the fastest route." I laugh and talk out loud to it, "The fastest route to where?"

I think of my children and wonder how they are doing. It is late back home, four hours ahead and I see each of them tucked in their beds and I long for my own. I have been away from them for three months now and am heading into my fourth.

So much time has passed, so many kilometres under my wheels. I would like them to be with me. I wish they were with me tonight to share the adventures I have been on, the life changing moments, to see what I have seen. I am lonely, tired, hungry and so far from home and apparently still on the fastest route going in the opposite direction from being there.

The blackness of the night has hidden all views of the mountains now and I can see the pink glow of the city ahead and I am anxious to get there. Pulling into town it is late, everything is closed and there is not much traffic. I drive the main road looking for a vacancy sign that I will call home for the night. There it is … Lake View Motel… Whoo Hoo!

Blip… "I am in Williams Lake. Checked into a motel"

"You must be tired."

"Yes I am, it was a long drive."

"I am glad you are there and safe. I miss you,"

"I miss you too."

"Sleep well; I will call you in the morning."

"Good night baby. XXX"

"Nite nite, xoxo."

I stare at my phone, waiting for one more text. But nothing comes. I want to send one but I have nothing to say. I am sure he is getting pretty tired of hearing me say "Wow Baby, Look Where I Am!"

CHAPTER SEVENTEEN

Stick to the Main Road ...

As I lay in bed thinking about my drive, it was a long one and I am having a hard time settling down. This morning when I left Alberta, I was excited about driving today, it is early Fall and I am on another adventure to a place I had never been before but have romanticized about for almost 30 years. I am singing to my favourite Melissa Etheridge CD, the windows are open, the breeze is warm and the fact that I am consciously aware that I feel something other than doubts and fears at this moment, that I actually feel an excitement about my next adventure, is huge to me. Even though I did not accomplish what I had set out to do back there, with Jack, have the conversation, I was not going to allow that to ruin my week ahead. I had to focus on letting it all go until the next time as I knew there was going to be a next time, there was always going to be a next time until I figured out what track to be on.

The drive through the Rocky Mountains is breathtaking and no matter how many times I do this drive, and I have done it several times this year, it always gives me the same feelings of awe. I want to park my truck and climb to the top of every mountain, or scale down the canyons to the rivers below, cast a line or just sit and ponder for a while. I have stopped many times along the way, just to sit and watch the waters flow, its powerful energy eroding the banks, ever changing the landscape, reminding me of how quickly my own landscape, the river banks of my life continue change and how most of the time I am not in control of those changes.

These roads are becoming familiar to me. As I am driving through the canyons I pass roads I have detoured down in the past and many that I have yet to explore. Then I pass a road that I did take the last time I drove through here and the memory of it makes me question myself, "Was I brave or reckless for how I reacted that day?"

On that particular day I had been driving for many hours and I needed a break. I turned left off the main highway onto a side road that was following a river. Following the road that winds down the canyon, I found the perfect spot to park. I ate my lunch sitting on the open hatch to the back of my truck then walked the short distance to the river.

I could not resist the desire to take my boots off and stick my bare feet in the water. It was cold, icy, numbing glacier mountain runoff cold and I could not keep them in there for long. The river was wide but shallow. I could walk across to the other side if it was warmer. I sat down on a rock and started putting my socks back on when I sensed I was not alone. I looked up and down the river but I saw no one. I heard the words of so many people echo, "Do not take unnecessary risks, and do not go to remote places alone, stick to the main roads and only stop where there are lots of people." Oh, but I couldn't help it and if I waited for someone to be with me ... I would have had very few adventures in my life.

I was tying my laces when my foot slipped off the rock it was propped up on and the noise it made when it hit the ground was enough to startle the birds in the trees around me. The crows flew over my head and I looked up to watch them fly past. As I put my head back down I saw movement out of the corner of my eye, across the river. I finished tying my boot without taking my eyes off the spot where I thought I saw the movement. Sure enough, there across the river was a bear. I was not sure at that point what kind of bear it was, I just knew it was a bear. Then there were two, and they were walking the opposite shore line coming in my direction and I was frozen to my rock both with amazement and fear.

I think of my friend Mr. Aswell when I said to him, "I should have some bear spray just in case." He laughed at me and said, "If you need to use bear spray the bear is too close and further more ... think about how accurate your aim has to be and what if the spray comes back into your face?" Of course he would have to make it sound like such a futile frivolous accessory for me to have but at this moment I would like to have it. "But you know Suzanne I have heard it works really well on the two-legged kind of animal."

"I agree as those two-legged animals are the most dangerous kind."

And right now I believe I am looking at a female and her cub and I would like nothing more than to have a two-legged animal with me right now, preferably one with a rifle *and* some bear spray.

I know a few things about bears and this is not my first encounter with them. I know that grizzlies like to bat their food around until it stops moving and bury it until it rots, so if you are fortunate enough to survive the attack of the grizzly and can wait until he buries you then leaves, maybe you can survive ... I never want to find out if any of that is true. But what I know about black bears terrifies me more ... they like their dinner warm. I also know that bears are fast. If they want me, they are going to have me, there will be no time to turn around and run to my truck, and these bears are too close for my comfort.

I am thinking about all the programs that tell you what you should do if you find yourself face to face with a bear.

The horrific image of what damage can be done with one swipe of a bear claw is instantly brought to mind. I remember thinking about the wind direction, and I wonder if I am downwind from them? It didn't matter because I knew, they knew I was there; they had stopped and were looking in my direction. Black bears … looking at me.

It is easy to say what you would do if you found yourself in my position, from the safety of your easy chair. You would run, and that is probably what I should have done but I did not. I slowly started to raise my body from the rock I was perched upon. I wanted to keep myself close to the ground in a crouched-over position and not make myself appear tall and threatening to them, but at the same time I needed to keep my balance. I do not take my eyes off them and for sure they are looking at me now. I am wondering why they are not running in the opposite direction from me? Most wild creatures do, so what's up with these two? I back up slowly making sure I keep an eye on them and watch where I am stepping. The last thing I want to do is trip and create panic in me or them.

My heart is pounding so hard and my knees are knocking but strangely enough I am not afraid in the sense I should be. I am excited and want my cameras, but they are in the truck. My thoughts are now about getting my cameras. I want the bears to come closer, and I want them to stay where they are. I know that all it would take is 50 lunges or less, if that is what bears do, that's all it would take for them to be across that river and I am dinner. Now I find myself not wanting to scare them off but of course they are much smarter than I am. They know better than to hang around tempting fate, and they turn away from me and head back into the forest. I was disappointed when I should have been grateful.

Back at my truck I know I should be feeling lucky that I was not dinner for two black bears but lucky was not how I was feeling, I am annoyed with myself for not taking my cameras with me. "Next time." And I say that to myself as if I know there will be a next time.

Back on the main road wanting to call someone to tell them of my encounter, I realized I had no reception. I wonder about myself when I am in places like this. No reception, back roads, no one knowing where I am, no one knowing where I just left, or where I am going. "Am I Brave or am I reckless, risking my life to take pictures?"

I also think, "What if the bears came from behind me or they smelled the food in my truck and they were there when I walked back. Yes it was scary, but am I going to stop going off the main road? Probably not, I will just be sure to take my camera everywhere from now on.

Alone in the Chilcotin Mountains

Before leaving Williams Lake with enough groceries to last me a few days in the wilderness if I should happen to find myself lost in the Mountains, I sit in a parking lot with my drive thru coffee, sending out text messages to my family and friends telling them not to expect to hear from me for at least a week. My brother, Greg, fired back a message that made me laugh out loud.

Blip … "Gits, (one of his nicknames for me.) You will never be able to last that long without a phone!"

"Yes I will!"

"No… you won't! You have not been without a phone attached to your ear since you were 13."

"Well this will be a test of will power for me won't it?"

"You are going to go through withdrawal from not being able to text message."

"What?! That's ridiculous. Of course I will be able to, I have done it before."

"When?"

I have to think about it. When was the last time I was without communication, without access to a phone for more than a few hours? I can't remember.

"I don't remember but I am sure I have. There is a satellite phone if I really feel the need to call someone."

"Oh great, I can see it now, you will rack up thousand of dollars of air time on Mr. Aswell's phone on your first day!"

"No I won't!"

"Ok Gits, good luck with that. I look forward to hearing from you over the next day or two."

"I'm not going to call."

"Well if it's not me it will be someone."

"Listen, if you do not hear from me by next Tuesday, send out search and rescue to find me."

"Okay Gits, but I know I will hear from you."

I give him the direction I am heading in and the approximate area I will be in and he sends back, "That is only about three hundred thousand square kilometres of mountain terrain … but okay … watch out for the grizzlies."

"Thanks for reminding me. Good bye Gregory."

"Good bye,… *Gits*. Haha."

He is so funny and he is right. I do get a little panicky when my cell reception goes out of range. I have become dependent on it.

Blip… "Where are you?"

"I am leaving Williams Lake."

"Ok, have a great time."

"I will. You have a great week."

"Be careful. Have we gone this long without communication before?"

"Yes, several times. Remember, last Fall and winter?"

"Oh yes, I remember."

I think to myself "I will never forget."

"Stay safe and I look forward to hearing all about your adventures when you come back down the mountain."

I can feel emotions through the text as I have always been able to feel them, but I would like for him to express them, good or bad, just so I would know what they were. I wonder to myself what if he did, what would I do then?

I get another coffee, consult my directions and put my

truck into drive. I do not know when I will lose reception so I make one last call that I know will last until I slip out of range.

"Hi Lee."

"Hey you … where are you?

"Just leaving Williams Lake. Not sure how long I have to talk but wanted you to know where I was going. If you do not hear from me by next Tuesday, here is my brother's phone number. Call him to see if he has heard from me."

Lee is the closest connection to my children. I have kept in contact with her almost everyday and she would know where to go if anything should happen to me. It was a plan she and I made before I left Halifax. "If anything should happen to me, go to Carly first."

"You must be excited to be going into these mountains."

"Yes, I have waited many years for this very moment."

"You don't sound very excited. What's up?"

"Oh Lee I wish I could shake this feeling. I can't stand not feeling excited when I should be. I hate it! I think I am still in shock about leaving home."

"It's been three months or more."

"Yes I know. You would think I would have adjusted by now. I probably would be excited if I knew what to feel, and not just about Jack, about everything. Who knew that getting so much freedom would be so difficult to get used too? I have no one or anything to take care of but me. You would think I would feel like the luckiest person on earth but I don't know this feeling. I don't recognize it; it's not sad, I'm not depressed it's a melancholy feeling and it's awful. I am sure at times the homesick feelings get to me and it's easy to get overwhelmed especially when I think about the events that have happened that I will have to deal with when I do come home—Blake's death and my granddaughter's birth and everything in between. How long is this transition going to take?"

"It's a process; I can't believe how many people around us are suffering some sort of crash in their lives."

"I know! Every one I speak with has something that is either breaking their bank, their heart or their soul or all three! They all want to be free of it."

"Free is a state of mind. Speaking of free, how is it going with him? Are you free of that yet?"

"I loved being there and he liked it too, but I left so quickly, what does that mean?"

"Suzanne, if you were meant to be there with him, you would not be going where you are."

"Really? I don't know about that. I don't like to think Mr. Aswell would give up our friendship if a girlfriend felt odd about us, and it has happened, he has had girlfriends, and I still show up. It is funny, when I think about where I am going and who I am going to be with. In the past, as you know, I would have been going there with a completely different mindset."

"It's pissing me off that Jack has infiltrated your brain this way. I wish you'd had that conversation with him."

"Well let's hope that the Mountain Gods provide some answers for me before I come down."

"I hope they do too…What I really hope is that you once again see Mr. Aswell in the same way you have always seen him. He is really the one you're in love with."

"Lee don't go there."

"Well it's true. I finally saw it for myself when I was there. You just don't want to admit it."

"No Lee that is not true, I do admit it, you are right. I have adored him for as long as I have known him but not like you are suggesting. Its funny Roslyn says the same thing. She has always thought he was the perfect match for me. She thinks I am the female version except I don't know how to skin a deer and never will. But right now … I could never entertain thoughts like that about anyone, especially Mr. Aswell. Besides, he does not think of me that way, I have to purge this emotional obstacle first. Get control of my senses and my mind again, Hello … Helloo … Lee … I am going to lose you."

"Go have some fun … Let er rip! Wow! Look Where You Are! Call me when you get back in range. Take care …"

Only 7 kilometres out of Williams Lake and I lost reception. I feel exactly what Greg had suggested I was going to feel—panic. I start talking to myself again. "No big deal, you can do this." I look at my phone several times looking for a signal but there is nothing.

"Ok this is going to be something new, maybe it will give me the patience and the discipline I need to get over him. Maybe enough time will pass that I will not want to contact him when I come down. Maybe I will finally be able to enjoy this journey without the expectation of hearing from him … maybe I should stop thinking about him." I also lose radio reception so I push the play button on the CD player and there is Bob Proctor telling me once again, "I can have any thing I truly desire." I have to turn him off because what I truly desire at this moment is cell phone reception. Eject!

I cannot listen to anything at this moment, every song has too much meaning, the lyrics, as any homesick, lovesick person knows, make me think too much. I curse out loud because now my inability to remove this emotional obstacle has interfered with one of my greatest pleasures, listening to music.

Soon enough and thank goodness I am distracted by what has suddenly become my view. The road I am driving is winding me through some of the most incredible scenery I have ever seen, and it only seems fitting that I am singing Janis Joplin and John Denver tunes to myself.

The hills and valleys are scenes out of the movies. Rugged cliffs carved by the river that flows swiftly below, barren valleys, arid fields of scrub brush. I know I am really far from home now. I am far from everything.

Every kilometre taking me higher and higher, at every turn I want to stop and take pictures but the shoulder of the road is not conducive to stopping and I cannot help but want to look over the edge. I want to see the river that is raging far below, but there is no guardrail to stop me from plummeting to my death should I veer too far onto the shoulder, so I resist the urge to gawk myself to my death and pay attention to the road, knowing eventually there will be a safe place to pull over.

I see off in the distance my first landmark, a long steel bridge crossing the river then it dawns on me that this is the Fraser River. I slow down as I drive onto the bridge. "Wow, Look Where I Am!' I pick up my phone to call my kids to say, "Your momma is crossing the Fraser River!" But I cannot … no reception.

I stop on the other side, get out of my truck and stand looking down at the water crashing against the sides of the canyon. I am speechless. I cannot believe how many times I have felt this way. Just when I think I have been somewhere that has made me feel insignificant, and that is a word I keep coming back too, I am somewhere new feeling it all over again—insignificant. I look around, there is no one else in sight, no one to share this moment with me, I wish there was, even a stranger, but there is no one.

Making my way through the switch back turns in the road that lead me even higher, but not high enough to see the peaks of the Chilcotin Mountains yet, I make my first turn off the main highway. My directions say 120km until the next turn off. The road turns to gravel and I think to myself, "I hope this turns back to pavement soon." It does not. "This is the reason it takes so long to get there." The terrain is surprising flat. Wide open fields for as far as I can see, but I can see no mountains. I am getting creepy feelings as I leave the main road, not liking that I do not have reception. Is this the start of the withdrawal my brother said I would experience? I wish he had never implanted that suggestion in my brain. What should take a little over an hour takes me over two hours. I have been driving for four hours since I lost reception.

Rounding a bend I step on the brakes and I slide on the gravel. In front of me is the forbidden zone … Elkin Creek Bridge. Mr. Aswell's words are ringing in my head and are written on my paper … "DO NOT go over Elkin Creek Bridge!" It is written twice as he said it twice. I look in the direction I am told to go and shake my head, looking at what has now become my "trail." I laugh to myself saying, okay, here we go … into the wilderness of the Chilcotin.

It is at this point, when I turned on to this trail, that I let go of everything. The outside world cannot affect me, cannot get to me. I will not know, nor do I want to know, what is going on out there. I am truly alone now. It is not long before the trail turns into decent roads and I am able to relax and soak in exactly where I am. I am in the middle of a vision I had for years. It had only been an idea, only a dream, but look at me now, I am living it, I made this happen.

I was happy to come across a fork in the road and I consulted my directions. Okay good, another landmark.

Keep to the right. I am climbing again and I can see ahead that the road narrows and soon I will no longer have fields but dense forest and far off into the distance I see what I have been looking for. Stretching from Tweedsmuir Park south to the Lillooet River Valley and east to Fraser River and the Caribou, I see the spectacular, mountain wilderness … the snow-covered glacier peaks of The Chilcotin Mountains.

The road is washboard in many places and it forces me to slow down. I have passed a few farms that look abandoned and there are cattle roaming free and at times I have to stop and wait for them to move out of my way. So far they are the only living things I have seen. I roll my window down and watch them watch me. It's funny to see and I take more pictures.

After I pass the cattle I come upon a small First Nations village and I am relived to see people. It gives me comfort to know should I have to ask directions I can. But I don't, I wave to the children playing in the school playground and I carry on with the challenge, trusting my own directions on paper.

I remember Mr. Aswell telling me of horses that roam the region, free and wild. So when I turned a corner and saw horses in the middle of the road, standing single file, waiting to move onto a trail on the side of the road that leads into the forest, I wasn't surprised.

At first I thought these have to be domesticated, this can't be the wild horses. But they are and they are huge and not so inclined to move out of the way to let me pass. I roll my window down and holler, "Come on big fellas, get a move on." The largest one of the bunch turns and looks at me as if I had just asked him to do the most unthinkable thing and he removes himself from the line and starts to walk towards me. I grab my camera and start taking pictures. He walks right up to the front of my truck, leans his giant head forward and starts sniffing my engine. I put my truck in reverse and he starts following me, going as fast as I am. Now his buddy is coming too, walking beside me keeping up with me. The rest of the herd is now making its way behind them and now I have eight horses surrounding me as I am driving backward, which is very unnerving.

"Enough." I said out the window and I stop. They stop too. They are not looking agitated or threatening, just curious. The big guy in the front walks around to the passenger side of my truck and I roll down the window. Sure enough he sticks his giant head right inside. I press myself against my door trying to keep as far away from him as I can. Camera in hand I start snapping pictures and he snickers horse spit at me. I reach out to touch him and he pulls back and bumps his head. I put the window back up and put my truck in drive and slowly they disperse to allow me to pass.

I look in the rear view mirror as I pull away watching them disappear into the forest. I found myself wishing once again to have someone with me. "That was weird." I shake my head in amazement at what just happened. Timing is everything. If I had been a few minutes earlier or a few minutes later I would not have seen these wild horses and they would still be legend to me.

I pass a few more landmarks and I am confidant I will reach my destination before dark. I have been driving for just over five hours when I come to another fork in the road, I consult my direction and this fork in the road…not on my paper. The next landmark I do have tells me I will have to travel 65km from that point but which way do I go from here? I do the eeney meeny miney moe thing and it comes out pointing to the right. I find myself thinking about all the maps I have consulted but none of them defined any roads leading to the cabins so all I can do is hope I have chosen the right road.

I am no longer feeling as confident as I was. I am now thinking I am going to be spending the night in my truck and hoping the flare I have is not a dud. The sun is setting in the sky and my mind starts to become overactive with images I do not want. The road has narrowed and at times it is just wide enough to get my truck through, then, back again to wider trails. I am going uphill, getting higher into the mountains, as I know I should be, but now traveling with only faith that I was going up the right mountain. Fresh tire tracks ahead of me provided some comfort that I was not alone on this mountain, but it also gave me the creeps to think, if I break down or get lost, I *am* alone on this mountain except for the people who made those tire tracks, and who are those people?

It is easy to conjure up images when you start doubting your decisions and you are hundreds of kilometres from civilization with no cell reception. Every horror movie and every scary book I have ever read came to life. I am suddenly the star victim in every scary scene. Little Blonde woman, alone, no cell reception, no one knows where I am, except I am going into the Chilcotin Mountain Range. No one expecting to hear from me for days. Even my friends were not sure when I would be showing up. I think about the grizzlies, the cougars and the wolves.

I think about the last person I spoke to, Lee, telling her to contact my brother but that was not for six days from then. So I knew no one outside these mountains would even begin to look for me for days. I continue to consult my directions that were given to me in a two minute phone call a few days before hoping it will jog something I did not write down, and several times I find myself doubting the road I am on. How bizarre is that? Questioning myself about the road I am on I laugh out loud at myself and my own philosophical analogies. Then I relax thinking, "Of course Mr. Aswell will come looking for me if I don't show up tonight or tomorrow. This is just part of the adventure. This is just a test of bravery, this is just a test."

Two hours later I come across a bulldozer in the middle of nowhere. It sits there ominous in the fading evening sun, years since its engine cracked the silence of this place, now becoming part of the landscape as the weeds and trees are growing up around it. Beside it I can see the reason it was here. I can see the work it had once performed. There is a long stretch of land that has been cleared. I am so relieved just seeing a manmade thing in the middle of nowhere, and as it is getting close to dark I figured this looks like a good place to stop for the night. I did not put it together that this long, open stretch of cleared land is the air strip I had written down and would come across, as it too has many weeds, but this is my last landmark. I did not realize I had arrived and where I was contemplating stopping for the night was two minutes from the cabin.

By this time I had come to terms with the fact it was getting late and I would be spending the night in my truck. I drove a little further to turn around when I saw a truck coming from my left. The man in the truck had his window rolled down and was waving to me. I backed up, turned and pulled up beside him. I knew I recognized him but at that moment I could not remember his name. I was a still caught up with being the star in my own horror flick.

"We were starting to wonder if you were going to make it or if you had gotten lost."

I just looked at him and said, "Are you Jack?" Jack is a

friend of Mr. Aswell's who has a cabin somewhere in these mountains too.

I knew this wasn't Jack as soon as the words came out of my mouth. He laughed and said, "No Suzanne, are you alright?"

"Yes I am now. Sorry Mr. Parker, just a little weirded out from the drive. Where do I go from here?"

"Just follow this road where I just came from, you will see the cabins on the hill. Didn't happen to see the dogs along your way, they took off a while ago and have not come back."

"No, I wish I had, I would have felt better seeing them, I would have picked them up to spend the night with me. I thought I took the wrong turn 100km back."

"Mr. Aswell put out an APB for you and the dogs to the rest of the cabins around so no worries, you were being looked out for. Grizzlies have been sighted so at least we do not have to worry about you. I am heading down to Jack's cabin, so we will see you there later."

As I pull up to the cabins I want to fall to the ground and thank what ever gods may be for getting me there safely and not having to spend the night alone in my truck, although I know I would have been fine. I am just happy not to have had to have done it.

As I am getting out of my truck Mr. Aswell is walking out of the front door of the main cabin.

"Hi,"

"Hi." He says back smiling at me. "Did you see my escapees?"

There were no comments like, "Glad to see you, I was worried, did you have any problems. Glad you found it okay." I just stood there watching him walk towards the ATVs parked near other cabins.

"No, but I met Mr. Parker on the airstrip and he told me they were on the run,"

"Yes. Come on, you hop on that machine. Let's go take a look this way to see if we can find them."

I look at him, and without saying anything I get on the "machine," the 4 wheel quad, like I did it everyday of my life, he points to the starter and I push it. He had no idea this was my first time as a driver. I have always been a passenger. I follow him out of the yard in the opposite direction of where I just came from. The sun is dropping quickly behind the mountains and I can sense his urgency to find the dogs before it gets dark.

It does not take long for me to get a handle on driving the "machine" and I have no problem keeping up with him. I can't believe I am doing this. After a short drive down a trail we come across the dogs bounding towards us heading back towards the cabins and the relief on Mr. Aswell's face is evident. It would be the same as a parent finding their lost child.

Back at the cabin, it is dark now as the sun just drops behind the mountains, like turning out a light. He tells me we are going to a party at another cabin. Jack and Joan's place is about 15 minutes drive. All I want to do is sit and take in where I am, and all that I have gone through to get here but I have no time. We are going to a party, a party in the Chilcotin Mountains.

We take his truck and when we arrive I meet several people I have never met before and some I had not seen in many years. They are laughing and I say, "What's so funny?"

"When Mr. Aswell told us to be on the lookout out for a blonde driving a Mercedes we thought he was joking. I told him *we were all* on the lookout for a blonde driving a Mercedes.

We didn't think it was true. Mr. Parker told us you arrived. "How was the drive?"

I laughed, "Fine, except for the missing part of the directions. The fork in the road 100km back … not on my map."

I look right at Mr. Aswell. No reaction. I wondered if he was checking out my survival skills.

After the party I am feeling extremely tired and on the drive back I say to him, "Did you leave out that fork in the road on purpose?"

"No, why would I do that?"

"I don't know but I get the feeling you did."

"If you had turned left it only went a little way. You would have turned around."

"That would have been good information to have three hours ago."

"You made it. I knew you would."

Back at the cabin I unpack a few things for the night and settle in. We sit at the kitchen table, having cold drinks and I tell him how happy I am to be there. He looks different to me. Suddenly this man I have known most of my life looks different. He is in his true environment. The stress of his life outside these mountains is not evident on his face. He moves about his mountain home as if he lives here everyday. There is running water in the summer months, thank goodness. Electricity is provided by a generator on the front porch and some of the lights are battery powered. There is an antique cast iron and nickel-plated wood stove and oven, the kind my great grandmother used, and the most delectable meals I have ever eaten, breakfast, lunch and supper have come out of this oven. He even bakes pies! Over the years I have stopped asking what I was eating until after I was done. I have not cooked one meal when I am with him, ever! It has become our way; he cooks, I clean up. My motto with him has become the K's. "You Kill it, you Klean it, you Kook it, I Konsume it, I Klean up. (I know they are not spelt properly.) I do not need to see the process of how it gets on my plate.

There have been times when I would show up at his home and he would just look at me. I never had to say a word, he just knew I needed to rest and be fed back to being well. No one does this better than he does.

Walking around the cabin, with my drink in hand, I am totally oblivious to anything beyond this moment when I see the "ghetto blaster." It is a clunky thing from the 80's. I plug it in and push play, content to listen to what ever CD is in it. I look over at him and chuckle, and start dancing to his music, legends of the 60s and 70s.

On the walls are the prerequisite mounts, trophies with eyes that watch every move we make, horns that curl and if stretched out straight, would be over 2 feet long. "What are they? Who shot them?" My jacket is hanging on a four point antler rack, next to his father's hat. The doors of the cabins are framed with antlers of moose, deer, elk, caribou and other animals I do not know. Everywhere I look, cabinet door handles, antlers, book ends, on shelves, in corners—antlers. Outside nailed to trees and laying on the ground bleached from the many years of exposure—antlers. I think to myself, "Ros would shiver at the sight of every one of these."

Then I see "it" and my heart skip a beat. Sitting on a side table in the living room, in a small silver suitcase, looking like something straight out of a James Bond, 007 movie, open for me to see, is the satellite phone! I look at him and he laughs, because he also knows how addicted to the phone and texting I am. I am as excited about this as he would be about seeing a big buck in the crosshairs of the scope of his rifle.

I tell him about what my brother said and he asks me if I want to call someone. "No! I can go without contact for a week … it's only a week…" He looks at me watching the conflicted conversation I am having with myself. I dance away from it, distracting myself by asking more questions. But it does not take long until I have danced my way back. Standing looking at it I say, "Perhaps … you should show me how this works …just in case there is an emergency and I have to call some one … like a helicopter."

Mr. Aswell is the modern day Renaissance Man. He exudes confidence in this wild, unforgiving wilderness, just as easily as he does back in the other world, and I have never felt safer, but at the same time I feel extremely vulnerable at not having the creature comforts of communication. He likes his rifle, I like my cell phone. He has only adopted a cell phone recently and has no add-ons; no message center, no text messaging, no call waiting. It is strictly to make calls. He does not use a computer and has a hard time accepting doing business unless it is done by fax machine. Whenever some one says, "give me your e-mail," he proudly proclaims, "I do not have one."

So, now I am standing looking at this phone in a suitcase. He walks over and stands beside me, picks up the receiver, and starts to show me how it works in the same manner as he gave me directions to get here, quickly and only once …. "push this, look at this, make sure it says this, watch that, then push the numbers." He places the receiver back down and looks at me.

He can tell I am vibrating, "This isn't funny!" but he laughs anyway. "Perhaps we should make one phone call just so I know how to use it." I want to fight using this phone more than anything at this moment. I do not want to accept that I am addicted to the phone. My brother cannot be right! I feel ridiculous having this battle with myself and Mr. Aswell can tell by the way I am fidgeting, that I am about to give up this battle and sure enough he becomes ... my enabler.

"Who do you want to call?"

"There is only one person on this earth that we should call!" I look at him. "Who do you think that is?"

"Ros."

"Yes!"

I pick up the phone and push all the right buttons in the right sequence as if I did it a million times before and seconds later, like she is right next door, I hear her voice... "Hello?"

"Hi."

"Hi! Where are you?" She always sounds so excited to hear from me. We do not even have to start talking and we are laughing. "I thought you were at the cabin."

"I am and it comes complete with a satellite phone!" We laugh our heads off. We talk for a few minutes, me doing all the talking, letting out all the suppressed energy of the past few months and especially the last ten days. It just spills out of my mouth.

I am giddy, babbling, feeling drunk from the thin air. I am trying to explain the drive here, the mountains, the horses, the feelings of being lost and the plan I had if I had gotten lost; the trophies on the wall, the remoteness of where I am both physically and mentally. I tell her I feel so free here that I never want to leave. I look at Mr. Aswell as those last words come out of my mouth. I know he has never seen me let loose like this. He has never heard me expose myself like this before and I don't care.

When I hang the phone I look at him and with as straight a face as I can muster I say, "I'm never leaving here and you

can't make me. I want this feeling to last the rest of my life."
I turn up the music and sing like nobody's listening and … I
dance.

Over the years he has seen me in many phases of my
life. Single, married, not married, pregnant, not pregnant,
fat, thin, healthy, sick, happy, sad, pensive, the world on my
shoulders and at times with not a care in the world. He has
always been consistent, strong and private. He opens his home
to me and allows me to do what ever I need to do, mostly rest,
eat and poke fires on his beach, never questioning me and I
do not question him. He sends me back home with renewed
energy to carry on with my life until I show up again.

We rarely spoke about our personal lives. It just never
seemed to matter. As I was only going to be staying for a short
time, it just never made any sense to become involved. We
are sure every one who knows of our relationship thinks we
are more, and we do not care what they think. It is no one's
business but ours. We like it this way. For me, I never wanted
to tempt risking what we have by crossing any lines. Why
would I risk it? He has been the most constant man in my life
and he cooks and lets me be me!

Sure there were times over the years when I wondered
about us. Why have we not crossed the line? And I have
thought about telling him every time I go to see him, that I
have had a crush on him my whole life, but when I get there,
I don't say a word. I can't. I am afraid of the unknown. What
if he has never thought of me in the same way? Then I will
have exposed my feelings and we would never be the same.
The dynamics of our relationship would change and that is a
risk I have been unwilling to take.

I have often looked at him across the table or across the
room, and wondered what he thinks when he is looking at me

and I have concluded that if he felt something other than what our friendship is, as it is, he would tell me or there would be some physical action to let me know. But he has never made a move or said a word. There have been moments when our eyes have locked and the words were so close to coming out of my mouth, but I excused myself and left the room until the moment passed, but other than those few moments, we have remained the same.

When I am back home, for the first few days, I have to resist the urge to call him, to tell him I miss him and the peace his place provides for me. But that urge soon passes and I am thankful that I did not succumb to my weak moments, until I find myself making plans to be in his home again and it starts all over again in my head. I tell myself… "I will not leave there with this…unfinished." But as always I leave without saying a word.

Now as we are both getting older, I want him to know how I have felt about him, since I was 18 years old. I do not want to die, as we know this happens, without him knowing how he affects me, how I have felt about him, how I still feel about him.

"Mr. Aswell … I have been curious about you from the moment you sat across from me that morning at the Riverside having breakfast with our friends, and you kicked my chair leg, jokingly asking me, "When are you going to leave that guy?" … motioning to my husband who was sitting next to me. Over the years as our relationship has grown, I have come to adore you and you have looked after me like no other, unconditionally accepting me whenever and however I show up. When I am with my friends and we start describing the perfect man, as women do with each other… I always describe you." Now he knows. I have written it. And he has read it. I will not speak to him about this and I do not expect him to respond. I do not expect our relationship to change because I do not expect this to come as a complete surprise to him.

When the ladies in my life would hear I was going to be visiting with him, before I left they would always say to me, "Suzanne you have to tell him, maybe he feels the same way." When I get home and I see them or speak on the phone with them, the first thing they ask is, "Did you tell him?" The answer is always the same … "No." Now these same ladies are heading for their phones, right now, to call me to see if I have heard from him, to see what his response has been to me exposing my feelings for him, in this way. If you and I happen to meet … please feel free to ask me if he responded and what his reaction has been.

Now here I am, in his most private place, in the wilds of the Chilcotin Mountains, a place I have romanticized about for as long as I can remember. The night is black, the stars and the moon are closer to me than I have ever seen. You would think we would be seduced by the atmosphere alone but we are not. There is no question; I am not emitting any vibrations to Mr. Aswell that would suggest to him that I am wanting to explore our relationship any differently that it always has been and I am not in a frame of mind to even pick up any from him if he was sending any to me. As a matter of fact, I am sure he can feel the wall that is built around me with a big "For your own safety … NO TRESSPASSING" sign attached to it.

I have finished dancing and he has gone out to turn the generator off. Climbing into bed I am exhausted from my day of thinking too much. I have finally turned my cell phone off, after checking it several times, just to make sure it does not have super powers to draw reception. The silence that surrounds us is only broken by the sounds of our own breathing and I succumb to the warmth of the duvet covering me.

Falling asleep I find myself wondering, why the Universe has put these two completely different men in my life. And furthermore, what are the reasons I feel so conflicted whenever I am with them?

I sleep so soundly and I am only slightly disturbed by the sounds of Mr. Aswell waking up and going upstairs. I opened my eyes only long enough to realize it was still dark. I rolled over and slept until the smell of coffee and bacon stirred me awake again.

I feel refreshed and excited about my day. I am so happy to feel excitement, and continue to be astonished that I am consciously aware of the difference in my feelings. I promise myself I will not dwell on trying to figure out anything about Jack right now. I just want some coffee and that bacon.

I put my hair up, pull my wool socks on, and over my night gown I put on one of Mr. Aswell's shirts that were cast offs that Roslyn and I rescued, several visits ago, from a bin that was going to go to Goodwill. This is my favourite outfit and I wear it often.

I walk up the stairs and the sun is shining through all the windows that take up most of the wall space in the cabin. I stand looking out at what I could not see last night ... the sun is warming my body and my mouth is open allowing my breath to escape in small increments, but words are not part of me. I cannot find them. What I am looking at has literally taken my breath away.

I look at Mr. Aswell who is looking at me. Mr. Parker is sitting at the table, also looking at me, I slept so soundly I did not hear him return from the party during the night.

Mr. Aswell's eyes are wide and the smile on his face tells me my reaction is everything he wanted it to be. I am sure every person he has invited into this world reacts the same way and he never gets tired of seeing this reaction. I walk into the kitchen and bump against him, "Thank you for this."

"For what?"

"For that." As I point to everything around me. "Suddenly I feel like no other world exists."

"It doesn't."

My coffee cup is sitting on top of the stove in the warming oven along with our plates. I cannot take the smile off my face. He pours my coffee and I say "Yes!" to breakfast.

While he is busy in the kitchen, an image I love, I chug back the orange juice he has poured for me, and take my coffee from the stove, just like I have every single morning for the past 30 years whenever I have woken up in his home. I step into my hiking boots and without doing up the laces, I tuck them in, and wander out the front door looking like a young Granny Clampett.

The air is still and pure, I take many deep breaths, filling my lungs with pure mountain air. I walk to the middle of the yard. Several cabins circle me. Smoke is rising straight up from the chimney of the main cabin, from the stove that is cooking my breakfast and warming the water for my shower.

I turn slowly, looking at all I could not see in the dark. I have to consciously make the effort to close my mouth. He comes to the door and I say to him "Oh My God! Look Where I am!! I can't believe where I am! This *is* another world; this is the most fantastic place I have ever been! And … it comes complete with a man in the kitchen to cook for me! What more could a girl ask for?" I am laughing as I say this. He just shakes his head and returns to the frying pans.

I am surrounded by mountains, and I am looking at glaciers. The summer is turning to autumn and the colors that I can see in the valleys between the mountains, rising as far as the edge of the snow, are an artist's dream palette … purples, whites, greens, golds and reds. I think of my friend Deborah, who is so talented with a paint brush. She would love what I am seeing. I miss her.

Fishem Lake is steps away, down a small hill. It is still, not moving, with the reflection of the mountains and trees, mirrored upon it. I walk to the edge of the hill looking down at the lake and I see a pasture with a corral. Two horses are munching on the hay that has been freshly spread for them. There is a building there I assume is the barn for the horses, Murphy and Striker. I come to find out it is also the ice house. Mr. Aswell comes up in the winter, cuts ice from the lake, many blocks, and stores it in this building. This is how we keep our food preserved and our drinks cold. The ice we used last night in our drinks was cut last January. I am impressed with this.

After breakfast, after I clean up, I go out to see what is going on as Mr. Aswell and Mr. Parker have been coming in and out and collecting things out of the other cabins. The horses have been brought up and are saddled. I look at the stuff they are tying onto the saddle. Tents, sleeping bags, heavier clothing, rifles and food.

"Are you going some where?"

Mr. Aswell looks at me like this is a question I should know the answer too.

He points his finger to the mountains across the lake. "See that ridge, just to the right of that valley, that open space?"

I look and I think I see where he is talking about but I'm not sure.

"Yes."

"That is where I am going and Mr. Parker is going a little further beyond that."

"And … you're staying overnight?"

"Yes."

No doubt the look on my face needed no explanation. I cock my head to right, and my eyebrows knit in question. The reality that I am going to be alone in the cabin for the rest of the afternoon and all night, does not take long to register, and I find that the prospect excites and scares me.

"Is there anything I can do to help?"

"Nope, were ready."

"Now? You're leaving now?"

"Yes, I want to get there while we still have daylight."

"How long is it going to take to get there?"

"About four hours."

"Call me on the radio to let me know when you get there. I will try to find you with those gigantic binoculars."

Further discussion reveals they will sleep on the mountain so they can hunt first thing in the morning.

"Um … would you show me how the generator works before you leave?"

We walk to the front porch and just like everything else I need directions for, he points to it and says, "Turn this, pull that, make sure you plug this in first and just do the opposite when you shut it down."

"You're so funny Mr. Aswell … I hope you shoot something. I'll be hungry when you get back."

"I will check in on the radio in a while." He walks about ten paces and turns to me. "Are you going to be ok?"

"Are you kidding? Of course I am! I am going to read, write in my journal, take pictures and wander naked all around your property!"

"Watch out for the grizzlies!"

We laugh but it really is not funny to me. I don't have a rifle or … bear spray.

I watch them climb up on the horses, tug the reins and head out of the yard. I am mesmerized by this whole thing, real mountain men. I walk to the edge of the hill, look out over the corral, the barn and the ice house, watch them get off the horses to walk them across the bridge made of logs that cross the river at the end of the driveway, I watch them until I can no longer see them. I turn in the spot I am standing, arms crossed, take a deep breath and walk back to the cabin. It is so quiet. I am not used to this quiet. I have been alone, a lot, but quiet, like this … never heard it before.

I wander around inside the cabin, humming to myself. I refill my coffee cup and wander back outside. The sun is high in the sky and I suddenly feel the heat of having too many clothes on. I walk to the steps of one of the other cabins, put my discarded clothes on the top step, sit down on them and lean back. I am not a sun worshipper but right now I am worshipping every element in the Universe. I am feeling the freedom of being completely exiled from every problem, every anxious moment, and every prying eye that has ever been upon me. I hear my own words confirming "I am a freak of nature." Never in my life have I walked naked in the sun without something in my hand just in case someone shows up. Today, no one is coming and even if they did … I would not care.

As I am walking around I see spirals of smoke from a pile of brush that Mr. Aswell spent his day yesterday cleaning up and I pick up my clothes and walk there. I pull my shirt back on and start to throw a few more sticks onto the smouldering ashes, thinking I will hang out here for the afternoon, doing one of my favourite activities, poking a fire.

When I finish burning the brush he had piled up, I am leaning on the stick I was using as a poker, staring at the ground, deep in thought, when my brain suddenly sends a signal to my eyes.

It had been raining the few days before we arrived and now I can tell how they knew there were grizzlies in the area. It takes me a few minutes to really comprehend what I am looking at because I have never seen animal prints this big before so it seems unreal to me. The impressions that are now dried in the mud are big enough to encompass a small child's head. The imprints coming off the end of these impressions that have pierced the ground, looking like someone purposefully took a nail and pushed it into the mud, are clearly claw impressions.

When you are looking at something you have never seen before it is easy to miss what it is that you are looking at but this was unmistakable. I immediately looked around. The fear factor was suddenly on high alert. Even though the tracks were dry and the grizzly was probably long gone I did not want to hang around without something solid behind me, like the walls of the cabin. Again all the scary movie and book scenes are in my head as I am walking quickly back to the cabin.

Once inside I pace from window to window. I look up to the mountain where the hunters are going and I curse them for not leaving me a rifle, but then I think Mr. Aswell would have had to show me how to use that too. It does not take long to talk myself down and I go out again but I do not stray too far from the front door. I tell myself there have been no reports, ever, of a bear attack here, no cougars or wolves either. I am not going to be the first. Somehow all this talking to myself does not placate my uneasiness as much as I would like it to.

In the late afternoon I take my dinner of leftovers Mr. Aswell put together for me, outside and settle into the captain's chair at the giant binocular station scouting for the mighty hunters. I see nothing, I hear nothing. I eat in peace wondering if the bears are smelling my dinner. The sun is setting and I know I am going to have to turn the generator on. I walk to it on the front porch, I turn this, I pull that, I plug that in and poof … I am set with power for the night and I head inside to clean up and settle in for the long dark night ahead.

In the living room I sit down in the big easy chair and I stare back at the eyes of the Big Horn Sheep mounted on the wall. As I am sitting there I become conspicuously aware of how I cannot see out into the blackness but anyone or anything could be looking in at me and see me clearly. There are no curtains to draw, nothing to hide me and I am convinced this is another test from Mr. Aswell. Why do I think like this? Roslyn would be straight out of her mind at this point. She would have insisted on going with them. I remember her being afraid of walking around my yard at night and was always amazed when she would call me and I was out in my yard at night alone.

I pick up my journal and start to write but the writing only confirms how remote and alone I am and I put it down. I pick up my book but cannot concentrate on the words in front of me, so I put it down. Pulling my feet up, curling myself into the chair my mind wanders to Jack. I walk to the kitchen to get something to drink and when I walk back into the living room … there it is … the satellite phone. Its ON button is glowing alien green. That is a sign to me if I ever saw one— green is for go. I pick it up, push this button, watch for that and push the buttons that will connect me to him.

"Hello?"

"Hi."

"Well hello there. I didn't expect to hear from you so soon. Where are you?"

His voice is comforting and I close my eyes and see his face, thinking he would love it here too.

"I am at the cabins and I am alone for the night."

"Why, where is everyone?"

"Gone hunting until tomorrow after noon."

"I did not recognize the number. It's an odd combination I have never seen before."

"Satellite phone."

There is a moment of uncomfortable silence before I say, "I did not like the way I left. I don't know why I continue to feel so unfinished with us every time I leave. I am still finding my way I guess."

"I didn't like it either, we are both finding our way. You okay there by yourself?"

"Except for the fact I have myself convinced that every grizzly, cougar and wolf is circling the cabin just waiting for me to step outside, yes I am fine."

He laughs with me and I feel better.

"Are you still planning to head North to Alaska when you leave there?" I expect him to break into a Johnny Horton tune after he said … "North to Alaska," but he does not. I play it in my head instead.

"Yes." And I think to myself, "Okay, this is the time for you to say, I want you to come back here." He does not.

"Well that will be exciting."

"I am looking forward to seeing Cheryl and Kenny too."

"Right, how long has it been since you have seen them?"

"17 years."

Another moment of silence, I want to tell him how

incredible this place is but I don't.

"I guess I should get off this phone."

"Text me when you get with in range. When is that again?"

I don't know why but this questioned irked me. Whenever he was anywhere I would remember exactly when he was going to be in contact with me again. Why could he not remember when I said I was coming back down the mountain? This was a significant separation of time and communication for us … I would remember every detail of when to expect to hear from him.

"Sunday."

"Okay, I miss you."

"I miss you too."

"Take care."

"You too. See you."

"Bye Bye."

Hanging up the phone I look around and think, "Now what?"

Out of the silence I hear a voice that makes me scream like someone just snuck up on me. "Suzanne, are you there?"

I stare at the radio receiver on the wall in the kitchen, walk over to it and press the button on the side. I resist the urge to say, "Copy that great white hunter, this is woman alone in dark cabin, go ahead."

Instead I say, "Hey you, are you tucking in for the night?"

"Yes, everything okay there?

"Oh yeah, me and my imagination are just fine."

"You can bring the dogs in for the night."

"I looked for you earlier but I saw no signs of life."

"In the morning maybe you can look again and see if there are any big bucks roaming around."

"Oh yes, for sure, that's what I will do."

I am sure he heard the sarcasm and will expect no such call. He knows the only time I want to see anything shot is by my camera. He knows I have no desire to see how my dinner gets to my plate and I especially do not want see it walking around just prior to being on my plate, nor do I wish to be the one responsible for sending it to its death.

"Okay, we will talk in the morning."

Again I want to answer back, "Ten four good buddy." But I don't.

"Sleep well up on that there mountain John Boy."

"Yip … good night."

It is early, too early for me to go to bed but I want to end the noise from the generator. I want to hear nothing again. I go out to bring in the dogs that have been in their kennels and after shutting them inside, giving them their dinner, I turn to shut down the generator.

I should have lit candles or turned on one of the battery powered lights before I did that but of course, there is a reason for every thing.

As soon as the power went off I could see nothing. The space around me was black. I could not see my hand in front of me. I could visualize what was around me and the walk to the front door was only steps away but I could not move from where I was. I waited for my eyes to adjust and took a few steps. I felt the hand rail of the porch and followed it until it ended. I walked off the porch— there are no steps—onto the ground.

The moon had not risen above the mountains and it was the darkest, blackest night I have experienced. You would think your eyes would adjust but it was just too dark. I walked to the middle of the yard and looked up at the most magnificent night sky I have ever seen. I forgot about being concerned about the wild animals, I forgot about everything. I sat down in the middle of the yard, felt the grass under me and laid back.

My eyes to the sky, I crossed my arms across my chest and just breathed. I could not help but start thanking whatever gods may be for bringing me here. The stars were not just falling from the sky; they were bursting, exploding from the heavens, brilliant orange, white, yellow and scarlet tails, trailing for so long before disappearing behind the mountains. As I lay there I felt myself starting to become overwhelmed with emotion and I couldn't help myself. This was the most spiritual event that had every happened to me. I start thinking about my journey.

I have done almost everything I have wanted and so much more, since leaving home. I have spent time with my family on the West Coast. I have visited with old friends all across the country and made new ones along the way. I have caught the biggest fish of my life. I have spent time alone exploring towns and villages and have driven to remote areas because I liked the name, names like "Head-Smashed-In Buffalo Jump, Alberta. I have had moments when I thought I was going to die and moments of bliss that I wanted to last forever. I have stood naked under waterfalls in the Rocky Mountains letting the freezing glacier water wash me clean and slept in a tent in a canyon listening to coyotes howl. I have explored under the Pacific Ocean picking sand dollars off the sandy floor, and chased eels and crabs into hiding spots in the underwater mountains of rock. I spent a month alone in a little guest home on a river, fishing, gardening, taking long walks, sleeping, reading, writing and meditating. I have had encounters with bears, deer, elk, caribou, moose, and coyotes and heard the threatening cry of the cougars. I have done all of this and more and I have only been gone three and a half months. What more could I possibly want to do? Alaska. I am going to A*laska*, when I head out of these Mountains in six days.

Then I started talking out loud to the gods. "What am I doing here? Why am I here? Why am I here alone?" As I lay in the grass looking up to the sky, I am overcome with emotion and tears are slowly sliding down my temples, soaking my hair and I do not try to stop them. I wonder to myself, "How does a person get used to being alone? How do you get used to doing things for no one but yourself? I don't know where to go, I don't know where I belong. All I am seeking is a little peace of mind and direction. I am not ready to go back and I do not know which way is forward. Why am I alone on this mountain? Why do I feel so weak one moment, unable to pull myself together and then feel like I can do anything the next?"

After a while the light show in the sky slows down and I find myself getting impatient. I do not recognize this person lying here, and this new woman who is trying so hard to emerge better hurry up because this emotional rollercoaster that has become my state of mind has to stop.

I start to think about Jack again. I wonder if he is taking advantage of this time alone to think about his own life. Does he ask himself the same questions? Do men ask them selves these questions? Probably. I wonder if he is aware that as I continue to drive further away from him, it is because I see that he is going through his own transition and it is a perfect opportunity for him to figure out what he misses in his life without my influence. I hope he is doing what he says he needs to do … "I need to be Free to figure it all out." I hope he is. I hope he does not continue to struggle as we both have been doing, wondering when all this living "in-between lives," is going to stop and we have it figured out. I know we will find some peace about us so we can move from this place of purgatory; I just want it to happen before I go down off this mountain.

When I get up off the ground, the moon has risen high in the sky, and I walk around the yard unafraid. I sing as loud as I dare "If Today was your last day" by Knickleback and the mountains echo back at me and I laugh at myself. I wonder if the hunters hear me too.

Back in the cabin I pick up the flashlight that is by the door and stoke the stove. It is still early for me to go to bed but what else is there to do? The dogs and I tuck in for the night. As I close my eyes I reach across the bed but there is no one there. I fall asleep knowing there will be no one there for a long time.

"Suzanne … are you there?"

It is barely light in my room and I hear this voice off in the distance calling my name.

I open my eyes and listen.

"Suzanne?"

I head up to the kitchen and pick up the radio.

"Hello, good morning!"

"In four hours, bring my truck up the road and meet us at the fork in the road. It's only a horse trail, where a tree has fallen and has freshly chopped wood chips all around it."

"The fallen tree with the wood chips."

"Yes."

"How far up the road would that be?"

"About fifteen minutes."

"Okay, see you in four hours."

I hang up the radio and shake my head. The fallen tree with the wood chips … that's funny considering I am in about three hundred thousand square kilometres of horse trails with forks in the road and fallen trees are everywhere.

Four hours later I meet the hunters at the fallen tree and find out they had no luck. My dinner was not compliments of the mountains but I was not disappointed.

Over the next few days I became an expert four wheel driver and the mountain trails we spent our days exploring have left me with an appreciation of how wild, remote and dangerous the wilderness really is. Driving along the side of the mountains, every bend in the trail brought me something new to take pictures of and I was grateful for Mr. Aswell behind me, fully armed and prepared to shoot our supper or anything threatening, should it appear on our path.

It is strange to meet anyone else when you are in the middle of nowhere so when we came upon a man walking the trail we were on it surprised me. He had been hunting for about five hours and told us he had seen grizzly. He accepted a ride with Mr. Aswell to take him back to his camp. As I look back at the pictures of that day, I smile remembering I did not have one moment of fear of Grizzly Bears or anything else as the two men on the quad behind me were so heavily armed nothing had a chance on that mountain.

When it came time to pack up I did not want to go. I had adjusted to living in the seclusion of the mountain quickly and was not ready find out what had happened in the outside world. Mr. Aswell and I had talked a lot about the remoteness of where I was contemplating going—Alaska. He was not concerned about my ability to take care of my self, it was the fact that I was going to be alone that concerned him. He had never voiced concern for me before and because he had this day, I was starting to think twice about where I was going. He too talked about the stretch of highway that has been dubbed, "The Highway of Tears," and although I would not be driving it on my way to Alaska, I could be driving that way on my way back. This is the kind of reality I have to take into consideration as I will be completely alone and no one will be expecting me.

For the past week I had stopped thinking about my cell phone and found I liked not being so attached to it until … we started down the mountain. When I got in my truck I turned it on even though I knew it would be many hours before I would have reception. There was a strange excitement in anticipating the *Blip* of messages coming in. I wondered if he remembered that I would be in range today.

Getting back into Williams Lake and watching Mr. Aswell and Mr. Parker drive in a different direction gave me an odd feeling. I wanted Mr. Aswell to be going with me and bringing his rifles. Knowing I was driving into the remotest part of the province then out of Canada into the Yukon then Alaska was scary. I suddenly felt an apprehension I had not experienced. I called Cheryl to let her know I would be arriving in Mackenzie late that night. After I hung up the phone I could not shake the feeling that going North was going to be a defining moment for me but I could not tell if the feeling was good or bad. I just knew I had to go.

CHAPTER NINETEEN

Alaska Bound

Seven kilometres from Williams Lake my phone starts to make the sounds I am clearly addicted to. I did not realize how much I missed the sounds and it is like getting a hit of adrenaline injected directly into my brain.

Blip, Blip, Blip … I pull into town to get a drive thru coffee and return a few calls and text messages.

After letting those who have been wondering how I am and where I am know, I call him.

"Hi, I am back in civilization."

"How are you? How was being in the mountains?'

"It was fantastic! It was more than I thought it would be. I have never experienced such isolation in my life. I adjusted to it quickly as it is such a simple way of living. It certainly is not for every one but once I got the hang of how everything worked I was fine."

"Where are you headed now? Still heading North?"

"Yes, I will be in Mackenzie late this evening. Baby … I really miss you. I tried really hard to be free of thinking about you but it was impossible, I wanted you to be with me experiencing everything I was. We would have laughed so much."

"I am sure we would have. It was hard for me too."

"I am feeling uneasy about going to Alaska alone."

"Then don't go. I feel uneasy about you going there alone too."

"I have to go. Something is drawing me there."

"Maybe spending time with your friends will help you get comfortable with your decision to go there. Being so close to Alaska you will know what you are supposed to do."

"I know what I am supposed to do. My heart keeps telling me to drive to you but my head tells me to keep driving away so you have your space to figure out what you need to do for yourself. So until you decide what your heart truly desires, I will keep driving away."

"I want you here right now."

"I want to be there right now but we both know it would only be a matter of time until I leave again because you feel so strongly about finishing your plan without distractions from me. I hope you have been working like you said you wanted too."

"I have been but it is tough to keep motivated some days."

"Yes, you have no idea how difficult it is to keep driving away from you and I am so homesick for my kids I nearly lose my mind with the feelings of loneliness. I am going to go now. I have another 5-6 hour drive ahead of me and I just drove for five hours coming out of the mountains."

"Ok, text me when you arrive. Sooz … I miss you baby. Be safe."

I hang up the phone and cry my head off in the parking lot. I want to go home but I have no home to go too. I want to be held by him but he is too far away. I start talking to myself again.

"Get it together Suzanne, you cannot stay here. Just drive."

A few hours later I am standing at a gas pump, in Quesnel, British Columbia, I look across the parking lot and there is a man standing there watching me. He is dressed in motorcycle leathers next to his very fast looking motorcycle. You know the feeling when someone is watching you and you can tell they are deciding whether to approach you or not. Well he made the decision to approach me. He walked across the lot and I was just about finished pumping my fuel when he said, "Hi, I thought you were a friend of mine. She drives the same vehicle, blonde hair and she is about your size."

My spidy senses were on high alert.

"Nope, I am not your friend."

He glanced at my license plate and Marc's comments come flying back into my head. "Be careful mom, little blonde, out of town plates, your going to attract attention you do not need."

"You are a long way from home."

"Yes we are."

"What brings you so far from home?"

I want to tell him to buzz off but you never know how people will react to aggression.

So I say, "My husband and I are taking our sons to compete in the Ultimate Fighting Challenge taking place in Prince George." Such a lie but I want to make him think I am not travelling alone and I have fierce protectors with me.

I am praying he does not look inside my vehicle as it is easy to see no one could possibly be travelling with me. The back seats are down, covered with my luggage and the front passenger seat has my cameras and road maps laid out.

"They are across the street picking up a few things from that little store."

Then I see his eyes look inside and my heart rate starts to increase.

I find myself staring at him trying to remember every detail about him, his face, the color of his eyes, color of his hair, does he have facial hair, how tall he is, just in case I have to describe him.

"So you are not staying in this area?"

"No."

"Well good luck."

I know he knows, I am lying.

When I pull out of the gas station I pull across the street to the little store. I go in and watch out of the window until he drives away. I pick up a few things and get back on the road. Just as I am pulling out of this little town I hear the sounds of a motorcycle coming behind me. My knees start to shake uncontrollably as I see in my rear view mirror the unmistakeable colors of the leather jacket he was wearing. There is no question in my mind as I pull into a parking lot and swing my truck around to head back into the town I just left, that this man on the motorcycle is following me. He goes by and as I am driving back and punching into my GPS directions for the nearest police station, he comes up behind me again.

My GPS tells me I am 3km from the police station and he is right behind me. I find myself wanting to slam on the brakes but resist the urge. As I turn, he turns, until I pull into the parking lot of the police station then he flies right by me.

Having this happen was more than a little unnerving but I was not going to allow him to think he could get away with following me, and even if it was just a case of him going in the same direction, which I do not think it was, I felt better knowing he saw me go into the police station. I left Quesnel feeling I did the right thing.

It is raining and very dark as I pass through Prince George, the road to Mackenzie narrows and with new black pavement making it even darker and harder to see, it forces me to slow down as there are no lines indicating the middle or the side of the road. Signs indicating wildlife, specifically moose, also forces me to slow down as I have seen enough moose on the sides of the roads to know they are around.

I am two hours from where I will be spending the night and I am so tired my eyes are starting to hurt again when car headlights flash by me. Rounding a corner I see a flash of white in my headlights, I slow down almost to a crawl because whatever this is, is in the middle of the road. I creep closer to the white things until I almost run into it. The white things are the bottom legs of a Bull Moose standing in the middle of the road. I am now completely stopped and he does not appear concerned at all that I am there. I cannot believe how big this beast is; he towers over my vehicle and is apparently not in any hurry to get out of the way. I honk my horn and he slowly turns his head to stare at me like he is completely bored and I am disturbing him. When he starts to move it is the most intimidating sight I have ever seen. The velvet of his antlers is peeling and hanging shaggily from scraping his antlers against trees. I know they do this when they are rutting as a show of dominance. I also know that when moose are in this rutting state they will not hesitate to jump on just about anything. I back up and honking my horn again the big Bull Moose is startled into doing a little two step that looks like he is drunk and clumsy but he regains his balance and slowly walks off the road and into the dark forest. I carry on once again wishing someone was with me to witness this.

I pull into Cheryl and Kenny's driveway at 11:00 p.m. It is so good to be here, Cheryl answers the door and tells me Kenny is away hunting and is not expected back for a few days.

Over the next few days my loneliness increases. Along with text messages from Jack the phone calls from friends and family back home make me want to get in my truck and drive east. Marc has been in constant contact with me as his girlfriend has gone into labour and I am about to become a grandmother again. As I speak with each person I try to make it sound like I am having a great time, which I am, but the loneliness is so hard to keep at bay. My stomach is so knotted with anxiety I can hardly eat and sleep comes with dark lonely dreams of me driving up mountains that never seem to go down the other side. I cannot keep my eyes off the exit but I tell myself to be patient and I keep myself busy helping Cheryl put away her summer gardens. The physical activity feels good and the days slide away.

It is the middle of September and the temperature in this Northern British Columbian town has dropped and snow is already starting to fall and accumulates on the grass. I am standing in the backyard thinking about all that is going on back home and all the momentous things that have taken place since I left home. I wonder about my decision not to go home to be with my children during the birth of my grandchild. I did not go back when Blake died and that was tough and I find this equally tough. Talking with Marc, I can hear the fear and excitement in his voice and I wish I was there with them.

As I am standing near the edge of the yard, trying so hard to keep the loneliness from encompassing me, I am keeping an eye on a dog that Cheryl has brought home from the pound to live its last days with her. "Sheppy" is old, blind, deaf, had been shot twice, and abused badly. She is crippled to the point she has to be carried up and down the steps. I carry her out and plop her down on the grass to do her business with great trepidation as the night before there were Grizzly bears in the carport. We know this because they helped themselves to liquid fish fertilizer Cheryl has stored there. I am on high alert listening for any sounds coming from every direction and as we are backed onto the forest I am more than a little freaked out they may return for the rest of the fish fertilizer.

The local radio station does a regular report on wildlife sightings and apparently it is not uncommon to hear of bears, elk, moose and the occasional pack of wolves waltzing down Main Street. I think to myself, "Of course, there are always wolves walking down Main Street in Northern towns … in the movies." I liked hearing the wolves howl, at a distance. It is so solitary, so lonely. Their howls described my state of mind perfectly but I did not need reminding. It was a constant feeling, this loneliness, the sadness and it was magnified by the thoughts of my children being without me during the birth of my second grandchild. When was it going to stop?

The conservation officer lives next door and had told Cheryl a few days earlier the bears were in the area. The mother bear and her three cubs had been spotted several times and the conservation officer and his team were setting out large green containers, bear traps, to lure them in to return them far into the mountains. The concern was that this was not the first time this mother bear had come back to town, and the fact that she had her cubs with her made her even more dangerous.

As I am standing at the edge of the yard, staring off into the night and keeping an eye on the dog who cannot reciprocate, I hear excited voices hollering and see lights flashing back and forth scanning the forest. I pick up the dog and turn toward the house just as a shot rings out breaking the silence of this sleepy village. I take the dog into the house and go back outside. I walk to the edge of the yard behind the house and I can see three trucks with the containers moving along a dirt access road and I know my worries about the grizzlies are over. Then it dawns on me, these four bears were just a mere 500 meters away from me or less and had been for days. My heart skips a beat thinking they may have been watching me and the dog every night. I find out the next day they had to kill the mother as she had become aggressive and had returned to town for the third time. The cubs were over a year old and able to look after themselves so they were returned to the mountains.

Kenny arrived home and the next day they took me for a drive up the highest accessible mountain in the area. They told me they wanted me to have a look at where I am contemplating going. Although Fairbanks Alaska is still over 3000 kilometres away, a 36 hour drive from their home, they think my seeing the mountain range between here and there will give me a good idea of what I am in for.

The road up the mountain ends but Kenny continues to drive straight up the rock face of the mountain until we reach the peak of the mountain. As we do this the truck is on a vertical climb and I cannot see beyond the hood of the truck as it is straight up and down, it's exactly like my dreams. They both laugh at me making little screeching holy shit sounds! I am starting to pray to whatever gods may be because I feel as if the truck is going to flip back wards and we will be squished.

We settle on top of the mountain and I thank the gods for getting us there safely. I get out of the truck and I am immediately hit with a gust of freezing wind that nearly knocks me over. We are so high that we are now looking down at the clouds that kept the town shrouded in grey.

I walk to the edge of the peak we have driven up with the blistering cold and powerful gusting winds pushing me around. As I stand there working very hard to keep my balance, I look out across at the vast expanse of the most isolated, desolate, scariest place I have ever seen and I think to myself: I am already isolated and in a scary place … in my head—so why am I considering taking myself physically there. As far as I can see in every direction there are snow-covered mountain peaks.

I have always wanted to go to Alaska and it is where I have told everyone I am going. In my mind it represents freedom. However, that day, standing there, looking across that mountain range, it suddenly became the most isolated, desolate, scariest place I have ever contemplated going as I shuddered from the freezing wind and fear as I stared out at so many mountains, so much snow, and so few towns to provide a safe comfort zone.

Since leaving home, I have stood on top of many mountains; always hoping they would work their mysterious magic on me, and some of them have, including this one. I am so grateful to have heard the wisdom in the wind that was knocking me around. Today the winds of change were not just gently wafting warmly over my skin, I was being bullied by the freezing North Wind and it was trying to push me to the ground as if it was trying to turn me around, sit me down, telling me to … "Stop! Stop running!" I held firm in my spot and I hollered back, "No! Not yet, I am not ready to stop running!" I wrapped my arms around myself, hugged myself tightly, and whispered into the wind, "But, I am getting there."

As we descended the mountain a strange feeling of accomplishment came over me, I felt as if I had gone as far North as I should. I was having a discussion in my head about my desire to continue going to Alaska and a very concrete feeling that this was not the right time to go there came over me. For the first time since embarking upon this journey, I was afraid of the unknown and I made the decision not to go to Alaska. I felt okay with my decision not to go, telling myself I will get there but I want to go there with the image I had of my self when I made the decision to go there, when I first left home. I saw myself happier, laughing, being more self assured about my life, and more in control of my emotions. I saw it as the turn around point, where I would make my U-turn in life and start heading back East to a life I was excited to start living. But it was clear I was not even close to being happier nor did I have any idea what I wanted to do for work as I had not secured a publisher yet nor did I know where I wanted live.

Back in Cheryl's kitchen I get a phone call telling me I am now the grandmother of a baby girl. I look at Cheryl and I start to cry. She congratulates me and hugs me. She has no idea how I want to run out of the house, go to the nearest airport and fly home, but I tell myself I have to stay the course. I cannot go back until I purge all these feelings of disconnection with my life, because I know if I go back now I would only want to leave again.

When I packed up my truck to leave Mackenzie I felt happier because I had spent time with my friends and I made a decision. As the weather was turning nasty quickly, it was time to head back to the coast, to Vancouver where the weather would be warmer.

My phone rings and it is Jack, "Are you going to Alaska today?"

"No, you know what …it scared me. As I stood on the Mountain, looking across at thousands of kilometres of mountain peaks and snow … it scared me. Something is telling me not to go there."

"I am happy you are not going today. I did not want to say anything to discourage you from going but I am relieved. I have no doubt you will get there when the time is right. I want to go with you when you go."

"Really baby ... that would be great!"

"What are you doing now?"

"I was going to head back to Vancouver. Winter is starting to settle in and I figured I better find a place to tuck in for a few months. I have secured the little cottage in Oyster River for the month of October so I can prepare for the writer's conference the middle of October. After that I have no plans. My sister has offered her place in Vancouver in November and I think I may take her up on her offer."

"When are you going to arrive in Vancouver?"

"I am leaving now so I should be there late this evening."

"I will be there too. Do you want to meet me there?"

"Yes! Of course I do."

It is amazing how my insides suddenly felt light and happy. He also sounded excited too.

I meet Jack in Vancouver and our brief visit is as it always is. We spend a few fantastic days together then in the last few hours we start to decline into the conversations that make us both want to run but we never do. As I drive away heading back to the Island my thoughts are that I will spend the winter there, that I will spend my winter on Vancouver Island in the little cottage I rented in August.

This time being there is not as it was in August, like I was on vacation. I am alone although I have friends down the road, but I cannot bring myself to be with anyone. The darkness in my mind is heavier than it has ever been making it impossible to think and feel positive. The overwhelming feeling that after two years of being patient and believing in him and his words but not seeing or feeling any closer to knowing if we have a future together is wearing on my nerves. I am tired of hearing him once again tell me, that he needs more time with himself to figure out who he is but at the same time saying all the right words to keep me hooked.

Having spent the weekend at the writer's conference together as he has a conference in the same city, I have all the information I need to successfully write my children's books and secure a publisher so I head back to the little cottage on the Island. As I am driving I evaluate our relationship, particularly this past weekend together. I get the feeling he did not like the fact that I was busy and had very little time to spend with him. I feel myself drifting further away from him, I am starting to feel a purpose and a strength that had not been there before and I know he saw and felt it as well.

Once I am back on the Island I try to occupy my mind and hands with writing but I cannot shake the constant feelings of melancholy and loneliness and I become aware of the symptoms that start me slipping into darkness again. I can feel that my life is on another downward spiral and you would think that recognizing this would help stop the darkness from creeping in but regardless of what I do I cannot settle my emotions down enough to concentrate on anything, let alone writing. I do all the right things. I listen to my CD's and read my books that have continued to inspire me, I exercise, I go for long walks but nothing is stopping the blackness from settling into my soul again. I cannot shake the feeling that I have a man in my life that is keeping me at arm's length because he has things he does not want me to know about him and I have been so consumed with blissful thoughts I continue to ignore my instincts, which goes against every thing I have taught my children to do.

I call him to just to hear him, I do not let him know how adversely affected by him I have become and although he says all the right things and we make plans for him to come over to the Island for Thanksgiving Weekend, I still feel no closer to feeling the security I seek in my relationship and my life. As he continues to push his own deadlines ahead and keeps me on a hook with comments like, "In two months I will be done this program with work and I will then be free to spend time on my personal life," and "I see us together for the rest of our lives but just not today," and "You have to get on with your writing." As he continues to throw me these bones, the further and further I slip into myself. So many "two months" have come and gone and with each passing day the expectations of the pending moment he is ready to concentrate on his personal life—our personal life—plays heavily on my mind and my heart. I have to face the reality that it may never happen and as this reality starts to sink in, and no matter how hard I try to fight off the blackness, the blackness settles in and I am suddenly not feeding myself again or sleeping and I spiral into a depression that takes me so deep inside myself that once again my thoughts turn to going to sleep and never wanting to wake up.

I call my sister and she convinces me to leave the Island and come to her in Vancouver, so at the end of October I pack up my truck and leave the Island.

In the middle of November I meet with Jack. He is in town for a meeting but only for the day, so I pick him up from where he is to drive him to the airport. I have not told him of my downward spiralling state of mind or my thoughts of ending this relationship, because I can no longer believe his words. I say nothing because being with him feels so right to me when we are together and he says the same thing. It is when we say goodbye that we feel unsettled and he starts with his "I need to be free speech," and I also say "I need to be free too" but I do not understand if we both agree it is difficult to leave each other, why do we do it, why do we cause such stress to a relationship that elates and calms us both? Being apart makes little sense to me, but I am soon going to find out exactly who he is and why the Universe has continued to keep us apart.

Having him sitting beside me as I drive I want to keep driving. He reaches across to hold my hand and we do as we always do, we sigh with desire, but as we draw nearer to the airport we both feel that distance that always seeps in and surrounds us those last few hours before we separate for unknown periods of time. I tell myself that this feeling has to stop, I can't stand it any longer and it is keeping me from living my life. So just as I feel brave enough to tell him, that I am ready to let him go, that I must let him go if I am to get on with my life, and he will start confirming that this is what I must do by reiterating to me plans for his own life, the Universe once again steps in and acts for me.

While I am driving up to the airport departure doors I am listening to him tell me of his plans for his future, and once again, how he is not going to make any changes in his personal life for another "two months," until he is finished the current project he is working on in his business. I know I must accept as reality that he and I have different agendas. Although he tells me all the time he wants the same things I want, it is clear to me now, his words and his actions do not match and I have to accept that they may never match. I cannot take the chance with my own life, waiting and believing he will "someday" be able to work and have a relationship too, when there have been so many kilometres between us over the two years, presenting him with so many opportunities to be alone to search his own soul to figure out what he wants. But I cannot say the words, "We have to let this relationship end."

I can feel his distance as well. I know he can feel the insecurity I am emitting and I desperately want him to be the strong man he has led me to believe he wants to be in my life, the man who would understand I am in a black place and need him to help me through this period of adjustment, the new life I have created by leaving all that is familiar and as he has been the man in my life for the past two years, and we have helped each other through some really tough emotional moments, I have come to depend on him being that stable person of understanding as I have been for him, but clearly at this moment he is unwilling to be that person.

The Universe steps in and my phone rings, it is a number from back East and I do not recognize it. Thinking it is one of my children calling from an unfamiliar number I answer the phone. I have my hands free unit turned on so he can hear the person's voice as I answer it.

"Hello?"

"Hi there, how are you?"

It is Dee, a man who has been my friend for many years. My heart sinks even though Jack knows this man is a friend and has been for several years, I can tell instantly this is not going to go over well.

"Dee, I cannot talk right now, can I call you back?"

"Sure, call me when you can."

"It is really late there, what are you doing still up?"

"I was asleep but I woke up and starting thinking about you and wanted to call and see how you are."

"Okay I will call you back shortly."

"Okay Baby. Talk to you soon."

I look over at him and I see the agitation in his face.

I hang up the phone and remind him of whom that was.

He clearly wants to get out of my vehicle but I stop him.

I say, "Please don't get all weirded out because he called me baby."

"How can I not? I don't want to hear some other man calling you baby. I don't want any other man calling you at all, but I don't have the right to stop you from communicating with anyone."

My heart is sinking fast. The Universe has done it again, has put an innocent phone call right in the path of an already insecure moment for us.

Looking at him and looking at the clock I know he has to go, his plane leaves in 35 minutes and he has to get through security. My mind is racing, searching for words but there are none. I tell myself we will have time to talk this through but I know the damage has been done.

He lips quickly brush mine as he gets out of my truck and as he walks away I know we are further apart than we have ever been since I left home.

I get back to my sister's home, where I have been staying and I tell her what happened and that I believe that phone call has just ended our relationship.

Within days of that phone call, and he and I have spoken many times, trying to piece together what we are supposed to be doing, I get wind that he has spent time with another woman.

I call him, "I have heard something that I don't want to believe."

"What's that?"

"That you are involved with another woman."

"What?"

"Yes, this woman has been heard to say she is dating you."

"What? No if that were true I would tell you."

He tries to ease my mind but I can tell by his words there is some truth to what I have heard.

"I know that since I last saw you we have agreed to give each other space but this is not what you said you were going to do. You said you wanted time alone, not to be with anyone, to see how it was to be alone and just concentrate on work so we can eventually be together and now I hear this."

"I did have dinner with someone and I cannot believe how quickly you found out."

At that moment, hearing those words of confirmation, regardless of how innocent he tried to make it sound, that she is just someone he works with, I knew the information I received was true.

The panic that struck me was unreal. I wanted more than anything to believe his words of denial, but I know him so well I can tell he is lying.

"Sooz, I think it is time we let this relationship go. I need time to figure out a few more things without feeling guilty. You need to go and write your book, you have a contract now and a deadline, you need to concentrate on that. I am not with any one, you have to believe that."

That was it, those words—"I need time to figure things out without feeling guilty"—were words I had heard before when he left me the first time to go back to his life, so I recognized the signs and I knew right then he was not being honest with me. His voice was shaky, his words were quick and sharp, and his tone was serious and unsure. I was sitting with my phone clutched to my ear listening to the man I adored lying to me, trying to tell me to let him be free but at the same time telling me he loved me but cannot have a relationship right now because he must concentrate on work.

"What? We have been having a relationship for over two years this way! What makes it so different now?"

"My company needs me, my team needs me. I am building a network across the country and I need to focus on that. I have no time for a relationship. When you and I are together it is all I want to do, be together. It is distracting and we have a hard time saying goodbye. I need you to let me go. I need to let you go. You need to be free to write and I need to be free to work without worrying about what you are doing. If I start to see someone else, I will tell you, you will be the first one I call. Whatever you heard is not true." I cannot believe what I am hearing … I will be the first one he calls? What the hell is he thinking? What would ever make him think I want to be the first to know he has started to see some one when we are still so attached?

"Jack, are you out of your mind? Nothing you are saying to me is any different than what we have been saying to each other for so long it is practically joke between us now. This is different. Spit it out! What is going on?"

When you believe with all your heart that you are doing the right thing, no matter what it is, and you are willing to allow the time it will take to manifest in the right way, you take pride in yourself for being strong and patient, loyal to the extreme, discarding all the negative signs and words from everyone around you, believing that every thing you have sacrificed is worth the pain and the wait because in the end you will be rewarded for this loyalty and patience. I was wrong.

I get off the phone and just stare at my sister.

"He is lying to me."

"How do you know?"

"I can tell by his words, the sounds in his voice. Oh my God Katie, it was not supposed to be this way. He said he wanted time alone and because of his business, we could not help but be apart, but it was not supposed to be this way. He kept telling me, for two years, I was all he wanted but he was not ready to commit, not yet, but he was getting there … I believed him … and now he is lying."

I stand up and look out the window, turn and look at Katie and my knees get weak and I sit down again. I have just been hit with the biggest dose of reality. I have been wanting to know for two years why my instincts are raging out of control about this man. I have refused to believe what everyone else in my life who knows me has said about him, that he is untrustworthy and it was only going to be a matter of time before he proved them right. But I refused to believe them. I just kept believing his words and kept the faith in us. I never wanted to believe anyone when they said, "Suzanne, he will never do as he says he wants to do. If you spend your life with him it will be just like it is today, a life of constantly waiting for him to finish some program. He will never get to a place where he can build his dream life with you. He has been saying that to you since you met him. Nothing has changed since he set himself free from his long term relationship over a year ago; he still continues to keep you on a hook with the hope of a life together in one hand, "but not right now" on the other hand.

Over the next few weeks he continues to deny any involvement with another woman but I have received so much information from a source that is close to this woman that I cannot deny this is happening.

I cannot believe how the Universe has smacked me in the

face. Is this its way of telling me to smarten the hell up, that I have continued to ignore all the little signs, and there have been many, telling me to run like hell from this man, telling me to give it up, and I have ignored all the signs so it had to step right up and smack me hard?

The Universe has continued to keep us apart for reasons I could not see, but now I have to look at reality and I do not like what I see. How could I have been so blind? Why did I continue to ignore these feelings of doubt? I trusted him with my heart when the whole time my instincts were telling me he is not the man I want him to be, he is not the man I have created in my mind, he is not the man I have fantasized about for two years because that man would never allow me, not once, to ever doubt his feelings for me. Why did I do this?

Even though I want believe this is the first time he has been with another woman since leaving his long term relationship, I cannot say for sure. I still know nothing for sure but I do know this. There is no doubt this is why the Universe has kept us apart; it has kept me safe one more time. Even though we have often said "we need to be free," we were never free of each other. If we were free, we would have left each other alone long ago. I loved him and he said the same thing. So this happening and the way it happened once again broke me down to the very core of my soul sending me deeper into that black place, so deep in fact that had I been alone, without my sister there to feed me and help me with her words of love and support, I would have died, I would have starved myself to death.

Speaking with him I ask him straight out, "Are you seeing some one?"

"No"

"Well this is what I have heard." I tell him I have heard

that he is telling some other woman that he is in love with her, that he sees her in his life forever, building his dream ranch together, building his dream life with her. He knows I now know it is true, that he has said these words to someone else as these are words he has said to me and the only way they would be said by some one else is if they were said by him. But he continues to tell me what ever I have heard is not true.

November and December are dark days in Vancouver; I cannot believe how my life has been affected both by the weather and by this situation with Jack. When I left Nova Scotia it was supposed to be different, it was supposed to be a time for me to find some joy; it was supposed to be freeing of all the drama that had already broken me down to the very core of my soul in the first place. It was supposed to be fun and exciting, full of hope, love and adventure. It was supposed to be a time to allow the new independent woman to emerge, happy and carefree, in love with life, and free to love the man I thought I loved.

Now it is filled with deception and despair. I feel beaten up and bruised, used and abused. I am wild when I think about my time, my unwavering loyalty and understanding for his need for more time. I feel manipulated by his words; I feel all my energy has been wasted. I am infuriated by this blatant act of deliberate humiliation and I feel like my insides are going to explode with rage.

"How could you do this to me? To us?"

He continues to deny all of it saying, "We have always said we are free, remember, we are always saying good bye, you are always telling me this may be the last time we see each other. But you have to believe me, I am not seeing someone."

"Yes but did that happen? Did we ever break free? Did you ever feel that we were apart? We were together less than two weeks ago! We were never free of each other, no matter what you say, this is a serious relationship, and no matter where we were in the world we have depended on each other every day! We have never been apart; we have been in contact if not physically then by phone or text almost everyday for over two years! Both of us believing and talking as if we will be together someday for the rest of our lives! There is no way in hell I would have continued on a daily life with you had I ever for one minute thought we would not be. You are lying!"

As I am raging on the phone to him he is still in denial.

"Jack, I just want the truth. I need to know the truth no matter how bad it is, no matter how hurt I will be I always just want the truth. The truth gives me something concrete to work with."

"Suzanne, I am telling you the truth, if there was someone else I would tell you."

Not really having any real solid evidence to work with, no one actually seeing them together and him being so adamant, I hang up the phone. My spidy senses are on fire because some big part of me wants to believe him still.

CHAPTER TWENTY

Oh what a tangled web we weave
When first we practice to deceive

—Sir Walter Scott (*Marmion*, 1808)

"It was like watching someone coming off of heroin." Those are the words my sister used to describe me. She says it was the most painful display of agony, of withdrawal she has ever witnessed and she has some history to back it up. She has witnessed someone very close to us come off of heroin and others close to her come off of alcohol but this she said was the most pain she has seen any one person suffer from deceit.

Even though I still had no concrete evidence, I still knew that everything I felt that Jack was doing was true. I tried to control the emotions. I tried to mask them with positive thoughts as I have been doing this whole journey. I tried to act as if all was normal but I could not. Everything came crashing down. Everything from the sale of my home to leaving my children, my career, believing in love, the past anguished relationships I believed in … all of it came crashing down and I had no idea how to deal with it.

This is what I feared the most when I was driving, why I did not want to stop driving. I feared facing the facts. I feared hitting the biggest Terror Barrier of my life. Even though every fibre of my being told me I was eventually going to be alright, that I was doing the right thing by getting away from everyone, exiling myself to figure my life out, never once, the whole time I was driving did I lose the feeling of imminent danger. I felt the vibration of impending disaster every day and every night but could never really put my finger on why

I felt like that. I just knew I was going to crash and I also knew that it was going to come via Jack. You are no doubt asking yourself right now, if I knew this why did I continue on pursuing him and why did I allow him to pursue me. Because for so long I believed in and was in love with the dream we had co-created.

November and December crawled and brought more sorrow and more pain than I could have ever imagined anyone could ever feel without actually being inflicted by some horrible painful disease or having been physically harmed in some horrible twisted accident. And every passing day as Christmas drew nearer only magnified the sorrow and the grief. And to add to the emotions I was already feeling, I felt so incredibly guilty for feeling this way. Every moment of every day I agonized about flying home to see my children, to spend Christmas with them but I could not get myself out of Katie's home to walk to the store. I was thanking whatever gods may be that I did not have small children to care for and be in this state and that I was exiled away from everyone.

Every waking moment was spent trying to piece together the deceptions that were coming over the phone. Every night was spent praying to sleep through the night, just one night, please, it's all I ask for—just one night—but I could not. I would fall asleep at 1:00 or 2:00 am then wake at 3:00 or 4:00 a.m. I would wake up in the most incredible slippery sweat gasping for air, replaying the last conversation in my head, replaying the last two years in my head, wondering how the hell everything went so wrong and how I had arrived in this place.

I was so angry this was happening to me but I did not have the energy to display this anger when Jack called. I still wanted him to tell me it was all just a nightmare and that he would be coming to make it better. But he did not come. His calls and texts continued in the same manner. "Just give me some time. I am going through some stuff too. No, there is no one else in my life."

Then a life changing phone call came in.

"Hello?"

"Hi, would you like to go to the cabin for a week or so?"

"Really? Do you have to know right now?"

"No but soon. I have to make sure I take enough supplies for you as I know how much you eat."

"You're funny! I will get back to you soon."

I hang up the phone and I look at Katie and I say, "Can you believe that? That was Mr. Aswell. He wants me to go to the cabins with him again."

"You're going!"

"Don't you find it just a little ironic that this is the second or third time that Mr. Aswell has just out of the blue called me and interrupted my life with Jack?"

"I am so fucking happy this has happened. You are going. We are going to go to town tomorrow and get you snow pants, hats, gloves and anything else you need to get you out of here. When does he want to go?"

"December 28th…. we will be there for New Years."

"Oh my god Suzanne, you are going to love it. You know you have to ski doo in pulling the cutters (sleighs) full of supplies. The dogs, you and Mr. Aswell, I can not think of a better place to be or a better person to be with!"

"We are going to spend New Years with Jack, Joan, the trapper, the trapper's wife and a few other people. It is hard to imagine all that taking place, it's so remote, so isolated. I can just imagine what this is going to do when I tell Jack where I am going."

Katie is so blunt, "Fuck him ... if I were you, and I hope you get to this point soon, I would never speak with him again let alone share any of the fantastic things you get to do. Fuck him and the bullshit he keeps feeding you. Go into the mountains, enjoy your time, come back down a different person, purge that arsehole and start living life again, the way you want too, the way you pictured it for yourself."

Christmas day, I receive an e-mail from Jack, outlining his plans for the next few years of his life. In the letter he says, "I regret not spending Christmas with you." Katie wants to reach through the computer and rip his heart out.

"Suzanne all that does is confirm how consumed he is with his own life. Regrets not spending Christmas with you ... you have so much ahead of you. You should type back you're grateful you spent it the way you did. Delete that and let's go shopping for snow pants."

I had an incredible 10 days with Mr. Aswell up in the Chilcotin Mountains. I do not know if he could tell that I was damaged or not but if he could tell, he said nothing. He never would, it is not our way; we just like being together without drama. We both understand that stuff happens in everyone's life and we are just so content at not creating it with each other. He and I just laugh, I read, he cuts ice for the next season, he goes on expeditions with the trapper, I wander around outside, marvelling at where I am once again, he kooks, I konsume the best food, I klean up, he keeps the fires burning, fixes things that need fixing, makes sure I have enough hot water for my shower, feeds me some more, we take rides on the ski doo, we sleep some more, he stuffs and bakes a big turkey we pack it in a cooler, put it in a cutter and travel through the snow covered mountains to Jack and Joan's to ring in 2011.

CHAPTER TWENTY-ONE

Grieving the Dream

*"The single biggest problem in communication
is the illusion that it has taken place."*

—George Bernard Shaw

I start to wonder if I have been going about this "finding my new life" all the wrong way. It appears to me that I have been running and running to get "back" to a dream life that was created when my life with Jack was new, fun and exciting. Going "back" to doing anything has never been an option before, so hence the conflict I continue to have.

After all we have been through, enough time has passed and I am done waiting. I have never been one to wait for someone or something to show up, if I had I would not have had nearly the adventurous life I have had. I am tired of wondering if I am doing the right thing, I am done watching someone else make choices for their life that have such profound adverse affects on my life. I am done listening to words that manipulate my emotions, wreak havoc in my mind and on my soul because the words are so contradictory to the actions I am seeing. I come to the conclusion that I have always been in control of my life, but because I was so emotionally attached, so involved with someone who shared their thoughts and feelings with me, I became attached to their words and I fell in love with the dream.

I know that all I have to do is let go, take control of my own actions and thoughts and stop grieving the dream of a life that will never be. I have to stop grieving for a relationship that could never be built on this kind of insecure foundation.

I have to stop grieving for this man, but keep the dream.

I still was holding on to the dream, if only by a thread, because I had at this point no concrete evidence for the second-hand news I had heard and I had not attained part of a goal I had set out to attain and that goal was for Jack and I to be on the same page about life without influence or intrusion from any other person or our careers and at times, I felt it was getting close. I thought that by being patient, going about my journey, letting him experience the time and distance apart while I figured out every other aspect of my life before committing to him was not only fair but needed by us both. This time and distance allowed him the space he needed without one second of concern or worry about me, to get his life and career balanced, ready for the beautiful vision we had created, before committing to me. And because I had faith that he would eventually get through his own life-altering transition, I wanted him to know and understand what faithfulness, loyalty and trust in a relationship looks and feels like. I continued to believe we would eventually fall into the easy way of living life together that happens when we are together, only without the ugly feelings that crept in just before we left each other, I thought for sure once we were on the same page all my doubts and fears would subside. I remained optimistic that we still had a future until that one more moment when the Universe just had to slap me again.

So to find out the truth, to find the concrete evidence I needed to break free, I purposefully put myself in his path by accepting an invitation to stay in his place in Calgary while he was away. I knew he would eventually show up and when he did, one look at him and I could tell he was a mess. After picking him up from the airport we got back to his condo and I sat on the couch looking at him, watching him pace around his home telling me what he needed to take care of over the next few days— bank, accountant, drycleaner … I watched him as he avoided eye contact with me. Then he came over and sat next to me.

I looked at him and said, "Jack, I know you better than anyone, something is going on and I need you to tell me. I need to know for me."

"I made a mistake."

"Yes, you did."

"I didn't mean for it to happen."

Such a ridiculous statement.

"Of course you meant it to happen. If you didn't mean for it to happen … it would not have."

The conversation is long and heart wrenching. I watch him confirm everything I had suspected, read and heard.

He had a relationship for several weeks but now he says it's over.

"Why didn't you tell me the truth when I asked you over and over?"

"I didn't want to let you go."

I am stunned, too shocked by reality to know what to do.

I looked at him in disbelief. Once again I could not, did not want to believe what was coming out of his mouth. He was clearly upset, confused and was visibly shaking from having to tell me the truth and I could tell that there was more he wanted to tell me and over the next few days, I did hear all about a relationship that turned his world upside down and so it should have—living several lives will eventually catch up with you.

It's funny how I reacted. Of course I was hurt and numb, I was in shock, but I was not surprised. You may think that all I wanted to do was to rip his heart out, but because so much time had passed and I had already gone through the madness and despair when the suspicions first came about I had no more angry energy to give and what I actually felt on this day was relief. I was now able to put my finger on the danger that I always felt was not very far away with this man. I do not want to believe I manifested this with my powers of manifesting whatever I give my time and passion to and as this is not what I truly desired, I believe that the Universe has continued to protect me by continually peaking my instincts, reminding me to be careful and not jump in as I have done in the past with relationships. My instincts kept telling me to wait just a little longer because something was going to happen and as I have always maintained … I was never sure if that something I felt was a good something or a bad something, I just knew it was something.

Jack looked at me and said, "There, are you happy now? You have wanted to know who I am and now you know!"

I looked at him as if his head was on backwards and said … "Are you kidding me? I don't think this is who you are! And if it is I want the extreme opposite of what I have found out about you." My head was starting to spin and I felt the tears starting to sting my eyes but I refused to give in to them.

"I believed in you when everyone around me said not to, I believed in you when my instincts told me not to. I believed in you when you said you wanted to be free, I understood what that freedom meant to you, I wanted to be free too Jack, and I am free. We were both free Jack … we were so free. We were free like no other two people we know. We were free to travel and work and still had a trust in each other to the point that we gave each other room to grow and explore the major changes we both deliberately made in our lives. We went about living our lives believing that no matter how bad, dramatic and hectic the outside world became, we knew we had someone in this crazy world that loved us so much that when we shut the door at the end of the day we could call them or when we met up after weeks apart, we shared our adventures, dreamed of adventures together, were happy and we calmed each others worlds. That is what it is all about Jack. To know that at the end of the day … unconditionally—I was there for you and you were there for me."

"It's over, you have to believe that. It was a mistake, it just happened."

"I want to believe it but I don't. You had the choice and you chose to risk us. Stop saying it just happened."

That evening he could tell I was different, and said so. He could tell I was stronger and that I was coming to terms with the new life I was seeking and liking it. I was getting used to being alone, doing whatever I wanted, whenever I wanted. My life was becoming the vision I created before I left Nova Scotia, and if I did not have to deal with the emotional relationship drama, there is no question; I would have been living the dream.

After he left, I called my sister.

"Katie…I think I am ready to leave Alberta."

"Wow that is great news. I am surprised you stayed but you know what… I get why you did. You said you were going to stay until you finished your book or until you felt stronger and attained a goal you set for yourself … so am I to assume you have finished with Jack?"

"No not yet, but I no longer feel the uncertainty. I don't feel so fragile anymore. I don't have the desire to run away from anything any more."

"Really? … What does that mean?"

"It means I did attain a goal that I set out last May to

attain. It means that I can now remove the emotional obstacle that has been in my life for two and a half years."

"Yes, but what does that mean Suzanne? Now that you have met this goal … what are you going to do?"

"It means I will do as I always do Katie … Now that the danger that I have feared has presented itself and I no longer feel that fear and the doubts that have plagued me, I am going to leave Alberta and start living. I see myself back in my truck, not today but soon, and I am laughing, going places that not only am I excited to go to, I am happy to be wherever I am and I won't be looking for the exit. I can't tell you how different I feel. The heavy black cloud is moving away."

"Oh my god Suzanne that is huge! You must be so relieved to be rid of that feeling."

"Yes I am relieved but look at the cost, look at what it has cost everyone involved. I don't know what to think about what has happened; it seems unreal to me, like it is not happening to me … I just want to move on. But Katie … even though I still have the feeling Jack and I are not finished ... I do know this, whatever it is that is coming my way… I am ready for it."

"Suzanne just finish what you are working on, pack up your truck and go see Al and Sue in Lethbridge for a while. You do not need to find out anymore."

"I am going to do exactly that, I have already called them to let them know I want to spend my last week of my Alberta winter with them."

For several more weeks I sit in Calgary, in Jack's beautiful Condo, writing, watching the snow rage through the nights and the sun shine during the freezing cold days and I shake my head at what could have been, but again I have to remind myself … no matter how beautiful the picture is in my head, no matter how easy and perfect I see life being, I cannot make anyone see or do something they do not want to do. I have given it my best shot and I am looking at the exit door one more time.

Now that I have the truth or enough of the truth to allow me to make decisions for the next phase of my journey, I know that before I make any serious moves or decisions, and all the guru's will concur, it is important to allow some time to pass to process the truth before I can accept it and move on. I do not want to take this drama with me, I do not want to travel with this on my mind, I want to purge it and leave it here in Calgary, purge this from my soul. I find myself wanting to be alone to process this but this time I do not feel the desire to sleep forever, I do not feel fragile … I feel determination to purge this part of my life and get it behind me quickly so I can be free to enjoy my life without wondering if I left any part of this life with Jack unfinished.

I leave Alberta on a sunny winter morning and drive back through the Rockies to Vancouver. I have a whole new perspective for my life and a strength which at one time I never thought I would have. I have a clearer mind and determination to build on the positive aspects of my life of which there are many. Having created all that I had in my life, and then letting go of it has allowed me to find out what I would miss in life but it has also shown me that I was not living as I truly wanted to.

After leaving the West Coast, driving slowly East, I stopped and stayed with some of the same friends and family that I had stayed with on my journey West. They all comment on not only the physical changes they saw in me, they told me I looked healthier, less stressed and they could tell that I had changed mentally. They told me they saw some of the old me but with more experience and wisdom. I told them that I prayed everyday to the " keep this feeling gods." And then I tell them, "I do not allow one day to pass with out spending some quiet time and some noisy time. I don't care what is going on, I spend time shutting my eyes and visualizing what it is I truly desire for my life. I will make my current vision, this dream I have today a reality and it is going to be fantastic— it already is- and I have made sure I follow one of my own rules. I make sure I add all the details because I am tired of my visions showing up with missing parts."

CHAPTER TWENTY-TWO

There Is a Reason for Everything and a Season for Everyone

I believe that Jack is one of those people who have come into my life for just a Season. He came into my life to help me grow and become the strong woman I have been portraying to myself and others for my whole life and now that I am that woman, life just had to throw me one more curve ball just to make sure.

Again … I have to caution everyone…be careful what you wish for because you just might get it all. I had arrived in Ontario and was away at a cottage with some girl friends for the weekend. I had driven for many days alone to get there and had resigned myself to the fact I would never see Jack again when my phone rang with his familiar ring tone.

He tells me he wants to see me and I allow myself to be taken one more time. He flies me back to the West coast and asks me to marry him … Oh my god! I got exactly what I asked for. I had been dreaming and manifesting this day for as long as I had known Jack and now it had arrived. I had dreamed about this very day when he and I were both on the same page with no outside influences or distractions to concern ourselves with. I believed enough time had gone by, that he was well over the brief relationship that he says gave him such a reality check and now he wanted me to marry him … but first … he needs to finish working on a few things … then perhaps in the Fall, in another three months, if we still feel the same way, we can discuss in more detail how to go about blending our lives.

Well needless to say, I was elated about the marriage proposal as it was a true desire of mine to marry him. In my mind we would have had the most incredible life—not too much drama as we both dislike it, lots of traveling for work and pleasure, spending time with good friends and quality time with our children and grandchildren—and lots of sexy love! I truly loved him and wanted all of this for us and I could make all of this happen and more … with my eyes shut.

I get freaked out when I think about how everything has come full circle with Jack, from meeting him to the marriage proposal. Oh I guess your wondering … Did I accept the proposal …. I did not. I did not want to wait another three months to start working on it. Do I still love Jack …yes I do. Just because someone messes up in life doesn't mean we instantly fall out of love with them. I wish it was that easy, it just means we have choices and when you know someone or something is not right for you, when your instincts and spidy senses continue to rage out of control … listen to them.

I wish Jack the very best. I wish him success in all he does. I know he regrets what has happened and has told me often, "If I could take it all back, change what has happened I would. But I can't."

Even though I would not wish what I have gone through on anyone, and unfortunately Jack and I are part of a huge statistic now, and no matter how twisted this sounds, I believe the Universe put us through this so we would grow and become better people, I also believe that I have not found the love of my life yet, that he is out there making his way to me and he will come from a place I least expect him to … straight out of left field.

Today when asked what have I learned on this journey one answer is hard to give. My head swims with moments and adventures I can't even begin to describe and lessons that only with time will I be able to share. What I can share is a lesson I learned from my sister Katie, a lesson she learned after suffering a stroke … "I can only focus on the task at hand, the one task that is right in front of me. It's not that I can't multitask, I just don't want to … today."

This summer of 2011, after not seeing my children for thirteen months, I am back in Nova Scotia. They are all fine and life has not been easy for anyone but they are survivors and they have proven they have their mother's tenacity.

I am going to sit with my children for a few weeks, cuddle my new baby granddaughter, fish with my grandson, visit with Blake's mom Gail and we will cry and laugh, see some friends, switch some clothes around, I have had the same clothes since I left … how many woman could live this way? Then the Warrior/Gypsy is going to get back in her truck and this time … I *am* going on the adventure of my life, the one I envisioned so long ago because today I no longer feel that scary feeling of fear or that constant feeling of being UNFINSHED …

I *am* free and I am going to write another book called FINISHED, then I will do what I have come to find is my passion. I will continue to write my children's books, the ones that make me and all the children of the world happy. I will write all about adventures of … The Lippy Cats.

Blip…

"Are you there?"

"Yes"

"Where are you headed today?"

"I am heading out to explore the world!"

"Really? Which way are you going?"

"I am not sure maybe across Canada or maybe down

through the Southern States. Which ever way the winds blow me. But I can only go North, South or West because I am as far East as I can be before falling off the continent."

"Wow…you're so lucky!"

"No, luck has nothing to do with it. It is what I truly desire to do…. so I am doing it."

"And you have no destination?"

"Well actually I do … I am going to Alaska!"

"This time I know you will make it."

"Yes I will!"

"Let me know when you get there."

"You know what … I don't think I will, which is really unfortunate because I really liked the way we used to talk. Wow Baby … Look where I am! I am Free!"

Look for the follow up book "Finished" to be released March 2012.

Follow along with Suzanne on Facebook: OntourwithSuzanne
Blog : Ontourwithsuzanne.blogspot.com
e-mail: Ontourwithsuzanne@hotmail.com
twitter: tourwithsuzanne